THE FIGHTING FRENCHMAN

THE FIGHTING FRENCHMAN

MINNESOTA'S BOXING LEGEND

Scott LeDoux

PAUL LEVY

UNIVERSITY OF MINNESOTA PRESS
MINNEAPOLIS · LONDON

Copyright 2016 by Paul Levy

Published by the University of Minnesota Press
111 Third Avenue South, Suite 290
Minneapolis, MN 55401-2520
http://www.upress.umn.edu

ISBN 978-0-8166-9719-9 (hc)
ISBN 978-1-5179-0170-7 (pb)
A Cataloging-in-Publication record for this
book is available from the Library of Congress.

Printed in the United States of America on acid-free paper

The University of Minnesota is an equal-opportunity educator and employer.

22 21 20 19 18 17 16   10 9 8 7 6 5 4 3 2 1

Dedicated to the memory of Patricia Ellen Meyer Levy,
who taught me to talk to the flowers, but listen to the rocks . . .
and to Scott LeDoux, forever the People's Champion

"Float like a buffalo
Sting like a tank
You couldn't hurt me
If you were swinging a plank
You may be big
You may be fast
You fight me
You'll end up last."

—Scott LeDoux, to heavyweight champion Muhammad Ali,
at a press conference to promote their December 2, 1977,
five-round exhibition match in Chicago

———————————

"Not bad for a white boy."

—Ali to LeDoux, at the same press conference

CONTENTS

Introduction

FIVE MINUTES TO GO

$\mathcal{S}$cott LeDoux's face once read like a road map that bobbed and weaved through boxing's final golden era of the twentieth century. George Foreman bloodied LeDoux's nose and opened a twelve-stitch gash above his left cheek. "George Foreman," LeDoux said with a wince, "hit me so hard my ancestors in France felt it." Larry Holmes, who stopped LeDoux in seven rounds in their 1980 heavyweight title fight, jammed his thumb in LeDoux's left eye, damaging his retina. Ken Norton's savage uppercut to the chin lifted LeDoux's feet off the canvas. Mike Tyson, having learned that the then-retired LeDoux was broke, hired the forty-two-year-old as a sparring partner—and then secretly had the stuffing removed from his gloves, pummeled LeDoux's face, and opened an eight-stitch gash above LeDoux's left eye. And Muhammad Ali? The Greatest verbally singed Le-Doux's ears.

But beneath the tough-guy facade and a nose mashed so badly that it seemed void of bone structure, the only man to step into the ring and go toe-to-toe with eleven heavyweight champions bore emotional scars that no boxer would dare let the outside world see.

"He eats rusty nails for breakfast, punches holes in concrete with either hand, bobs and weaves like a giant Rocky Marciano, and can fight," the legendary boxing promoter Don King wrote early in LeDoux's professional career, as King tried to create a mystique about a kid from the heartland who preferred denim overalls and milking cows to the bright lights. You can almost see King's thousand-watt Cheshire-cat smile and electric hair stand at attention as he tried to turn this miner's son from a small northern Minnesota Iron Range town near the source of the Mississippi River into boxing's next great white hope.

"I was white and hoping," LeDoux said.

"The name—Scott LeDoux—this 220-pound towering chunk of French Canadian stock . . . loves to fight with the purpose in mind to destroy the other guy," read King's one-page essay, the words apparently pounded from a manual typewriter, some of the characters practically piercing through the thick parchment glued to the inside cover of one of the many scrapbooks kept by LeDoux's mother. LeDoux, according to King, was a modern-day Paul Bunyan who "immensely enjoys chopping trees" and "can usually be found in the north woods of Minnesota tracking deer, hunting, or just chasing bear cubs for the fun of it."

But in dingy, mildew-scented dressing rooms in minor-league towns like Utica, New York, Sioux Falls, South Dakota, and Billings, Montana, where sometimes a single lightbulb swaying from a water-stained ceiling would illuminate the layers of dust settling over cracked concrete floors, LeDoux would nervously lean against the trainer's table, every bead of sweat running down the side of his face representing another worry. Sometimes he would gaze beyond the shadows and simply watch the dark. He was safe there—secluded from the social deviants, scandals, and incurable diseases that threatened to destroy his career and family.

His name once illuminated the marquee at Madison Square Garden, prompting his college buddy Glenn "Chico" Resch to gush, "That's Madison Square Garden! That's your name, Scotty! Can you believe this is happening?" Resch, the hockey goalie who became an instant folk hero in New York after leading the Islanders to two improbable Stanley Cup playoff series comebacks in the mid-1970s, wanted this midwestern farm kid, whose parents never even made it to high school, to bask in the moment.

"Scotty! It says 'Scott LeDoux' up there in lights," Resch shouted in March 1977 as the pair stood outside the Garden before LeDoux's battle with Pedro Soto for the Garden's version of the American heavyweight championship. "My name has never been on that," Resch told LeDoux, "and I've played here a hundred times. Scotty, it doesn't get any bigger than this."

Yet the larger LeDoux's world became, the more his ring began to shrink. "They saw me bleeding from the outside," LeDoux said softly, his husky voice fading into a muffled whisper. But that was all the most popular boxer from Minnesota allowed fans to see. Never a world champion, he was always the people's champ, just a big, good-natured kid, charitable to a fault and willing to take us all on a ride he himself found hard to believe.

Who could resist a guy who was willing to spar verbally with Muhammad Ali during a televised appearance before their 1977 five-round exhibition in Chicago? When Ali, the reigning heavyweight champion, who had secretly agreed to defend his title against LeDoux six months after the exhibition, told LeDoux that he had better watch out, that Ali and his "brothers" might burn LeDoux's house down, LeDoux quipped, "Then I guess I'm staying at your house."

When he wasn't rubbing elbows or trading left jabs with boxing royalty, life's sucker punches came hard and often. There were the career-defining, head-scratching moments that made him a media curiosity. He knocked askew sportscaster Howard Cosell's toupee on national television, triggered a federal grand jury investigation in 1977 when he cried "fix" at the U.S. Boxing Championships, and innocently became a pawn in the biggest sports and bank scandal in U.S. history when he accepted a fifty-thousand-dollar advance—one-hundred-dollar bills in a brown paper bag, delivered at a Minneapolis–St. Paul airport restaurant.

Outside the ring, life threw one haymaker after another: a horrifying childhood encounter that would haunt LeDoux for decades, death threats and rumors of hit men, alcoholism and clinical depression that triggered thoughts of suicide.

Sandy LeDoux, Scott's first wife and one of the two great loves of his life, could put a glow in her husband's eyes, even when they were battered shut. But in those dim dressing rooms—often crowded dins of chaos with managers, trainers, and other fighters champing at the bit, waiting for their big chance at a decent payday or, at least, relevance—LeDoux was left alone with his fears.

"I was terrified," LeDoux said. "Before every fight, I worried about everything. I don't think fighters like to admit the fear factor very much. I was scared to death up until five minutes before they rang the bell. Then someone would knock at the door and say, 'Five minutes to go.' That's when I lost my fear. I knew I had to go in the ring. It was too late to be afraid anymore."

1

THE GREAT MILFORD MINING DISASTER

*E*ighty-five years later, words that once reverberated in the womb—words that nobody else seemed to hear—continued to haunt Katherine Perpich. Her Balkan-born mother, Mildred Magdich, was three months pregnant with Katherine that cloudy, frigid Tuesday morning of February 5, 1924, and just beginning to show. But no day would ever shape Katherine's life like this one, and maybe the same could be said for all of Crosby, Minnesota.

"My mother told my dad not to go to work," Katherine recalled in March 2009. "She knew something bad was going to happen. But he went to work anyhow. We didn't have much money, like most of the miners' families back in 1924. And there was good ore under that lake. They were mining under a lake, Foley Lake. And those engineers wanted that good ore."

Tiny Crosby lies deep in the land of the windchill factor, where the gentle ripples of ten thousand lakes mesmerize tourists, and the Paul Bunyan statues in every other town hint at legends that are bigger than life. This is the heart of Crow Wing County, where twenty-first-century beer commercials are filmed, where in Brainerd vacationing celebrities blend with auto-racing fanatics, and where on February 5, 1924, the greatest iron-ore mining disaster in American history changed a town's landscape in a way the prehistoric glaciers never could.

Men had been mining the Cuyuna Range since 1911, just sixteen years after surveyor Cuyler Adams discovered traces of magnetic ore on this range between the nonmining communities of Brainerd and Aitkin. Named by Adams's wife, who combined the first three letters of her husband's first name with the name of their dog, Una, the Cuyuna Range was rich in manganese, an ore valued for steel production and coveted during World War I, when America stopped importing the suddenly precious mineral. By 1918, the twenty-seven Cuyuna mines, owned by mostly small, independent companies, had yielded two and a half million tons of ore. Miners who came to the range in search of work began settling in places like Crosby and Ironton.

"You came to Crosby to do open-pit mining," said Judy Wynn, Scott LeDoux's sister. Their father, Allen Glenroy LeDoux, and maternal grandfather, Frank Stangel, worked the mines. "Most of them worked six months, and then they'd be laid off six months. They didn't live in fancy, expensive houses. They didn't have money. But they mined. If you lived in Crosby, you worked the mines."

"That's what drew my folks to town—the underground mines," remembered Frank Perpich, a distant cousin, by marriage, to Katherine Perpich. At seventy-seven, he was still living in Crosby in 2009. "It was cheap labor," he said of mining, "but we were all raised on the work ethic. And when the miners got paid, good times prevailed. Let's leave it at that. We're simple people up here and we're impressed with simple things. 'Who caught the biggest fish? Who shot the biggest buck?' Yes, the men got paid, cashed their checks at the grocery store, and, well, the bar was right next door."

Simple people? Minnesota native Garrison Keillor talks about a place where "all the women are strong, all the men are good looking, and all the children are above average." And northern Minnesota, where you would expect nothing but lumberjacks and maybe Babe, Paul Bunyan's blue ox, certainly has produced its share of good-looking résumés. The voice of a generation, Bob Dylan, and basketball Hall of Famer Kevin McHale grew up in Hibbing, birthplace of baseball slugger Roger Maris. Show business legend Judy Garland was raised in Grand Rapids. Two-time Oscar winner Jessica Lange is from Cloquet. Legendary aviator Charles Lindberg grew up in Little Falls. Baseball Hall of Famer Chief Bender was born in Brainerd and raised on the White Earth Reservation, later the home of international activist and two-time vice presidential candidate Winona LaDuke. Film star Jane Russell, one of the first pinup girls, was born in Brainerd. Seven of the twenty members of 1980 Olympic gold medal Miracle on Ice hockey team were from northern Minnesota.

For thousands of immigrant families who settled in northern Minnesota, the underground mines were like stepping-stones to a better life.

The miners might go days without ever seeing daylight, but in the dark, they were immune to the shadow of bigotry that followed people with foreign dialects, some of whom spoke little or no English. And with money from the mines, they could not only fill their families' stomachs but maybe fulfill the dreams of educating their children.

It didn't take much: Fourteen-year-old Frank Hrvatin Jr., who shoveled dirt that was carted away from the Milford Mine, was paid $3.80 a day. His father, an expert blaster who worked at his son's side, made $6 a day. It seemed like enough. Maybe more than enough. Yes, a baby boomer like Scott LeDoux, whose grandfather worked the mines, and whose father, also a Crosby miner, never made it to high school, could actually realize his dream of going to college.

Many Crosby homes were bilingual, Frank Perpich recalled. The LeDoux family was typical: Scott LeDoux's grandfather Edward LeDoux, spoke French, and Edward's wife, Tillie, spoke German. "They'd yell at each other in two different languages," Scott remembered. "They were great arguments because neither one knew what the other was saying."

Language barriers aside, the immigrants who toiled underground, side by side, against elements they often could not see, learned to trust one another, as if their lives depended on it. "A man's handshake was his word, and if tempers flared, well, settle things and then forget about it," Frank Perpich said. "That's how it was."

Then came February 5, 1924, a day nobody in Crosby would soon forget.

Katherine Perpich's father, Peter Magdich, ignored his wife's plea and went to work that morning at the Milford Mine, seven miles north of Crosby. Of course, he did. The mine was rippling with precious metal.

"I would be scared to go down into an underground mine pit day after day, but my grandfather [Stangel] was a tough, hard-nosed guy, who maybe smiled once a year," Scott LeDoux recalled. "I asked my grandfather what it was like to go down into the mines. He said, 'You know, I had a job and I worked the job every day. I never thought about anything going wrong.'"

Stangel didn't work the Milford Mine on February 5, 1924. But Frank Hrvatin Jr., a big, husky kid, was deep in the pit that day, alongside his father. "Everything was working," Hrvatin said. "They couldn't get the ore out of that mine fast enough."

Forty-eight men worked the day shift that Tuesday. One of them, Joe Sabyan, a maintenance worker, was called up from the mine around two o'clock "and wasn't too happy about it," his daughter, Gloria Perpich, recalled in June 2010. It was twenty-eight degrees below zero above ground but a tolerable forty-five degrees inside the mine.

Peter Magdich's shift was to end at four o'clock. Shortly before quarter to four, a powerful blast of warm air whisked through the mine. Suddenly, darkness extinguished the lights.

"Look at the water, Harry," young Frank Hrvatin said after dumping some ore down a transfer chute.

"Water?" his buddy Harry Hosford, responded, assuming his friend was joking. "You're nuts."

A fraction of a second later, the mine exploded in mud, "sounding like a thousand automobiles coming at you," said Matt Kangas, one of the miners. The weight of the bog water above, water from Foley Lake, caved in the mine's wall, sending a rush of thick, murky water through fragile passageways, and tremors through the veins of the men being washed away with each gush. Water poured in at a rate of one hundred thousand gallons per minute. Timbers fell. Workers were slammed into walls. Emil Kainu, a pump man at the bottom of the two-hundred-foot-deep mine, heard a booming noise.

"Oh, my God! My God!" Hosford screamed.

"For God's sake, run! Faster!" young Hrvatin pleaded.

Clinton Harris operated an electric hoist that dumped ore from one of the cars into a bucket that was lifted to the surface, then emptied and returned. That day, Harris was at the bottom of the mine, filling in for another worker. Harris could have attempted to escape when mud began swirling through the mine. Instead, he yanked the rope of an alarm, warning miners up above of imminent danger. For four hours that warning signal sounded. When Harris's body was found, no one was certain if his body had become tangled in the rope, or if he had tied himself to it.

Fifteen minutes. That's all it took, and forty-one miners were dead. Frank Hrvatin Jr., days shy of his fifteenth birthday, survived. His father, working at his side, was gone. Just like that. Some of the bodies were not discovered for months. The last body was removed on November 4—nine months later. It took that long to pump out the mud and water.

Thirty-three women were made widows. Eighty-eight children were fatherless—including one child who had yet to be born, Katherine Perpich. Her father's body was recovered six months after the walls caved in.

"When the women found out the men had drowned, they came to the mine and wanted to jump in there to be with their loved ones," John R. Perpich, Katherine Perpich's husband, recalled decades later. Mildred Magdich, Katherine's mother, never jumped. She worked the hayfields instead, to support her six kids. "There were a lot of widows that were left," Katherine said with a sigh. "They didn't get much money. I think they got $10,000 plus a little every month to live on." Historical records say it may have been even less—a total of $7,500, with weekly payments between $8 and $20. Relatives of single miners were given no compensation at all.

Theodore Christianson, governor of Minnesota, declared it an act of God. Decades later, federal magistrate and Ironton native Miles Lord questioned such logic. "An act of God?" asked Lord. "An act of God when you dig into the bottom of a lake?"

Disaster couldn't close the Milford Mine, but the Great Depression did. When the demand for steel waned in the early 1930s, the mine shut down. The debate continued for decades—until they finally shut down the last of the Cuyuna mines in 1984.

John Davies, the Crosby-Ironton High School football coach, who came to town in 1957 and whose first all-state player was an undersized lineman named Scott LeDoux, remembers his teams playing on a field near an underground mine. "If we scored a touchdown, the miners underground cheered," he recalled. "You could actually feel the echo."

Nothing shakes the foundation of a community like sudden disaster of unprecedented magnitude. "A devastating affair for our community," Gloria Perpich called it in 2010. "For years, my father wouldn't talk about it. Like a soldier who comes home from the war, there just wasn't much for him or the others to say."

Yet, nostalgic Crosby natives remember the mines with pride. Like the ore that once sparkled beneath the surface, the mines are part of their foundation. Nearly a century later, old miners still meet for coffee at the SuperValu in Crosby or at the Miners' Diner in Ironton.

"If you're from Crosby, you stick with the mines," John R. Perpich said. "And you stay there."

2

DOC AND MICKEY

*T*he young boy had never seen his father fight. But from the street—through thick saloon doors and walls and above the boisterous roars of the animated betting crowd—he heard his father's blood-curdling screams. They terrified him.

"My father would let out this gut-wrenching scream at the top of his lungs, screams that must have echoed across the Cuyuna Range," Scott LeDoux recalled. "These were primal screams, the kind that send chills down your spine. Sometimes, my dad began screaming before his opponent even showed up."

Some men fight for pride and honor. Some fight for survival. Some fight with dreams of one day becoming the heavyweight champion of the world. LeDoux's father, Allen Glenroy LeDoux, was forced to fight by his own father, who took him from bar to bar, betting money that his adult son could beat someone else up. Often, Edward LeDoux had his son, who was in his early twenties, fight two men at once. On at least one occasion, he ordered him to fight four "or he'd kick his ass," Scott LeDoux remembered.

"And if Dad lost, Grandpa would beat him up," Scott's sister, Judy Wynn, said with a shrug. "How's that for a sad story?"

"That's true," Wayne Wynn said of his father-in-law, "but I don't know that Doc ever got beat."

Doc! Everyone called Scott LeDoux's dad Doc because he could fix anything, except, maybe his father's expectations. The newspapers never referred to him as Doc, at least not when they wrote of his arrests for Saturday night brawls. His name was often misspelled—as the LeDoux name had been for decades following the family's nomadic journey from Quebec to Minnesota.

"But make no mistake about it, they all knew who Doc was," said John Davies, the former Crosby-Ironton High School football coach. "Scott LeDoux was my first all-state player, but it was Doc LeDoux who was legendary around here."

Doc, a World War II veteran, was one of those tough miners who probably could chew iron ore for breakfast and sweat rust before lunch. Once, rather than wait for a hoist to lift an engine from a truck, Doc lifted the engine with his bare hands. Doc drove a stock car. His big ol' Farmall tractor was the envy of Crosby. Other families in Crosby owned recreational vehicles, but when Doc retired, he went elk hunting in a converted school bus he customized himself. As a miner, he operated a Monaghan, the biggest shovel in the world. "It took trucks to move that shovel," Wayne Wynn remembered. "I can't imagine anyone else but Doc operating it."

He stood a hair under six feet tall and weighed no more than 190 pounds. But Doc was a bigger-than-life character that everyone in Crosby knew.

"Every Saturday night they'd go out dancing, and, I swear, every other week there'd be a brawl and someone would go to jail," Judy Wynn remembered. "They'd come back from the war and that was a typical Saturday night for them, the fist-fighting."

Doc didn't leave his temper in an empty glass at the bar. After one bar fight, Doc chased his opponent out of the bar to an apartment building "and beat the crap out of him," Scott LeDoux said. Years later, he decked a snowmobiler who tried to make a trail on Doc's property.

Once, when Doc and a very young Scott were fixing a fence, a group of deer hunters and their dogs wandered onto the LeDoux property. Suddenly, the dogs took off after Doc's springer spaniel, Stubby. As one of the hunters' dogs broke over a hill, Doc threw his hammer from thirty feet away and nailed the animal on the head.

"I told you guys, 'You get those dogs out of here, or they'll be dead,'" Doc shouted.

He was a simple man, a creature of habit. Doc owned only springer spaniels and named every last one of them Stubby. He never made it to high school, never learned to read or write, but he could tear down an engine and build a house.

"Doc was brilliant," recalled Glenn "Chico" Resch, who forged a lifelong friendship with LeDoux when both were freshmen at the University of Minnesota Duluth. "But one thing about Doc seems to run through the family. The LeDoux boys all have short fuses. If Scott had been docile, he'd never have reached the heights. But Scott got that short fuse from his dad. And that created a few situations."

Doc, apparently, inherited his temper from his dad. Edward LeDoux hailed from Montreal, moved to Winnipeg, then to North Dakota, and, finally, to Brainerd, Minnesota. His height at five feet six, Edward's shoulders may have been as wide as he was tall. He always carried thick bolts in his pocket, and sometimes a tire iron, and wasn't bashful about using them.

"I always thought my dad was so cool, but my grandpa scared me," Scott recalled. "When I was very young, I heard some loud screams coming from the kitchen. My grandpa was trying to beat on my dad. And he meant it. I was so scared. I jumped on my grandpa's back, trying to stop him while the two of them were swinging away."

Judy recalled waking up at home one night, with Edward standing in the yard, cussing and challenging Doc to come out and fight him. Doc tried to quiet him down, and Edward responded by hitting Doc. Judy said she was about ten years old at the time, Scott, maybe seven.

"Mom, Scott, and I would be huddled together in the porch, watching and crying," Judy said.

Doc and his wife, Mickey, moved the following year to the neighboring community of Deerwood. For reasons unknown to others in the LeDoux family, Edward never again came to Doc's house to pick a fight with him. Still, other stories of violence emerged. Judy recalled Doc telling her that Edward often beat up his wife, Tillie. Doc and his older sister, Gloria, would intercede, with Doc jumping on his father's back, often to no avail.

Matilda "Tillie" Blanck LeDoux was a tall and loving woman who raised eight children, pretty much on her own, Judy remembered. She spoke English and German and asked for very little out of life. Tillie didn't drive, taking the bus to the grocery store and spending hours sitting on a bench outside, where she would visit with other women friends. That was the extent of her social life—that and visits from her grandchildren, for whom she made fried pork chops for lunch. The grandchildren came by almost exclusively when they knew Edward wasn't there.

"That was pretty much the extent of her social life," Judy said. "She was a lonely woman."

Edward and Tillie likely arrived in Brainerd around the same time Mickey's parents, Frank and Georgia Woods Stangel, arrived in Crosby.

Like Edward LeDoux, Frank Stangel hailed from Canada, but the similarities ended there.

Edward LeDoux worked for the Burlington Railroad in Brainerd, in the roundhouse, running the overhead crane. Apparently, he wanted his kid to be as tough as he was. When Doc was fourteen, he spent the summer working for room and board on an uncle's turkey farm in Fargo, North Dakota. Doc then later worked at a Civilian Conservation Corps camp in Big Falls, Montana, sending every one of his paychecks to his parents, never seeing a dime. As an adult, Doc continued to roll up his sleeves, working in a missile plant in North Dakota and taking odd jobs in Missouri to make ends meet.

Doc would work thirty-seven years for the Hanna Mining Company, toiling on the Cuyuna Range for twenty-eight of those years, and the other nine years on the Mesabi Range. His first job was driving a truck. He came home one night, his face battered and bruised. He had rolled a Euclid truck into a ditch. The boom lift in the cab had come loose and kept hitting him in the face.

He later worked as an oiler on a shovel, oiling a boom in forty-degrees-below-zero temperatures so unfathomable that he had to hold the grease gun between his elbows and push his forearms together because his fingers had lost feeling.

"This is how they lived," Judy said of her father's family.

The Stangels' lives seemed so less complicated, an almost mythic tale of the great north woods. Georgia was a teacher, and she drove a horse and buggy and picked up students along the way to school in Blackduck, Minnesota. Frank and Georgia met at a logging camp in northern Minnesota, near Deer River. He was a laborer. Georgia was one of the camp's cooks. "A fantabulous cook," Judy said.

Georgia made cooking an art, with a style she passed on to her daughter, Shirley. Georgia was so talented a chef that later in life she was hired to cook for the wealthier families in Crosby. Georgia's expertise in the kitchen was in such high demand that she was able to convince Frank to spend autumns in Bigelow, Missouri, where they ran a club for a group of doctors who spent the fall hunting ducks and geese. Frank did the maintenance. But Georgia was the star. She did the cooking.

The LeDouxs and Stangels—with so much, yet so little in common—would unite as families when Doc and Shirley married.

Shirley, the fifth of the Stangels' nine children, was nicknamed "Mickey" because she was born the same year Mickey Mouse was created. She was the center of Doc's life. She kept their home spotless and, at least once a week, baked batches of cinnamon rolls, filled cookies, or assorted pies. She ran her own restaurant in Crosby—Mickey's—"where she cooked everything to death, I mean really well done," Judy recalled. Mickey worked full time, helping support the family through the tough winter months when Doc was laid off from the mines.

"There was always a lot of love in our house," Judy said. "Dad always acted like a no-nonsense, gruff kind of guy, but he really was a warm, big-hearted guy who loved his wife and kids."

He knew how to get a message across. When Scott was in grade school, Doc told him, "If you ever steal, I'm going to slap the snot out of you." Scott never told him that when he was eight or nine, he stole a candy bar from the grocery store.

"I did see Dad lash out at Scott once in a while, but Mom, knowing his abuse history, would always put a stop to it before it could escalate," Judy said. "She would put her hands on her hips and say, 'Allen!' And Dad would always settle right down. It was like they had this unspoken agreement that Mom would loudly say, 'Allen,' to remind Dad he was about to repeat his abusive past."

On Saturday nights, Doc and Mickey would go dancing with Mickey's brothers and their wives, and sometimes with Frank and Georgia. Judy was the designated family babysitter and remembered hearing stories at the end of the night about one or more of the family members going to jail because of a brawl.

Others remember only Doc's gruff side. "Doc was a tough guy, a street brawler, the kind of guy Scott never was," said David Martodam, who moved to Crosby when he was in ninth grade and became another of Scott's lifelong friends. But Doc never could escape the always-ready-to-rumble demeanor of his father.

Edward LeDoux remarried after his first wife, Tillie, died from a heart attack in 1965. "We don't talk much about Grandpa's second marriage," Judy said.

After the couple separated, Edward LeDoux bludgeoned his wife to death with a hammer. Then he shot himself in the head.

3

"I THOUGHT I HAD DONE SOMETHING BAD"

*F*or nearly four decades, Scott LeDoux kept his darkest secret to himself. As a child, he never explained his nightmares to his parents or sisters, fearing they wouldn't understand. He cringed at the thought of exposing them to the shame and anguish that tortured him inside. Getting pounded by bone crushers like George Foreman and Ken Norton later in life was excruciating, but those scars eventually healed. Not this one.

Victims like young Scott LeDoux often wear their past like invisible bull's-eyes on their backs, but somehow the bullies always know. In LeDoux's case, they may have suspected that he had been harmed or hurt and sensed his vulnerability. They would get off the school bus and follow young Scott home, or to the old camouflage-green World War II tank parked along grassy Crosby Beach, or to the Crosby Theater, or to Jim's Lunch, the twenty-four-hour restaurant that most days closed at 8:00 p.m. They followed him to the playground, where LeDoux, by far the smallest kid in his class, was often the last player chosen. The bullies hid behind the A&W or the Snyder Drug store, just waiting to jump him.

"There was this neighborhood kid, he was older, who got off the school bus just to beat up Scott," recalled LeDoux's boyhood buddy David Martodam. "Everybody knew that Scott wouldn't back down. He had to be hurt really bad before ever saying, 'Uncle.'

"Years later, when he got into the ring, that determination made him somebody you could really root for, a real-life Rocky. But as a kid who just wanted to fit in, that determination made Scott a target for bullies. And him being so bullheaded probably didn't help."

Doc LeDoux used to tell his son, "You land a good punch and they'll leave you alone."

But they rarely left him alone. Look at every one of LeDoux's class pictures from grade school and two lessons repeat themselves year after year: "I was always the smallest kid in my class," LeDoux said, "and in every picture, I've either got cuts near my eyes or a scab on my nose."

He was the smallest kid because he was usually the youngest kid in his class. LeDoux was three when he entered kindergarten. It wasn't because this future master of the "sweet science" was considered a child prodigy by his parents. At best he was an average student, claiming he never earned an A until returning to college after his boxing career was over.

"I was freshman class president three straight years," he often told audiences after he retired from boxing and entered local politics in the suburban Twin Cities.

Doc and Mickey never intended to set Scott up to fail, said Scott's sister Judy. But Doc was working in the mines, and Mickey had jobs as a cook and waitress. Together, they operated their own delivery service, the LeDoux Dray Line, with Mickey driving trucks from the train station to businesses or people's homes.

"When my dad was at the mines, my mom ran the truck, delivering anything you would want," Judy recalled. "My mom was awesome. During a time when many women wouldn't think of working, my mom was doing a million things for our family." But she couldn't be in a million places at once. The only way both Mickey and Doc could work was to send young Scott to school as early as possible.

The life lessons that followed came hard and often.

As much as it may have driven his dad crazy, young Scott never threw the first punch. It wasn't his nature. Bob Dolan, the Minneapolis lawyer who met LeDoux two decades later and traveled the world to watch LeDoux box, admits he was startled when he was introduced to LeDoux. "He was this big guy involved in a vicious sport," Dolan said, "and he was the softest, most sensitive guy I've ever met."

Sometimes, the skirmishes with bullies ended without young Scott ever having to throw or take a punch—when his sister Judy was around. She was three years older and determined to protect her little brother. "I used to get in fights with bullies that were trying to hurt Scott, all the way home from school," she said. "We were seven blocks from the grade school and there was always somebody who wanted to pick on him because he was so little," Judy remembered. "I ended up stepping in and boxing their ears. It went on like that for a couple of years. It was kind of funny that when I was in junior high, I started dating some of the boys I beat up that bullied my brother."

"The neighborhood we lived in, it wasn't rough like northeast Minneapolis-rough," she said, referring to a blue-collar section of Minnesota's biggest city. "But our neighborhood had its gang elements. Yep, right in little old Crosby."

If this wasn't the Small Town America that another Minnesotan, Sinclair Lewis, described with his satirical classic *Main Street,* that is only because Crosby was even smaller. Only 2,600 people lived in the Crosby area in 1960, when LeDoux was eleven years old. Fast-forward a half century: with a mere 552 families as of the 2010 census, Crosby was half the size of Lewis's hometown, Sauk Centre.

People raised animals right in the heart of Crosby, Frank Perpich remembered. The houses weren't fancy. Yet parents who grew up in the mines, through the Great Depression and in temperatures so cold that exposed skin could turn gray with frostbite minutes after you ventured outdoors, still believed dreams were possible, even in tough, northern Minnesota.

But these weren't completely innocent times either, as a glance at the *Minneapolis Morning Tribune* on LeDoux's birthday, Friday, January 7, 1949, reveals. Aside from the obligatory January-in-the-land-of-the-tundra front-page weather story, there were articles concerning President Harry Truman's "firm" policy toward Russia and of a new experimental program wherein food stamps would be distributed to low-income families. Grabbing the greatest amount of space in the paper that day, however, in the form of several advertisements, was one of the original fast foods: "Minneapolis witnesses mealtime miracles as Minute Rice hits town," the ads proclaimed.

"It seemed so innocent back then," LeDoux said a good half century later. "Without television or the Internet, you could let your imagination run wild. I'd sit behind the wheel of my dad's tractor and pretend it was a machine gun and that I was in a tank and it was World War II. We had a wood stove, and my dad would cover the wood with a big tarp and I'd go out there and just pretend" that the stove was a rival tank or enemy headquarters.

There was an ever-present smell of the fresh-baked cookies that lined the LeDoux kitchen counters. Scott's mother may have been no better than an "efficient" cook to her son and two daughters. "The meat was always so crisp, always well done," Scott said. But Mickey's cookies couldn't be beat. At Christmas time, there were piles of them everywhere. "It wasn't unusual for my grandmother to line the kitchen counters with as many as forty pans of cinnamon rolls," Scott's son, Josh, recalled years later.

Her chocolate cake was even better. Scott would place a slice of cake in a cereal bowl, douse it with milk, and admire the soggy mess before devouring it, as if he had just discovered nirvana. It was a slice of LeDoux etiquette others learned to stomach. Years later, when Bob Dolan had LeDoux over to his home in Minneapolis for the first time, Dolan's wife, Jeannie, baked a chocolate cake. To the astonishment of the Dolans and their four children, LeDoux helped himself to half the cake, placed it in a mixing bowl, doused it with milk, and then inhaled the whole thing. "I'd never seen anything like it," Dolan said. But he would again—many times. LeDoux was a bit more discreet with the oversized chocolate sheet cake at his sixtieth birthday party in suburban Minneapolis, a gala affair. "I'll wait until everyone's gone and see what's left," he said with a wink.

Long before their son was inhaling chocolate cakes, everybody in Crosby knew Doc and Mickey. When Scott was born at Miners Hospital in Crosby, he weighed six pounds, two ounces, and word spread through the mines that he was a sickly kid. "A bleeder," Mickey called him. Scott was born with a form of hemophilia, a disorder in which the blood doesn't clot properly. Doc began bringing his son to Miners Hospital for shots to combat the disease when Scott was a baby. "Always two needles, the second one bigger than the first one," LeDoux recalled. "I was still seeing Dr. Marshall and those big needles, still getting the shots when I was five years old. I was so small that my father would carry me out of Miners Hospital on a pillow."

Boxing has seen its share of bleeders. Chuck Wepner, a brawler from New Jersey who suffered cuts above both eyes and a broken nose in a gutsy fifteen-round loss to Muhammad Ali, was known as the Bayonne Bleeder. After years of treatment, LeDoux stopped bleeding often and profusely. This was long before he climbed into the ring. Still, nobody could have predicted LeDoux would one day become a professional boxer.

"It was the last thing that I ever thought Scott would do," Mickey said years after her son turned pro. "He's kind of a softy. He can cry real easy. I couldn't imagine him going in there and inflicting punishment on anyone."

But there was the day, when he was five years old, that young Scott was too frightened to cry.

In a small community, you know all your neighbors and learn quickly whom you can trust. Years later, when the family lived in the area known as the Deerwood Shortcut, Scott often walked from the family farm into town, and somebody would invariably pick him up. "One week I might go to the Catholic church, and the next week it might be the Lutheran church," he said. "It depended on who gave me a ride." His parents, who rarely attended church, didn't mind.

Nevertheless, Doc warned his five-year-old son about a neighbor, a young man who may have been around twenty at the time. "My dad always told me to never go out in the woods," LeDoux said.

But he did one day, out of curiosity, wandering maybe a half mile from home. Someone was there, someone who knew who he was. It was the guy Doc warned him about.

"He said I wasn't going to go home unless I did what he asked," LeDoux said. "He molested me."

As he told the story some fifty-five years later, LeDoux slowly reached for a chair, looking like a fighter about to go down for a mandatory eight-count. In a husky whisper, he recounted the incident, declining to offer details. He said, simply, that there was more than fondling involved.

"Then he told people," LeDoux said of his assailant. "I'm sure he told people, because kids teased me."

Diane Resch, who went to high school and college with LeDoux, said years later that she was convinced that other kids had to know something had happened—whether they were told or not. With sexual abuse victims, even casual acquaintances can sense that something is wrong. "I'm sure that has a lot to do with Scott being picked on," she said.

When he reached adulthood, LeDoux gradually told friends of the day he was sexually assaulted in the woods.

"I always thought I had done something bad," he said. "And then, one day, I came to realize I've done nothing wrong.

"When a child gets molested, they have to live with it their whole life while the molester goes on to the next thing. There's no known cure once you've been molested. That's why I've been such an advocate for kids."

He waited until he was forty-three before telling his parents.

"I was outdoors when I told my dad," LeDoux said. "And I went home and I called my mom. I asked her, 'How are you doing with this?' She said, 'I'm doing good, but your dad isn't.'"

Doc, the veteran brawler, cried for three days, Mickey said, devastated by the notion that he had failed to protect his son.

4

WHEN LIGHTNING STRUCK

*A*s a teenager, Judy Wynn did something that George Foreman, Larry Holmes, Leon Spinks, Ken Norton, and even the great Muhammad Ali couldn't do. She knocked Scott LeDoux out cold. Not with a left hook or a right cross. She hit her brother over the head with a vacuum cleaner.

"I was the oldest and always got stuck doing the cleaning," she recalled. "It never failed. If Mom and Dad were going to run some errands, they'd say, 'Judy, you clean up and vacuum while we are gone.'"

Her brother created an obstacle course while she tried to clear the way with that old Electrolux vacuum. Scott threw cigarette butts and assorted trash on the floor, laughed in his sister's face, and then ran away.

"I got so mad I hit Scott on the head with the metal vacuum cleaner hose and knocked him out cold," Judy said.

Then there was the time Scott threw trash at Judy's feet, enraging his older sister. She chased him through the house—until Scott locked himself in the bathroom. Judy was so angry that she put her foot through the bathroom door. Doc and Mickey weren't happy when they arrived home and discovered the damage. Judy and Scott lost their allowances for months. "I'm sure we bought the equivalent of at least ten doors before our allowance was reinstated," Judy said.

An extraordinarily close-knit family—everybody in grade school learned quickly that Judy had her little brother's back—the LeDoux clan could be volatile one night and darn-right combustible the next. Individually, they personified Minnesota nice, say those who watched Judy, Scott, and their younger sister, Stormy, grow up, but together they could raise a Midwest hailstorm. When it came to compromises that didn't meet his approval, Doc's head was as hard as the ore he mined. His children could be as unforgiving as January in Minnesota.

"They all had an element of Doc's temper," said Chico Resch, who embraced the LeDoux family as if it were his own. "Scott had a tumultuous life, and some issues with his sisters," Resch said. "It wasn't like you could sit those kids down. There were some explosive times. Stormy, too, says what's on the top of her head. They couldn't curb their tongues when they got into heated issues. Scott has a temper and will say things that are hurtful. And the girls would do things to deliberately get Scott going."

Still, they had each other. At times, they may have felt like family was all they had. But it was plenty.

Mickey LeDoux used to tell her children that the first house they owned in Crosby was so small that she had to place Judy's crib on the kitchen counter to keep her from the rats. (Until her death, Mickey was terrified of rodents.) Then the family moved from northeast Crosby to a modest farmhouse on Olander Lake, near the passage known as the Deerwood Shortcut. Judy and Stormy shared a bedroom. There was no bedroom for Scott. For a while, he slept on a mattress in a hallway.

He graduated from the hallway to a walk-in closet—about eight feet wide and twelve feet long, large enough for a small table and cot. It was only after Doc built a downstairs living room and bedroom on the lake side of the house that Scott finally had a bedroom of his own. He was fourteen.

But that bedroom couldn't contain him any more than the bib overalls he was beginning to outgrow. The little boy, who used to leap from a window into snowdrifts solidly packed five or six feet deep, could dunk a basketball and pretended to be Wilt Chamberlain. Scott was suddenly growing as quickly as his imagination.

The LeDoux family paid a price as Scott hit new heights—a price that went far beyond the cost of new clothes that fit. Scott's growth spurts played havoc with his sleep patterns. He began sleepwalking—and the rest of the family stopped sleeping.

The bedrooms were on the second floor, turning the modest farmhouse into an obstacle course for a sleepwalker. Stormy recalled a night in which Scott, apparently fast asleep, was standing by the wooden railing at the top of the stairs. He evidently was dreaming that he was about to dive into the lake. While terrified family members screamed in an attempt to awaken Scott, Doc stood below, waiting to catch his son, anticipating his sudden fall or jump. Scott never leaped or stumbled, but the family remained on edge every evening from that point on. After each sleepwalking escapade, Scott would have absolutely no recollection the following morning of the commotion he had created the night before.

Waking hours were spent playing baseball in a pasture, daydreaming in the hayloft, milking cows, or, in winter, hanging on to a rear bumper while someone's car or truck veered across frozen streets. There were tick races to watch at the Woodtick Inn in Cuyuna and turtle races in quaint Nisswa. There were Saturday matinees at the Crosby Theater, summer afternoons at the grass-covered beach at Serpent Lake, and mischief year-round. Scott and Judy threw tomatoes at cars, with Scott sometimes hiding in the tree house Doc built. There was horseplay with Scott's best buddy, Jim Rocca, who once walloped Scott across the head with a stick, according to their friend David Martodam.

That was nothing, Rocca recalled. Once, while he and LeDoux were supposed to be installing fence posts at Rocca's grandfather's farm, Rocca chased LeDoux with a chainsaw, leaving Grandpa Vincenzo Rocca to mutter, "If Christopher Columbus hadn't discovered America, I wouldn't be in this mess."

Grandpa Rocca and anyone else victimized by LeDoux's unbridled spirit and curiosity were in the same boat. Against Stormy's protests, Scott once mounted her small Arabian horse, Keyo. Scott was simply too big for the horse. While trying to take a corner with Scott in tow, the poor animal tipped over and rolled into a cemetery fence.

"Thank God the horse was never hurt," Judy said.

When it came to mischief, the farm seemed the perfect playground for Scott. He placed Doc's prized saddle on a cow, tried to mount the poor animal, and after being bucked and thrown to the ground, watched the cow bound deliriously through the pasture. Back and forth, like a pinball machine gone haywire, the cow trampled through the field until the saddle—dragged, kicked, chewed, and flung—was completely destroyed.

"There were certain things of my dad's that you didn't touch without his permission," Judy said. "His saddle was one. And, of course, his cars and trucks."

Doc worshipped anything with an engine. After World War II ended, he was stationed in Hawaii, where, as a mechanic, he was assigned to recondition a fleet of Jeeps and trucks. "He got them in top shape," Scott said.

"Then they took them out in the ocean and dumped them. All of them. He said it was one of the most disturbing things he'd ever done. He couldn't believe it. He said, 'Why don't they ship 'em home and give 'em to people?'"

It was one thing for Scott to drive around in his brother-in-law Wayne Wynn's old car, with Wayne's permission, but nobody could possibly be foolish enough to mess with Doc's cars or trucks. Yet, one day, when school was canceled due to a huge blizzard, Scott decided to visit his friend Diane in the neighboring community of Emily. Many of the streets connecting these towns that straddled the Mississippi River were gravel roads, and even the occasional paved roads were primitive by today's standards. There was no direct route from point A to point B. Getting from one city to the next often involved driving around the dozens of small lakes in the immediate area.

Still, Scott loved visiting Diane, and her parents loved having him over. Her mother once baked him a birthday cake. He ate half of it—all at once. "Then he stood on the table, started jumping up and down, and said, 'I'm packing it in, so I can have some more,'" remembered Diane.

The teenagers never drank, didn't do drugs, never got into trouble. They played the card game "500," watched *Shock Theater* on TV, and talked about the big world outside of Crow Wing County, a world in which eagles didn't soar above the fir and pine trees and loons didn't dance mystically on the surfaces of lakes. Their relationship was strictly platonic.

Scott, who worked on the small family farm before and after school, said he rarely dated in high school. "It was the fragrance of the gods," LeDoux explained years later. "After spending hours with the cows, no girl would get near me."

But Diane was his buddy, and on this snowy day, he was determined to get to Emily. He tiptoed out of the house, started Doc's '53 Buick—and skidded down off the road and into the lake.

"Where are you going? Look at this weather, Scott," Doc said, his tone frostier than fallen snow.

Hooking one end of a large chain to his tractor and the other end to the car's bumper, Doc pulled the vehicle, easing it out of the lake. But the second Doc unhooked the chain from the Buick, Scott pushed the accelerator to the floor and took off. As snow flew from the back tires, Scott looked through his rearview mirror to see Doc wearing a new coating of white as he stood waving his arms in anger and disbelief.

When Scott finally arrived at Diane's, she asked him what it was like driving through the blinding squalls on treacherous roads. "He told me he was more worried about facing Doc when he got home," she said.

Scott was grounded—again—after a few choice words from Doc, but virtually nothing could diminish the teen's spirit.

Maybe it was surviving a lightning strike to the house while he was in the bathtub. Maybe it was the growth spurt in which he shot up to six feet almost overnight. Maybe it was the confidence he was gaining at the playgrounds, where he no longer was the last player chosen—far from it. It wasn't that Scott had become more daring. He was always slightly goofy, Rocca said years later. But now, the kid who described his childhood as "near perfect, I had so much fun," was actually learning how to enjoy himself.

There were still fights. There was still an aura about Scott, a mysterious cloud that seemed to invite goading and teasing, regardless of his growing physical stature. During one of his visits to Emily, he confided in Diane, telling her he had been molested years before. None of the other kids knew, but they sensed that they could push his buttons.

And they did.

"All through school he was picked on or tested," Rocca said, somewhat bemused. "He was a little gullible. In gym class they'd razz him. They knew Scott had a temper. And Scott wanted to fight. Even if he knew he couldn't win, he wanted to fight. He wouldn't back down."

A kid challenged Scott in high school. Scott swung at him and punched poor Martodam, standing nearby, when the kid ducked.

"Some of my favorite memories with Scott came when we were duck hunting," Martodam said. "One day, we're chasing ducks with shotguns with that goofy spaniel of his. The dog was a pretty good retriever, but that day, the dog decided it wasn't getting wet. So there would be Scott—retrieving. He'd wade into the water fully clothed, retrieve the ducks, and come back soaking wet."

On another occasion, LeDoux stripped naked—presumably because the spaniel again had gone on strike. He began firing shotgun blasts toward the sky and, as luck would have it, connected with his prey. The duck dropped from the clouds—and landed on LeDoux's pile of clothes, making a mess that might have frustrated or embarrassed someone else. Scott shrugged it off, put on the soiled clothing, and smiled.

Nothing seemed to bother him anymore. If children and health are the great equalizers for adults, sports offered a kid once tormented by peers the chance to be somebody special. A first baseman and pitcher, Scott had become a baseball star and an American Legion tournament Most Valuable Player. He starred for the Crosby-Ironton baseball team and played on the varsity basketball team, too. He wasn't quite a star there. While most of the Crosby-Ironton fans chanted, "Go, CI, go," LeDoux had his own cheering section at basketball games. "Two for Le-Doux," they would chant. Yet they weren't necessarily referring to points scored. "Someone would bring donuts for the players after games or practices," Resch said. "Scott would grab two. Two for LeDoux."

But it was on the football field that opponents learned to take LeDoux seriously. He had done little to distinguish himself as a junior high school player, and during his sophomore season at Crosby-Ironton High School, "he wasn't noticeable," coach John Davies recalled decades later.

By his junior year, at nearly six foot one, you couldn't miss him. LeDoux had become a presence on the field. By his senior season, LeDoux "was a grownup boy," said Davies, who was so startled by LeDoux's physical development that he asked the youngster, presumably in jest, "Who are you?"

The summer before his senior year in high school, LeDoux worked in the rice paddies near Aitkin, driving a big tractor with a rototiller attached to the back. He also gained nearly thirty pounds.

It was more than the growth spurt, or the added muscle nurtured daily through long hours of work on the farm. The easygoing LeDoux became a terror the second he stepped onto the field.

He was Davies's first all-state player, a lineman who played on both sides of the ball. An extremely coachable kid who loved to work hard and was excited to play, LeDoux "didn't appear mean and tough" at first glance, Davies said. But in a conference game against Staples, LeDoux hit an opponent so hard with a forearm that a referee stopped the game and told LeDoux to remove his forearm pad. The referee assumed that without the protective padding, LeDoux would be less likely to use his forearm like a club. A few plays after removing the pad, however, LeDoux leveled a Staples lineman with a forearm shiver.

"After that," recalled Davies, "we tore them up."

Football was LeDoux's release valve, a way to channel any rage brought on through frustration. Mostly, though, it was just plain fun. For LeDoux, there was always a game within the game. He and Rocca played side by side on the line. LeDoux played guard, Rocca was a tackle. At 170 pounds and change, neither was a very big lineman, so they always sought an edge. LeDoux would tell the player opposite him, "I'm gonna run right over you." But once the ball was snapped, LeDoux would charge the player across from Rocca, and Rocca would go after the player opposite LeDoux.

"Other players are dragging from exhaustion or injuries, and we're laughing the entire way back to the huddle," Rocca said. "Other than when my grandpa let us use his 1953 Chevy truck, I can't imagine Scott and I having so much fun."

Martodam suggested that the boyhood moments LeDoux cherished most, however, were much quieter—in his kitchen with Mickey. "Saturday mornings were spent in the LeDoux kitchen with a bowl of cereal listening to Scott talk to his mom," Martodam said. "I think Scott was closer to his mom than to his dad. There was a tension in his relationship with Doc. Remember, Doc was a street brawler—and that just wasn't in Scott's makeup."

While Saturday mornings were reserved for Mickey, Friday nights were bonding moments for a father and son who could sit in front of the tiny black-and-white TV together and watch the *Gillette Friday Night Fights*. The ESPN generation that remembers LeDoux as a twice-weekly commentator for the sports network's boxing presentations may never comprehend the popularity and influence of the fights broadcast by NBC in the 1950s. Through grainy telecasts, often blurred by shadows and vertical-hold controls that sometimes needed the aid of a good slap to the side of the cabinet filled with all those odd little tubes, Madison Square Garden could be brought into homes as remote from the big time as those in Crosby, Minnesota. Rocky Marciano, Sugar Ray Robinson, Willie Pep, Rocky Graziano, Carmen Basilio, and the great Archie Moore—a man LeDoux would one day meet and treasure the memory the rest of his life— they were right in the LeDoux living room. They tore opponents apart. They allowed a father and son, who weren't always great at expressing how they adored one another, to bond once a week in front of the TV set.

The fight LeDoux remembers most from his childhood is one that may have changed the face of sports—all sports—more than any event other than the major-league debut of Jackie Robinson with the Brooklyn Dodgers in 1947. February 25, 1964. Cassius Clay versus Sonny Liston. The rising star of the 1960 Olympics, the undefeated Louisville Loudmouth who could float like a butterfly and sting like a bee versus the intimidating knockout artist, a champion with ties to organized crime who was so intimidating that British heavyweight Henry Cooper's manager said of Liston: "We don't even want to meet Liston walking down the same street."

Fifteen-year-old Scotty LeDoux couldn't wait to invite them into his home. The snow outside was at least five feet deep, and Doc and Mickey weren't home that night. LeDoux crawled onto a kitchen chair and worked the Philco radio until he found the fight. The broadcast wasn't live. In those days, fight fans listening to the radio still had to settle for round-by-round recaps. They could only imagine the lightning jabs the twenty-two-year-old Clay threw at Liston. When Clay entered the fifth round, blinded by a chemical solution that poured from his brow into both eyes with sweat, LeDoux, too, was in the dark, not quite sure what was happening. When Liston failed to answer the bell in the seventh round, the boxing world had been knocked for a loop. The Greatest was anointed. An era had begun.

LeDoux was hooked. Clay, the underdog, had done what underdogs like LeDoux dream about. And Clay did it his way.

"This was my first real boxing interest," LeDoux said. "From then on, watching the Friday night fights with my dad became something so cool."

Thirteen years later, LeDoux lived a dream when he stepped into the ring with the great Muhammad Ali.

"I crawled through the ropes, and who's looking back at me?" LeDoux recalled with a childlike glee. "For a kid from Crosby, Minnesota, it's just impossible to believe."

5

THE LAST PLACE ON EARTH

*I*t had been forty-three years, for goodness sake, Vern Emerson said, when reminded of a story that Scott LeDoux loved to tell. So, once and for all, for the record, Emerson said he couldn't remember lifting LeDoux over his shoulder and threatening to throw him through a big picture window.

"I may have dangled a rookie out of a second- or third-floor window, holding him by the ankles, when I was with the St. Louis Cardinals, as part of a hazing," said Emerson, who was listed at six feet five and 260 pounds during his three years of playing tackle in the National Football League. "I don't remember doing anything like that to Scotty... although I suppose it's possible."

According to LeDoux, Emerson, then a star senior on the University of Minnesota Duluth football team, had reached his limit with stories about LeDoux, the freshman who had been an all-state selection from Crosby-Ironton the year before as a high school senior. Emerson played his high school ball in nearby Isle, Minnesota, on the southeast shore of beautiful Mille Lacs Lake. The city has claimed to be the walleye capital of the world but is not known as a football power. Emerson, easily the best player UMD had in 1966, never made the all-state team in high school.

"He hated me because I made all-state," LeDoux said. "I played across from Vern in practice, and he just beat the crap out of me every single day."

Yet LeDoux often spoke of Emerson with great reverence, never with malice, and the admiration Emerson had for LeDoux was mutual. The two worked together with two other members of the UMD football team as night clerks, rotating shifts from 10:00 p.m. to 8:00 a.m. at the Viking

Motel near campus. The players lived together. They socialized with one another. The linemen watched each other's backs as they battled the Bulldogs' opponents in the trenches each Saturday. During practices, Emerson, arguably the greatest player ever at UMD (and that includes the 2008 and 2010 NCAA Division II national championship teams), knocked the stuffing out of LeDoux, who gave away forty to sixty pounds to a lineman who was as crafty as he was overpowering.

According to LeDoux, one evening at a party, LeDoux said the wrong thing at the wrong time to Emerson. (Decades later, LeDoux couldn't remember his choice of words, and Emerson couldn't recall the incident.) Emerson, who LeDoux insisted was really six feet seven and 270 pounds or more, lifted the 200-pound LeDoux as if he were an oversized stuffed toy Emerson had just won at the Minnesota State Fair.

"When Vern lifted me up, I saw my whole life pass before me," LeDoux claimed years later. "My whole world was moving in slow motion. I was stunned. If you can imagine what it's like getting hit by George Foreman in his prime—and I know what that's like—the shock of Vern lifting me was a lot like that."

For a kid who had been bullied for years—since the time he was molested—being hoisted into the air against his will was traumatic, LeDoux said. Whether Emerson was simply having fun with his younger teammate before coming to his senses and putting LeDoux down without harm, or whether the incident really did happen was fodder for debate in bars on either side of the harbor bridges that link Duluth and Superior, Wisconsin. But LeDoux's fears were real.

What is really shocking is that LeDoux was in Duluth and on a university campus at all. Nobody from the LeDoux family had ever attended college, but Doc sure in hell wasn't going to let his only son follow him into the mines. "You will never work there," he told Scott when he was sixteen. When the teenager asked why, his father replied tersely, "You might like it. And I don't want you to like it."

Still, college wasn't a given for LeDoux, regardless of scholarship offers. "I wasn't thinking about college till I was a senior, and it obviously showed in my grades," he said. "I just didn't care. I loved football, basketball, and baseball, and that's the only reason I went to school.

"My parents never said anything about college. They never paid too much attention to my schooling . . . as long as I passed.

"Then I took a class in algebra and a few other classes and got good grades. I raised my grade point average and went from a C-minus student to a B student because I made some effort. I wanted to go to college."

Making all-state didn't hurt his prospects. LeDoux claimed years later that twenty-six schools, including Dartmouth, offered him scholarships. LeDoux's improved grades in algebra aside, Davies questioned his first-ever all-state player's math. He recalled talking to coaches from several area schools, among them St. Cloud State and Bemidji State. Rocca remembered hearing from North Dakota State and assumed that his buddy LeDoux was recruited by that school as well. The University of Minnesota also courted LeDoux, "but I didn't want to be a little fish in a big pond," he said.

Davies thought UMD would be the perfect fit for LeDoux. UMD's coach, Jim Malosky, was a Crosby native, a no-nonsense disciplinarian much like Davies and something of a Minnesota football legend. Malosky was the starting quarterback on some great post–World War II University of Minnesota teams, when the Golden Gophers were truly golden. His teammates included wide receiver Bud Grant, later enshrined in the Pro Football Hall of Fame after coaching the Minnesota Vikings to four Super Bowls; Hall of Fame defensive tackle Leo Nomellini, the first-ever draft pick of the San Francisco 49ers and a two-time NFL Pro Bowl player as an offensive player and a four-time Pro Bowl pick on defense; halfback Billy Bye, the Gophers' Most Valuable Player and considered among the most versatile athletes in Minnesota high school history; and Verne Gagne, an All–Big Ten Conference football player who became better known as professional wrestling's world champion and the inventor of the stomach-claw hold.

"Billy Bye came to a few of our practices," LeDoux said. "You talk about hard-nosed. He quit grade school because they had a recess."

Six players on the 1949 Gophers team were first-round National Football League draft picks, but Malosky was their leader. He was an even better football coach. In forty years at UMD, Malosky won more games than any coach in NCAA Division II history, compiling a record of 255–125–13, a .665 winning percentage. His teams finished .500 or better in thirty-three seasons. Twenty of his players were named to All-America teams, and five played in the NFL. UMD's home field was renamed James S. Malosky Stadium in 2004.

Malosky retired in 1997, due to health issues. In 2009, the year he was honored with the Distinguished Minnesotan Award by the Minnesota Chapter of the National Football Foundation and the College Football Hall of Fame, he was eighty years old and in an assisted-living residence. A stroke had robbed him of his mobility. He spoke in a soft rasp. But his memory remained strong, his words delivered with confidence, grace, and power.

"Of course, I remember Scott LeDoux," he said one afternoon while lying in bed. "He was 196 pounds when he came to UMD, not very big for a lineman. But he was a strong kid and very determined. And he was from my hometown. The Crosby-Ironton High School coach, John Davies, loved him, and that was good enough for me, even if he was a little small for the line.

"I wanted to see how Scott would do against Vern Emerson in practice. Nobody could handle Vern, including Scott. But the kid survived. Thirty-four freshmen came out for football that year, and by the time we played our first game, only ten were still around. Three were from Crosby, including LeDoux. I had better football players, but I don't know of anyone who was tougher than Scott LeDoux."

You had to be tough if you were going to make it in Duluth, the gateway to the Lake Superior North Shore that some Minnesotans liken to a frozen San Francisco because of Duluth's drastically steep inner-city hills. For decades, there was a tobacco shop on Superior Street in downtown Duluth called "The Last Place on Earth." For the fainthearted who visit the city for the first time in January, Duluth is likely the last place on earth they would want to be.

The host city to the annual John Beargrease Sled Dog Marathon oozes charm and can take your frosted breath away. The UMD campus is lovely—even LeDoux's dorm, old Torrance Hall, peeling paint on the walls and all. The Duluth shoreline is absolutely heart stopping. No matter how many times you have driven north on Interstate 35 from the Twin Cities, or east along Highway 2, when you reach the hill that overlooks Duluth's harbor, that first glimpse of Lake Superior is simply mesmerizing. Like a freshwater ocean, Superior sparkles like a gigantic jewel that appears from seemingly out of nowhere, assuring midwestern travelers that they are not in Des Moines or Omaha. Mounds of taconite, recently hauled in from the mines, border the lake's edge. Downtown's Canal Park is loaded with trendy shops, restaurants, hotels, passing ships, and legends of the greatest of Great Lakes. The sound of its bellowing foghorn aside, this has never been your typical blue-collar Great Lakes port. By the end of the nineteenth century, Duluth was home to more millionaires per capita than any other city on the planet. Word of Minnesota's modest gem had spread—probably by sled dog.

But the sinister side of Highway 61, immortalized in song by Duluth native Bob Dylan, runs along Minnesota's North Shore and right through this city of eighty-five thousand or so. For sailors navigating the two thousand miles from the Atlantic Ocean to the Twin Ports harbor via the St. Lawrence Seaway, Duluth is the end of the line.

"I heard all the stories when the Seaway opened [in 1959]," Arvid Morken, president of Central Dispatch, Inc., which serves the Upper Great Lakes Pilots Association in Duluth, said in 1987. "People would see those ships coming into Duluth and Superior and say, 'Lord protect us and Lord save our daughters.'"

If downtown Duluth is the heart of the Twin Ports, then a five-block stretch of Tower Avenue in Superior is its liver. There's no doubt when you've crossed the state line. You can smell it in the tavern floorboards that have been drenched in beer night after night for decades. Bars are more than just cultural experiences in Wisconsin. Beer is the state's lifeblood, from Milwaukee to Green Bay, from Madison to Superior. For a couple decades, including LeDoux's tenure at UMD, if you were looking for something to drink in Superior, all you had to do was follow the neon signs and the three patrolling squad cars. There was the Dugout Lounge, Elbow Room, Franklin's Tavern, the bar at the Androy Hotel, Locker Room, Shorty's Bar, Who's Bar, and Palace Bar—right next to the Palace Jesus Loves You Theater. Also found in this brief stretch of Tower Avenue were the VFW, Yellow Sub, Labor Temple, Union Junction Food & Pub, Carnigan's Bar, Cove Cabaret, Brass Rail, Terry's Lounge, Lamplighter, Casablanca, Tower Bar, Tip Top Lounge, Anchor Bar, Betty Boop Saloon, Molly's, Classic Bar, Capri Lounge, and LaBelle. For nondrinkers, there was the Massage Parlor.

"Superior had one tough joint after another," LeDoux recalled. "There was a bar there, Tommy Byrnes's Bar, that had a lot of fights. When I was ranked seventh in the world, I was ranked twenty-fifth in Tommy Byrnes's Bar."

There were days during his freshman year, though, when the odds of surviving in the toughest beer joints seemed better than making it in the classroom. "That first quarter, I worked my butt off, thinking I'd be on the honor roll—and I wasn't," LeDoux recalled. "I had a 2.2 grade point average. I was working all the time, trying to study, and it kept getting harder and harder."

As if football practices and classes weren't enough, LeDoux worked three jobs—a clerical job through UMD's work-study program, the clerk's job at the Viking Motel, and a weekend job storing freight at an electrical warehouse. Few detected the pressure the young freshman was under, probably because he was somewhat stressed before arriving at UMD. Already nervous about leaving Crosby for college, LeDoux received this farewell message from his mother: "When you come back, you're a guest here."

LeDoux might as well have been pounded aside the head by future sparring partner Mike Tyson. The young freshman was shell-shocked, convinced that "I can't come back and stay anymore."

"Gosh, I couldn't believe it," he recalled. "I hardly came home at all. Christmas and summer. It wasn't my house anymore. My bedroom had changed. I'd waited so many years to have a bedroom, and now it was gone, taken from me. I felt like I had no place to stay. I was scared."

His inauguration to the world of college football wasn't much easier. Emerson remembered LeDoux as "a tough kid, willing to pay the price." Sometimes, the battles began before he left the locker room.

Glenn Resch, a UMD hockey player from Moose Jaw, Saskatchewan, met LeDoux when the two were freshmen. Crosby-Ironton had no high school hockey team, and when LeDoux saw his first game at UMD, a perennial national power, he was captivated by the sport's power, speed, and grace.

Resch and LeDoux, two fresh-faced kids from the heartland, clicked almost immediately. "You just didn't forget Scott," Resch said. "He challenged situations, but he also challenged himself. Scott could get explosive. He had these extremes. If someone cut him off, he might chase him and ask, 'Tell me why you did that. Why did your brain go there?' What got him in trouble also pushed him to great heights.

"But Scott was also the kindest person you could ever meet. Maybe too kind. And maybe too easy a target because of it.

"When he was a freshman, they taped him into a locker. They were bullying him. The guys on the team just taped him up. Now, I know what that's like. And I know there are different ways you can react. When I was in New Haven [playing for the minor league New Haven Nighthawks], they were gonna initiate Bobby Nystrom. He's standing in the corner with two skates in his hands. He said, 'Come on. Come and get me. But I'm gonna cut somebody.'

"But Scott, when they came after him, he took it. With Nystrom, it was different. With Scott, as big and strong as he was, the other guys knew he could be bullied.

"How much longer was he going to put up with it?"

6

"I'VE HAD ENOUGH"

*I*t had to be a misprint. When posters trumpeting a Golden Gloves tournament featuring Scott LeDoux began circulating around the UMD campus, classmates smirked, shook their heads, or checked their calendars to see if April Fools' Day had come early. A skeptic from Le-Doux's dorm decorated LeDoux's picture with a simple message, one undoubtedly shared by others: "This," the doubter scribbled over LeDoux's mug, "is a joke."

LeDoux, fighting for his academic life and, as an undersized, 220-pound lineman, battling for survival with each snap of the ball during every UMD football game, was ready to explode. "If you think it's a joke," he wrote on the defamed poster, "come to Room 212."

"When he started boxing, it kind of surprised me," said Diane Resch, his high school buddy, who followed LeDoux to UMD and later married his good friend Chico Resch. "He did have some kind of inferiority complex," Diane said. "I think, with the Golden Gloves, he'd found a turning point. I think he finally thought, 'I've had enough.'"

Jim DeJarlais, a six-foot-five UMD basketball player, was going through some growing pains of his own. DeJarlais didn't know LeDoux, but like few others on campus, DeJarlais understood LeDoux's urgent need to shed his emotional shackles, explode through a few walls, try something new, and become reacquainted with the dignity that others tried to bury.

After two somewhat indifferent varsity seasons, DeJarlais left the UMD basketball team before his senior year. Nobody ever mistook him for George Mikan, anyway, and if his friends and kin on the Iron Range were clamoring for a hoops hero, they would have one a decade later in

Hibbing's Kevin McHale. For DeJarlais, a lanky kid from rugged Keewatin, when it came to choosing between basketball and becoming a dorm counselor, the new job seemed like a slam dunk.

He still went to the gym, but instead of hook shots, DeJarlais was throwing right hooks. He had met another aspiring young boxer, a future UMD student named Craig Gallop, whose dad was once the state welterweight champion.

"I was going on my senior year in high school and started working out in the gym in August—and with some pretty good company," Gallop recalled. "Jim DeJarlais, with all that height, really had the prospect of being a good heavyweight. And then, in late October, this big heavyweight comes in."

It was LeDoux's freshman year, and the football season wasn't quite over, but the big kid from Crosby was already looking for ways to stay in shape during the off-season.

"You could see right away that he'd never been in the ring before," Gallop said. "Scott was raw. But my dad saw something right away. My dad told me, 'If this guy could ever shorten his punches, he could be a heck of a fighter.'"

DeJarlais, three years LeDoux's senior, would be the first to test the young prospect. They boxed three or four times, with DeJarlais throwing jabs and then backing away as quickly as possible. "That was my strategy, to stay away from him," said DeJarlais. "Three or four times in the ring with him was enough. I probably quit at the right time."

For Sammy Gallop, LeDoux represented yet another new beginning. Raised in Duluth, Gallop became a professional fighter in the 1930s. He left the ring for the jungles of New Guinea, where he was stationed for three and a half years during World War II. He and his wife, Pearl, would own the Kasbar Restaurant & Night Club in Duluth. But Sammy's heart was in the ring, and, for a while, so was Pearl's.

The fight game had seen better days in Duluth, however, and by the early 1960s boxing barely existed on the North Shore. Then Bobby Daniels and a few others started an amateur boxing program in 1966. Gallop, who would become the greatest fight promoter ever in Duluth, was about to take on the challenge of his life.

A no-nonsense competitor in the ring, Gallop didn't allow his fighters to sit between rounds. "If you're too tired to stand there and talk, you probably shouldn't be fighting," he would tell young fighters, jabbing them with nuggets of boxing wisdom at every bell.

When he watched DeJarlais and LeDoux, he knew he was witnessing a kid who had never sparred before. But Malosky had marveled at LeDoux's quick feet and toughness on the football field, and Gallop saw it, too.

"It takes a lot of nerve, a lot of guts to walk up those steps, duck through those ropes," said Denny Nelson, a referee who would work several of Le-Doux's professional fights and sixty championship fights in all. Nelson also refereed some of LeDoux's amateur fights. This was "one rough kid," Nelson said to himself, the first time he worked a LeDoux fight. But what really struck Nelson was LeDoux's desire to fight. "He never backed down from anybody," Nelson said. "His big thing was he just wore people down because they couldn't hurt him.

"Just about everybody is a nervous wreck before they make it into the ring. George Foreman, when he fought [Joe] Frazier, said that when he got in the ring, his knees were knocking.

"Scott came to fight. He took a lot of punches in the beginning. A lot of fighters complain. He never complained."

The ring became a safe haven, the one place LeDoux could escape life's sucker punches. The memory of being molested more than a de-cade before still kept him awake some nights. His mother's going-away speech—about being a guest when he returned home—also ate at him. He was only sixteen years old his freshman year: physically, he looked like a man, but he often showed the maturity of a high school junior.

His 2.2 grade point average his first quarter did little to settle his nerves. There were no family members he could ask about college life, because he was the first to experience it. He wanted to confide in his older sister, Judy, but she had married at fifteen and was living her own life.

So he pushed his way through the ropes and into a new world. His emotional baggage vanished in the ring. He was focused once the gloves went on, seldom overreacting in the ring. His fears disappeared, his tem-per was under control. Nobody enjoys being hit, Craig Gallop said, but LeDoux didn't seem to care. He treasured his time in the ring with DeJar-lais, whom he always credited for launching his career.

"I loved it the minute I started sparring with Jim," LeDoux told re-porters a year later. It was a way to stay in shape when football season ended, and "it gives me something to do in winter," he said, perhaps overlooking his studies and part-time jobs. "I'd like to keep on fighting for a while," he told the media. "Not professionally, just amateur."

He sparred with Glenn Diver, a middle-to-light heavyweight, who dazzled LeDoux with his speed and skill. "I learned so much being in the ring with Glenn," LeDoux said. "Mostly, I learned that he couldn't hurt me."

He also learned that he couldn't hide anymore. As a lineman on the football team, he was another tree in the forest, occasionally standing out, but often just blending with the others. But in the ring, he was alone, completely vulnerable with nowhere to hide.

And he loved it.

"In the ring, there's no team effort, and if you lose, it's all your fault," LeDoux told curious Duluth reporters. "You get a lot of personal satisfaction knowing you've done something yourself."

He was a raw talent with size—six feet one and a half inches and 220 pounds—and plenty of heart but with little polish. His Golden Gloves bout his sophomore year against Jim Herrin in Brainerd was typical of LeDoux's earliest escapades. Herrin decked LeDoux with a right to the jaw in the first round. But LeDoux came back in the third round, knocking down Herrin to earn a split decision.

The kid who never sat down between rounds was becoming a knockout with the fight crowd.

"I find that I can breathe a lot easier if I stand up," he told reporters, never mentioning that Sammy Gallop wouldn't have it any other way. "When I'm all hunched over a stool, I can't catch my breath.

"When I fought Herrin, a lot of my friends were laughing because they said my standing up bothered Herrin. I guess it might psych another guy at that, especially when he's over in that other corner trying to get ready for the next round."

Outside the ring, LeDoux's struggles in the classroom were becoming as predictable as A-B-C. A fire in his dorm further disrupted his life, forcing him to search for temporary housing. He moved in with the Gallops for four months. Craig, then a freshman, became a lifelong friend, the brother LeDoux never had. Pearl introduced him to Jewish cooking—and what was not to like? Sammy became a living boxing lesson, extolling the virtues of living the right way in and out of the ring. He didn't have to pound his boxing wisdom into LeDoux. The young fighter craved it.

"Sammy, can I get punchy doing this?" LeDoux asked Gallop.

"Probably not," Gallop responded, "but you won't get any smarter."

LeDoux won eight of his first nine amateur bouts. Yet by his second year in the ring, he was still something of an unknown, even in northern Minnesota. At the February 10, 1968, Northern Regional Golden Gloves tournament at the Wadena National Guard Armory, he was listed in the program as "Scott LeDeau."

Then he fought ten days later at the Minneapolis Auditorium, and everything changed. Boxing fans in the Twin Cities were absolutely knocked out by the charismatic newcomer.

"Scott LeDoux is a big, handsome youngster with curly blonde hair," wrote Lew Ferguson of the Associated Press. "On the street, he might be mistaken for a young actor imported by Hollywood for some of those muscle beach movies.

"A big smile spread across LeDoux's face under his bloody nose Monday night after he hacked his way to a unanimous decision over veteran Tom Runnels of Minneapolis to win the Upper Midwest Golden Gloves heavyweight championship in Minneapolis Auditorium," Ferguson wrote. "It wasn't a very artistic performance, but the crowd of 3,876 who paid $11,573 didn't mind. They cheered the wild swinging match from start to finish. And LeDoux's victory was a popular decision."

The love affair spread from the banks of the Mississippi in the Twin Cities to the North Shore, where columnist Dick Gerzic of the *Duluth News Tribune* wrote: "Just looking at LeDoux makes you want to like him. He's big [200 pounds] and rugged, has that Hollywood muscleman look and a personality which portrays a well-versed, considerate young man.

"Out of the ring, he's quiet and well mannered. Inside, he has the heart of a lion and a mind to destroy his opponent. . . . He's awkward and in [Sammy] Gallop's own words, he needs a lot of work. . . . The finished product will be something to see."

For all his guts, determination, and strength, LeDoux's greatest asset may have been fear. "I've never liked being hit," LeDoux would say years later. "I think I'm quicker in the ring for fear of being hit."

There were awkward moments, like the time LeDoux slipped when his opponent stepped on his foot. But later in that fight, Gallop recalled, "when the other guy went down, Scott really tagged him . . . about three times."

"We're not going to throw him in over his head," Gallop said. "When we get him in real good shape, we'll look ahead to national tournaments. If he looks good next season, we'll let him go all the way. Until then, he's going to learn more about boxing.

"Who knows? Maybe by summer, he'll be ready for bigger game."

7

SANDY

*W*ho could have predicted it? On the night that a date stood him up, Scott LeDoux may have discovered the love of his life.

LeDoux knew Sandy Tigue, who was a year ahead of him at UMD, only because he was dating her roommate, Pam Terwilliger. Sandy was pretty much off limits, anyway. She was engaged at the time, LeDoux said, but he couldn't help but notice her. Blonde hair. Brown eyes. "Snappy eyes," Diane Resch, Sandy's UMD dorm neighbor, liked to call them. "The kind of eyes that told you, 'This is going to be fun.'"

Not that Scott and Sandy had much in common. The little girl from northeast Minneapolis was "much stronger than my brother could ever have dreamed of being," Judy Wynn said. "And Scott would be the first person to tell you that."

Sandy's Norwegian mother, Thelma, was raised in Thief River Falls, in the state's northwestern corner, nearly in Manitoba, and about as far from the Twin Cities as you can get and still be in Minnesota. The nearest big city was Winnipeg, but Thelma moved to northeast Minneapolis, where the residents in the ethnic, blue-collar neighborhoods must have seemed every bit as tough as the folks of northwestern Minnesota. Folks in Thief River Falls would go ice fishing and ride their snowmobiles year-round if winter would only last longer than six months in this bone-chilling terrain where the ground seemed harder than survival itself.

Thelma met Ray Tigue, who drove trucks for Century Motors Freight, sometimes to destinations as far away as Alaska. When it came to being one tough customer, LeDoux said he had nothing on Ray. But long before LeDoux forged a loving relationship with his future father-in-law, he had to become comfortable with Ray's daughter—and vice versa.

"I'd go over [to see Terwilliger] and Pam would always be late," Le-Doux recalled. "Sometimes she wouldn't be there and I'd have to wait. So one time, Sandy answered the phone and I said, 'Is she there?' When she said, 'No,' I asked her if she was doing anything tonight. And she said, 'Nothing.' I told her to come on down here and we'll go to a movie."

Sandy reminded LeDoux that she was engaged, not to try anything funny, and, above all, don't get serious with her. "We'll just be friends," she told him. They went out to a hamburger place on Woodland Avenue in Duluth. They talked, laughed a lot, and talked some more. LeDoux fell in love with her that night.

They remained friends until one summer night, she called LeDoux. She had just been on a date with her fiancé, who had returned from Vietnam. "I'm Avis, I'm No. 2," LeDoux said, half-jokingly referring to the car-rental company's popular advertising campaign of the time.

"You're No. 1," she told him.

"She recognized that she liked me more than him," LeDoux said of the fiancé, whom he enjoyed meeting years later. "Things happen for a reason."

Sandy rarely waited for things to happen. Spontaneous and spunky, "she did things just because she wanted to do them," Resch said.

Her favorite song was "What a Wonderful World," Wynn recalled. She didn't have to sing that old song to breathe life into it.

"When you met her, you liked her," Resch said. "She'd look outside at Duluth and call it tundra. But when spring came to Duluth, it might be only sixty degrees, but she'd tell you to put on your bathing suit."

She could turn the simple into the sublime. She loved to hop in the car, get some smoked fish, sit on the rocks, and gaze at Lake Superior. She would go to quaint Two Harbors, immediately north of Duluth, and hit the antique stores, one time returning with a tea kettle, another time a funny hat.

Her favorite day was St. Patrick's Day, which never made sense to Resch because Sandy wasn't much of a drinker. They would go from bar to bar, ordering Tom and Jerrys. Later in life, she would make her kids green eggs and ham.

Dick Young, the legendary New York Daily News sports columnist, devoted an entire column to her in 1980, just before LeDoux's title fight with Larry Holmes. The column began: "I'm not going to make a pick in the Holmes–LeDoux fight because I've lost all objectivity. I have fallen in love with Scott LeDoux's wife. I want her to be the wife of the heavy-weight champion, just once, just for a little while. . . . Sandy LeDoux deserves something wonderful to happen to her."

Craig Gallop, who first met Sandy when they were students at UMD, described her as full of life, yet soft spoken. She knew how to make her point, and LeDoux usually listened to her. She disliked LeDoux boxing, but understood that that's what he wanted, Gallop said.

She tried to be the voice of reason for the couple—often in vain. When LeDoux was offered his first professional boxing contract, Sandy told him not to pursue a career in the ring. When LeDoux signed the contract, he said his wife "told me not to start, but she never told me to quit."

"He asked me what I thought and I said I didn't want him to do it," Sandy said. "He did it anyway and I guess I learned then that a man has to do what he wants to do, otherwise he wouldn't be worth having."

But there was no doubt about who ran the show. When Sandy fixed her husband's tie at Gallagher's, a restaurant in midtown Manhattan, LeDoux said with a laugh, "I can't even get dressed without her."

Even when she didn't know the answer, she had one. When Sandy and Scott visited Diane and Chico Resch in Boston, she arrived wearing a red fox fur coat. A stranger very loudly chastised her for "wearing a dead animal," Diane remembered. "She looked at him," Diane recalled, "didn't miss a beat and said, 'Every fox in this coat was sick and they were happy to be in my coat.'"

It didn't matter the situation; Sandy could break the tension, recalled Chico. For LeDoux, Sandy proved to be the perfect complement, exhibiting an emotional strength that matched his physical presence. She would look after him. He would be her protector.

Long before she began seeing LeDoux, Sandy was date-raped, LeDoux said. When LeDoux learned the assailant's name, he paid the man a surprise visit in northeast Minneapolis. His message was simple: If you ever so much as talk to Sandy again, "you're gonna have a limp for the rest of your life." The man immediately disappeared from her life.

They were married in December 1969 at the Deerwood community center, with a basketball backboard in the background of one of their wedding pictures. Scott was a few weeks away from his twenty-first birthday. Somehow, they made it work.

"If you talk about marriages and relationships, they're not all perfect," Chico said. "With them it was."

Sandy was "the stabilizing force in their marriage," Judy Wynn said. "She was beautiful, really pretty, with a good heart. Always positive about things. Just a wonderful woman. I adored Sandy.

"She was an awesome mother. She'd say, 'The heck with housework. I'm playing with the kids.'"

As Molly Lappin, Sandy and Scott's daughter, noted, "I've never met anybody who was perfect. But my mother was about as close as you're going to get."

8

PAPA JOE

By LeDoux's junior year at UMD, he was embroiled in a battle much more complicated than any he had encountered in the ring. He was fighting for his academic life. Everything was a struggle. He continued to work three jobs. On the football field, he became a starter on both the offensive and defensive lines—which meant downplaying separations of both shoulders to the coaching staff. By the fall of his junior year, his grade point average had fallen to 2.1. LeDoux said he needed a 2.5 GPA to be eligible to play his senior year.

"I took too many physics classes," he said. "I would have been better off if they were all phys. ed."

In May 1969—with the war in Vietnam splashed across the front page almost every day—LeDoux enlisted in the army for a two-year stint. He was on academic probation, a full semester behind his graduating class. He was still single. (He and Sandy would marry seven months later, on December 20.) He didn't know where Vietnam was, but enlisting seemed like the right thing to do. For LeDoux, maybe the only thing. His father had served during World War II, his grandfather in World War I. "I felt I needed to go, that it was my turn to serve my country," he said.

Friends said he had little choice. "He enlisted because I think he was afraid he'd be drafted," said Craig Gallop, who watched his buddy fall behind academically during the four months LeDoux lived with the Gallop family. LeDoux thought he might better control his destiny by enlisting instead of waiting to be drafted.

LeDoux was sent to train at Fort Bragg, North Carolina, and told that he would be ordered to Vietnam. During basic training, he confided in a sergeant who had already served two tours of duty in Vietnam. "How do you know if it's a Vietnamese or a Vietcong?" LeDoux asked his sergeant. "He said, 'You shoot them and then you ask,'" LeDoux said. "'Doesn't matter if they're friend or foe. They'll probably shoot you if you don't shoot them first.'"

As a teenager, LeDoux would walk three miles to church, just to listen to hymns and sermons he couldn't comprehend. When LeDoux got his orders for Vietnam, he turned to the Bible. "I thought, 'I'm going to Vietnam. I'm going to die. I want to find out what's going to happen to me.'"

LeDoux went home for Christmas—to marry Sandy, who had graduated from UMD and was working as a dental assistant. Recognizing LeDoux's insecurity, she assured him that she wouldn't dump him.

Two weeks later, his orders were changed. Instead of Vietnam, LeDoux was stationed at the army base in Fort Lee, Virginia. "It was a God thing," LeDoux said. "God wanted me to be with Sandy. He knew someday, I'd have to take care of her."

Sandy joined her husband in April 1970, calling a trailer their home until LeDoux's discharge in July 1971. Everyone knew her. "Shoes," they called her, because of a pair of red shoes she loved wearing.

"Scott was the nicest guy, but if he gets ruffled, he can be a hard head," recalled Doug Rollins. "He was pretty immature. Sandy had to settle him down."

Rollins had been stationed at the base for six months when LeDoux arrived. He remembered officers marveling at LeDoux's size and wanting to assign him to the military police. When LeDoux balked, there was talk about making him a cook. That discussion stopped when word spread that LeDoux had gotten into a fight, for which he was nearly thrown in the brig. He was transferred to a special services unit, where he became a physical-training specialist for sixteen months, a lifeguard at the base swimming pool.

"None of those Commies ever went swimming in my pool," he said.

LeDoux didn't spend that much time around the pool, either.

"We played a little golf," recalled John Carney, an army buddy who stayed in contact with LeDoux for four decades after both received honorable discharges. Carney, whose introduction to his lifelong friend came via LeDoux's elbow during a basketball game, was in charge of the army golf course at Fort Lee. That meant he and his buddies could play every day for free, "as long as we stayed out of the brass's way."

Among the creative ways they found time to play: Carney said he once dumped extra chlorine in the pool, forcing the pool's closure for several hours—long enough for LeDoux to get in another eighteen holes. Other days, LeDoux would sit by the pool for eight hours and then play a round. LeDoux claimed to have a handicap of four by the time his tour of duty ended.

"If I had reenlisted, I could have played golf forever," LeDoux said.

Golf, swimming, Wiffle ball, baseball games against other units—all part of the daily routine. Other guys in the barracks found recreation by smoking marijuana, with LeDoux being one of the few who refused to partake, said army buddy Bob Smith.

"It wasn't like *McHale's Navy*," Smith said, comparing his unit to the popular TV comedy. "*McHale's Navy* was fairly strict by comparison."

LeDoux participated in nearly every sport the army could offer, except one: He didn't box. There was talk of getting him in the ring, to literally fight for his army team, which would have meant a transfer. He declined. Instead, he ate. And ate. And ate. By the time of his discharge, he was a puffy 253 pounds.

He knew how to throw his weight around. During a baseball game, when an opposing player slid hard into second baseman Smith, first baseman LeDoux came over and forcefully lifted the base runner up with one hand.

Smith recalled another incident, at a Dairy Queen near the Virginia Beach church, where LeDoux, Sandy, and Smith and his wife were headed. When two young black kids approached the counter, they were told to go to the back of the line. This happened repeatedly, according to Smith. LeDoux stepped in and said he would order for the kids. He was told that if he did so, he would be fined. LeDoux left $16.09 on the counter—more than the total of his bill, which included ice cream for the youngsters—and told the manager to keep the change and put it toward his fine.

"Different era," said Smith. "By the time his tour was up, I think Scott and Sandy were ready to leave Virginia and happy to get back to Minnesota."

In fall 1971, LeDoux reacquainted himself with the gym and amateur boxing. He worked a night shift, loading and unloading trucks for

Consolidated Freightways, a union job his father-in-law helped him get. His afternoons were spent working out, sometimes at a gym on Hennepin Avenue and Seventh Street in Minneapolis. One of the regulars who pumped iron with him was professional wrestler Jesse Ventura, Minnesota's future governor.

"We were paupers then," Ventura reminded LeDoux years later.

LeDoux's decision to get back into fighting shape was applauded by his friends, but his family resisted the thought of him taking up boxing full-time. Sandy told him, plain and simple, that she didn't want him to box. Mickey showed indifference when her son told her he wanted to get back into the ring. (Throughout LeDoux's career, she rarely watched him fight, even when she attended his matches.) Doc merely shrugged at the notion of his son boxing again, telling him, "Do whatever you gotta do."

When LeDoux won his second Upper Midwest Golden Gloves heavyweight crown in 1973, he knew it was time to turn professional. At six foot one and 220 pounds, with burly shoulders, he looked every bit the tough guy he was becoming. With his golden curls, chevron mustache, sparkling blue eyes, and gift for tossing humorous one-liners, he was a promoter's dream. At worst, he was another in a long list of great white hopes.

He turned pro in 1974, becoming part of a Minnesota boxing legacy that began on May 20, 1871, when Dan Carr knocked out Jim Taylor in the eighteenth round in a bare-fisted bout in Winona—the first professional fight in Minnesota. Twenty years later, on February 17, 1891, Chicago's Tommy Ryan defeated St. Paul's Danny Needham for the world welterweight title. That battle, at the Twin City Athletic Club in Minneapolis, lasted a staggering seventy-six rounds. The five-hour bout was among the longest recorded in boxing history, but it wasn't Needham's longest. Needham, nicknamed "Iron Man," also fought a near-seven-hour, one-hundred-round draw against Patsy Kerrigan in 1890. The fight began at 8:30 p.m. and was called at 3:15 a.m. At the time, it was boxing's longest-known match. Amazingly, Needham broke his hand in the fifth round and continued to fight another ninety-five.

Former heavyweight champion Jack Dempsey fought an exhibition in St. Paul in 1931. During the 1920s, John Dillinger was a ringside regular at fights in St. Paul.

Fifty years later, LeDoux would help usher in a new boxing era in Minnesota. Leading the way through the ropes was the man to whom he would entrust his career: a portly character, who knew more stories and characters than nearly anyone in the business, Joe Daszkiewicz. (Over the years, LeDoux happily accommodated journalists by spelling his manager's last name, telling them, "When I can't spell that anymore, then I know I've been hit too much.")

Daszkiewicz was a throwback, a boxing lifer who seemed from another period, a good half century before his time. "Come by our gym any night and I guarantee you'll find twenty fighters," he said during an interview in 1990, sounding like the consummate promoter that he was. "This game takes hunger, and the kids on the streets today are hungry."

He was then holding court at the Northside Gym at Forty-Second Street and Lyndale Avenue in north Minneapolis. Sweat poured onto the cement floor, the stench of mildew was ever present, and the six fluorescent tubes and the 100-watt bulb hanging from the low ceiling illuminated the rusty lockers, dusty mirrors, and faded posters. Papa Joe was oblivious to it all. As long as he could sit on a stool as close to the ring as possible and watch his fighters spar, he was content.

"This," Daszkiewicz told a visitor, "is where the fighters is."

"Joe was an old curmudgeon, a guy who loved the sport," recalled Bobby Goodman, a promoter who worked with Don King. "He slept and drank boxing. He would call you at all hours. He always had the next guy who was gonna do it. 'Oh, wait till you see this kid.'

"He had a nice manner about him. He had a smile. I really loved Papa Joe."

Everyone called him Papa Joe. He and his wife, Rita, had ten kids. But he also embraced his fighters as if they were his own children, said his son Chuck Daszkiewicz. Chuck learned that firsthand. He was part of his father's ring team after his own fight career, which started with him using the name Kid Polack.

In many ways, Daszkiewicz reminded LeDoux of another father figure, Sammy Gallop, the trainer who gave LeDoux a home when he needed one in Duluth. Gallop died in April 1972.

"I know he's an honest guy," Craig Gallop told LeDoux, referring to Daszkiewicz. "Papa Joe," Gallop said years later, "had Scott's best interests at heart." LeDoux considered Daszkiewicz so honest that the two never signed a contract throughout LeDoux's fifty-fight professional career. "We didn't have to," LeDoux said.

The son of Polish immigrants, Daszkiewicz was born in Chicago but spent most of his life in Minneapolis. He boxed in the Golden Gloves for St. Philip Catholic Church in north Minneapolis and at DeLaSalle High School. After serving in the navy, where he was on the boxing team during World War II, the Mill City Polack—as he became known in local boxing circles—considered becoming a doctor. His father, who owned a bar and restaurant, quashed those medical dreams. "No, you're taking over the bar business," he told him.

He did just that while taking classes at the College of St. Thomas. In college, he boxed, played football, and earned a degree in business. He tried to pass those lessons in finances on to his fighters. "Before giving them their cut, he always told them, 'Make sure you invest this,'" said his son Chuck. "If they fought in Las Vegas, he wouldn't give them their money till they got home, because he didn't want them to gamble it away."

As a businessman and bar owner, he may have been too far ahead of his time. His bar was called the Northern Bar, which he renamed Papa Joe's. He claimed that his was the first bar in Minneapolis to have live rock 'n' roll. He renamed the bar Papa Joe's A Go Go and also opened a downtown club called Times Square with a partner. Blues guitar legend Johnny Winter played there. So did Janis Joplin.

According to Chuck Daszkiewicz, Joplin showed up at his father's bar after playing a concert at the Minneapolis Auditorium. Janis went on stage and gave the crowd a piece of her heart. "All she asked for was a bottle of Scotch and a bottle of vodka," Daszkiewicz recalled.

Papa Joe, the bar owner who didn't drink, quickly tired of the rock 'n' roll scene. The neighborhood was changing, and the restaurant business was failing, his son said.

The Minnesota boxing scene also was changing. Daszkiewicz was becoming a dominant local figure in boxing circles. His stable of athletes included Rafael Rodriguez, who won the state super welterweight title in 1974, and Doug Demmings, who fought for the U.S. Boxing Association middleweight title in 1977, losing to Sugar Ray Seales.

"You gotta get with Joe," Rodriguez told LeDoux. "You'll never get anywhere unless you train with Daszkiewicz."

Always the businessman, Daszkiewicz quickly sought the financial muscle he felt necessary to back LeDoux. He approached a couple of land developers and a Minneapolis lawyer—customers who frequented the

Northern Bar—and told them that he had a heavyweight "contender" that they could "buy into," recalled his son Chuck. "Man, you're gonna make money on this," Papa Joe told them, his son remembered. Chuck also recalled his father telling him, "These guys know nothing about boxing."

Minneapolis businessman Arnie Palmer saw enough in LeDoux to know he was worth the risk. "He had that right hand, that overhand right," Palmer recalled. "When he threw it, it kind of hurt people. And he had style."

Style? He wore bib overalls! Daszkiewicz called him a "clubber" and said he lacked finesse. He was stubborn. And he was determined. If Daszkiewicz called LeDoux and said he had a sparring partner for him if he could make it to the gym by three thirty, LeDoux would double-park his semi in the loading zone near Seventh and Hennepin—in the heart of downtown Minneapolis, with rush hour approaching.

The new investors loved LeDoux's determination. Palmer was the one who often worked with local boxing promoters, like Ben Sternberg. Minneapolis attorney Dick Gunn helped advertise LeDoux's fights.

Gunn, a highly respected expert on eminent domain cases, was a conservationist who loved the outdoors but probably knew little about boxing, said his son, Brad Gunn. Yet Brad remembered attending a number of LeDoux's fights at the Minneapolis Auditorium with his dad. Before each of those fights, Gunn would have someone in his law office make eight-by-eleven-inch posters advertising the bouts. He then had his sons distribute them around town.

But the key to LeDoux's team was unquestionably Papa Joe.

"My dad worked with everybody," Chuck Daszkiewicz said of his father, who was inducted into the Minnesota Boxing Hall of Fame in 2011, eight years after he died at age seventy-nine from Alzheimer's disease. "It was nothing for him to call up Don King, Bob Arum, Angelo Dundee."

Daszkiewicz had his little quirks. One of his eyes often twitched. Once, when he and LeDoux were at Muhammad Ali's home in California, the champ noticed Daszkiewicz struggling. "I think your manager likes me," Ali said to LeDoux. "He keeps winking at me."

Winking aside, everybody who dealt with Daszkiewicz found him to be honest—and in the boxing world, that in itself made him an unforgettable character. He told his son, "Chuck, this is an education that nobody could buy. You have to earn this. Just keep your nose clean, get a good reputation, and you can stay in this business forever."

LeDoux promised his manager, "I'm gonna get good at boxing so that I can give up this job" driving and unloading trucks. That meant often confronting LeDoux about his moodiness and work ethic. George Glover, a sheet-metal worker, was a corner man for Daszkiewicz. Over a half century, beginning in the 1950s, Glover taught nearly five thousand kids about boxing and discipline. He said he nearly came to blows with LeDoux after questioning LeDoux's effort following a fight.

Daszkiewicz knew he was in for a challenge, but months after meeting LeDoux, he insisted, "I'm telling you, I'm gonna make this guy a contender."

9

THE GREAT WHITE SHADOW

*T*he great Joe Louis defended his heavyweight title thirteen times in twenty-nine months, so often in fact that the phrase "the bum of the month club" was coined to describe his opponents and the frequency with which he manhandled them. Upon turning pro in 1974, LeDoux fought even more often than that. From February 4, when he knocked out Arthur Pullens at the Minneapolis Convention Center in his professional debut, to November 22, when he knocked out John L. Johnson, LeDoux fought a total of ten opponents, beating them all. He knocked out Reggie Fleming on May 5 in St. Paul, and on May 23, he knocked out Larry Penninger. His fifth-round knockout of John L. Johnson came exactly two weeks after he beat Lou Rogan, on points, in Crosby.

"I want to be recognized as a good fighter," LeDoux said after knocking out Ron Draper, a 1971 Golden Gloves champion from Kansas City, in the Minneapolis Auditorium on October 8. "Even better, to be known as a good competitor. That's what boxing is all about—competition. Isn't it?"

Competition? The public knew better. An estimated crowd of only six hundred attended the LeDoux–Draper bout. Just who were these guys LeDoux was fighting? After ten professional fights—nine in the Twin Cities and one in his hometown—LeDoux was undefeated, but his opponents were journeymen at best. Even die-hard boxing fans would have difficulty recalling their names.

"Perfect condition," said Rodney Bobick, a heavyweight from Bowlus, Minnesota, who would fight LeDoux in 1975, "is the best thing Scott has."

Bobick. Now, that was a name Minnesota fight fans knew. As an amateur, Bobick defeated LeDoux and later served briefly as LeDoux's sparring partner. But it was Rodney's brother Duane to whom LeDoux would be compared for much of his career.

In the early 1970s, Duane was boxing's great white hope of the moment. Once a gravedigger (as were his father and grandfather), Duane came from a family of thirteen children—twelve of them boys—who grew up poor in central Minnesota. When Duane was in the seventh grade, a bank claimed the Bobicks' house after Duane's father fell behind on monthly payments. "For us, a ghetto was where the rich people lived," said older brother LeRoy.

Duane fought through it. While in the navy, Bobick defeated future heavyweight champion Mike Weaver in a military tournament. After losing in an Amateur Athletic Union (AAU) tournament bout to future heavyweight contender Ron Lyle, Bobick won sixty-two straight amateur fights, including one with future heavyweight champion Larry Holmes. In 1971, the handsome, six-foot-three, 210-pound Bobick defeated Cuba's Teófilo Stevenson en route to the Pan American Games gold medal.

With his boxing résumé and movie star good looks, Bobick seemed set to strike it rich as a professional. "I'm talking about a lot of money," he said. "Not $100,000. I'm talking millions." At the 1972 Olympics in Munich, however—just hours after terrorists had slain eleven Israeli team members—Bobick lost this time to Stevenson, a defeat that for many defined Bobick's career. Losing that fight would hit Bobick's wallet as hard as it slashed his pride. Many of the boxing managers that eagerly recruited Bobick before the Olympics lost interest. His signing bonus with a Denver sportsman was reported as $25,000 by some. Bobick said it was actually a $50,000 loan that he received from investor Bill Daniels.

By the time LeDoux had turned pro, Bobick already was 16–0, although many of his opponents could, at best, be considered bums. Yet despite Bobick's impressive record, it was LeDoux who was beginning to grab the attention of fight fans in 1974—with his quick fists and quicker wit.

For instance, just minutes after the Draper fight, LeDoux regaled reporters with this anecdote: During a clinch in the sixth round, Draper told LeDoux, "I'm going to knock you out." "I told him he was crazy," LeDoux said. Once again, LeDoux would be the last man standing. He bludgeoned Draper, knocking him down for a ten-count in the ninth round, and not even the bell could save him. Draper lay unconscious, and under the rules, referee Wally Holm continued his count. According to the *Minneapolis Tribune,* Holm could have counted to forty. No way was Draper getting up.

"If he had gotten up, I would have had to leave the building," LeDoux said.

"Those three-minute rounds were getting awfully long," LeDoux said. "I planned to lie on him in the seventh and eighth rounds so that I'd have something left for the finish. I thought it would last ten rounds. But then I caught him with that right in the ninth round. It felt great."

After beating Rogan on November 8 in Crosby and knocking out Johnson on November 22 in Minneapolis, LeDoux fought professionally for the first time away from Minnesota. He took on C. J. (Bar) Brown, of New York, on January 18, 1975, at the storied Boston Garden, "just to stay busy," he said. LeDoux remained unbeaten with a six-round split decision. It wasn't easy.

For starters, LeDoux's fight team knew little about Brown, who was a last-second substitute for an opponent whose identity was never revealed to LeDoux by the Boston promoter. All Daszkiewicz knew about Brown was that he had only recently turned professional. That was it. There was no scouting report. In an era before the instant access of the Internet, Daszkiewicz was relying on familiar sources—and none had seen Brown fight.

"They ran in this Brown on us," said Daszkiewicz. "We didn't have a record on him, but he turned out to be a good one. His New York sponsor thought they had a good prospect, and I think they have. He's a big, tall guy who can box and punch."

LeDoux started well. "In the fourth round, he nailed Brown with one of those overhand rights," said Papa Joe. "Then, as usual, he shot everything for a knockout and just fought himself out. Brown landed a right in the fifth round, knocked Scott's mouthpiece out, and proceeded to work him over. He was lucky to finish the round.

"Before the next round, the last, I said, 'Scott, you've got the decision won if you stay out of trouble. Just jab and move and kill time.' Scott followed instructions, didn't get hurt anymore, and we won a split decision. But believe me, I was plenty scared."

LeDoux's next battle came after the fight, in his cramped dressing room. Let LeDoux tell the story:

"I fought in a lot of dumpy places—and the old Boston Garden had to rank right up there. There was a promoter named Sam [Suitcase Sam Silverman] who was like something straight out of the *Rocky* movies. You went into this little room that was like a closet after the fight. There's a lightbulb hanging down. The place stunk.

"And here comes this Sam. He said, 'Well, you got $250 for this fight, but . . . Now, you got a locker fee. And there's a towel fee, the physical . . .

"By the time he was done, I was left with $80. I turned to my trainer and said, 'What do I do now?' And Papa Joe says, 'Don't worry about it. Just take it.'"

(LeDoux could have done worse. Duane Bobick, who was undefeated at the time, earned a payday of $445.80 after winning his twenty-fifth fight. After Bobick's expenses were deducted, he said he was left with a balance of "about a minus $200 on my account.")

Eleven days after the Brown fight in Boston, LeDoux was back in the ring, this time in Rochester, Minnesota. With most of the 1,320 paying customers at the Mayo Civic Auditorium in his corner, LeDoux dispatched Larry Renaud—a last-day substitute for Pete Chiano, of Saddle Brook, New York, due to a January snowstorm—in the sixth round. LeDoux almost immediately began promoting a possible fight against Rodney Bobick, whose thirty-four wins against four losses included a victory over future champion Mike Weaver. Sign-holding fans shouting, "We want Bobick," raucously agreed. Bobick, also on the card that night, beat Terry Krueger, of San Antonio, by technical knockout in the third round.

"I've challenged him so many times I'm out of breath," said the 222-pound LeDoux. "The way Bobick fights, he couldn't draw more than two cents in a carnival. I'd be the one drawing the fight fans. From now on, if he wants to make the match, he'll have to come to me."

That night, however, it was Bobick who fought in the main event and won for the thirty-second time in thirty-five bouts. When he talked about his immediate future, LeDoux's name never came up. "I'll be back in Miami tomorrow, and back in the gym Monday," said Bobick, who trained under Angelo Dundee, Muhammad Ali's trainer. When Dundee talked about the promising future of Minnesota heavyweights, he ignored LeDoux.

"Scott's making a lot of noise, isn't he?" Dundee said after Bobick's fight. "If they want the fight bad enough, they've got it. But first there are other places. They want Rodney in New Orleans and out in California.

We're in no hurry. Mark it down, though, that both he and his brother [Duane] will be getting big heavyweight fights within two years."

Before Rodney Bobick, though, there was Roy (Cookie) Wallace, a journeyman from Dallas with an 18–19–2 record. Before his career was over, Wallace would lose to George Forman, Ken Norton, Earnie Shavers, Duane Bobick, Rodney Bobick, and dozens of heavyweights long forgotten before they ever entered the ring. He lost thirty-five of his sixty fights. So when he met undefeated LeDoux, at the St. Paul Armory on March 14, the boxing world assumed he would lose again.

Dundee wasn't so sure. He was among those who questioned LeDoux for taking the Wallace fight instead of concentrating on a fight with Bobick. "Wallace may be too clever for LeDoux," Dundee said. "He's been around and he's pretty smart. LeDoux may be sorry if he blows the Bobick fight."

Ben Sternberg, the promoter who had hopes of a LeDoux–Bobick match at the Met Center, also was a skeptic. "I think LeDoux is taking a chance with Wallace and I can't understand why," he said.

Daszkiewicz tried to justify the fight, saying, "I know I'm on the spot for taking Wallace, but I think Scott can handle him and he needs a good fight before facing Bobick."

When the Wallace fight finally arrived, LeDoux learned that the first cut truly is the deepest. For the first time in his career—after thirty-two amateur bouts and twelve straight victories as a pro—LeDoux was cut. Not by a left hook or right jab. LeDoux sustained a gash on the corner of his left eyebrow from a head butt as he and Wallace wrestled along the ropes at the end of the first round. "He butted me and I tried to butt him back," LeDoux said. "I didn't even know I was cut until I got back to the corner and Joe called attention to it."

The scheduled ten-rounder was stopped twice in the second round. While Dr. LeRoy Fox, the ringside physician, examined the cut, Papa Joe pleaded that the fight continue. It did, but only for a few seconds. Once the cut reopened, referee Denny Nelson stopped the fight. It ended with a minute and twenty-five seconds left in the second round. Wallace was declared the winner by a technical knockout.

LeDoux's manager, Arnie Palmer, was incensed. "The movies will show that Wallace butted LeDoux 15 times in that short period," he said days after the fight. "They will also show that the butt which opened the cut near LeDoux's eye was delivered clearly after the bell ended the first round."

LeDoux also was furious. This was a loss he would lament for decades. Changes to boxing rules that came years later would have disqualified Wallace for the head butt, he said more than thirty years after that bout. That night, however, LeDoux, who said he cried after the fight, was not easily consoled. "I've never been a good loser," a finally calm LeDoux said thirty minutes after it ended. "I'm embarrassed. I should know better than to try and wrestle with a wrestler." The cut, LeDoux said, "was not even big enough to require stitches." The fight should have continued, he said.

What stung most was that LeDoux was convinced, even in defeat, that he was the superior boxer. "I knew I could win, maybe by the third round, once I found I could jab him," LeDoux said. "Then I got that little nick from the butt. They might as well have taken my pocketbook. Professional fighting is my living."

Even before the Wallace debacle, a fight between LeDoux and Rodney Bobick was in the works. It was a fight that these two Minnesota rivals wanted as much as their fans. By now, LeDoux was nearly obsessed with Rodney and Duane Bobick. He took films of both fighters with him on an early April trip to New York.

"Rodney makes a lot of mistakes and I think I know every one of them," LeDoux said. "I want that guy."

But there were complications that had nothing to do with the fighters. Palmer, one of LeDoux's managers, asked promoter Ben Sternberg to forbid Dundee to go to the Met Center the day of the April 23 fight and tamper with the ring ropes. There had been reports that Dundee had tampered with the ropes to give his fighter Muhammad Ali an advantage during his title fight with champion George Foreman in Zaire.

The intensity between the LeDoux and Bobick camps was so volatile that Sternberg may not have been joking when he said, "I've got to get them in the ring before they end up fighting on Hennepin Avenue. There's some bad blood there."

When Duane Bobick warned that his brother had better be in top shape for LeDoux "or he'll lose," Rodney responded, "You can bet I'll be in shape for that guy. There's no one I'd rather beat."

Minnesota fight fans seemed just as anxious. The Met Center—home of hockey's Minnesota North Stars and the future site of Mall of

America—was the largest Minnesota venue in which LeDoux would ever box. Bobick, with a 32–4 record, was ranked among the top ten heavyweights in the world. Unranked brother Duane also was on the card.

"I assume that LeDoux would like the size of his paycheck, too," Sternberg said. Indeed, LeDoux and Bobick would each receive $13,717.79 for a night's work.

"This is just another fight, except for a big payday," said Bobick.

LeDoux saw things differently.

"I have studied films of some of his fights, have seen him fight, and I am not impressed," LeDoux said. "Give me trouble? Every fighter gives me trouble."

LeDoux probably didn't score points with Rodney by letting the world know that what he really wanted was a date in the ring with Duane, who was managed by boxing legend and recent champion Joe Frazier. Duane was the Bobick who seemed destined for a shot at the title.

"My dad told Scott that there's no money in undercards," Chuck Daszkiewicz recalled. Duane Bobick's fight was the main event on the card. "My dad told him, 'You gotta be the big event fighter to make any money.'

"It wasn't that easy to build Scott up," Daszkiewicz went on. "Remember, here was a guy who always wore bib overalls."

LeDoux was twenty-six. He had boxed as an amateur for seven years. He had been married for five years. He was working as a truck driver and dock worker. He would begin his roadwork, running with his sheepdog, at eight o'clock, then exercise in his basement, visit the gym, and take a few hours off before working from four o'clock to midnight.

"I waited seven years to turn pro because I wasn't mature enough," he told Larry Batson of the *Minneapolis Tribune*. "I wasn't ready for the type of fight where you're trying to hurt the other guy. And sometimes, you know, they do things just to be cruel.

"The press, the writers aren't always nice, either. Or even fair. You have to be tough mentally. I waited until I was sure I could handle everything they threw at me.

"I'm glad I did. I was the type, if I'd gone pro four or five years ago, who would have been caught up in the real, real dream world of boxing. You see the kids around the gyms, out of touch with reality, visions of titles and wealth dancing in their heads and not a quarter in their pockets.

"Right now, I'm still a dreamer. I'm a believer. I can punch. I can knock out anybody. I think of Rocky Marciano. He lost a lot of fights for thirteen rounds, then won. One punch is all it takes. But if you never get it, you lose. You have to be ready to face that possibility, too. I am, and in the meantime, Sandy and I have a wonderful time from boxing."

LeDoux certainly was ready for the 227-pound Bobick when their Wednesday night battle finally arrived. The largest crowd ever to watch a Minnesota boxing card watched LeDoux score a decisive upset, dominating Bobick from the start, to win a unanimous ten-round decision. The 9,256 fans who paid a Minnesota boxing record of $70,148 to witness LeDoux's coming-out party also watched Duane Bobick defeat Raul Gorosito in ten rounds.

LeDoux dominated his match with Rodney Bobick throughout. At one point, Bobick was battling his own corner, as well as LeDoux. Bobick's glove became untied. At the end of the round, he put his arm on the ropes and asked Gene Fesenmaier, a promoter, to tie his glove. Fesenmaier tied the strings around the top rope, as well as the glove, Daszkiewicz said, more than twenty years later. "The bell rang and Rodney started to come out of the corner," Papa Joe said. "His left arm was tied to the ropes. LeDoux ran across the ring and clubbed him. Then, Rodney turned around and punched Fesenmaier."

It was only in the ninth round that LeDoux's corner got a scare, when Bobick and LeDoux accidentally bounced heads against one another. A cut opened over LeDoux's left eye, the same eyebrow that was cut in the Wallace fight. "I didn't even know there was bleeding," LeDoux said. "And being late in the fight, I was sure it wouldn't be important."

After the fight, the only marks LeDoux had were above each eye. LeDoux's right eye was very swollen, but when Daszkiewicz told him to put an ice pack over his eye, LeDoux countered, "Which one?"

Bobick's ribs were so battered that two of his brothers had to help him to the shower and then shielded him from the media after the fight. LeDoux never got a chance to visit with him immediately after the bout.

But another Bobick—Duane—couldn't wait to see LeDoux. After watching the final two rounds of his brother's fight with LeDoux, Duane seemed ready to step into the ring with LeDoux himself. "I thought LeDoux tired in the final two rounds and ran out of gas," Duane said.

"LeDoux has a good overhand right. But that's about it. He has a fair jab and he comes to you. I know I can handle Scott LeDoux any day."

Daszkiewicz, for one, was game. "We'd love to get in with Duane," he said. "They got to test him with a puncher sometime. Why not Scott? I doubt if they will, though."

There was talk of a May 22 date. "This fight is hot now," said promoter Sternberg. "We could do $100,000 on May 22."

"We're ready to fight Duane Bobick any time," Arnie Palmer said. "I think it would be an easier fight for LeDoux than his fight with Rodney Bobick. Duane took some good shots from Gorosito. He won't take such shots from LeDoux and survive."

But after the Bobick fight, LeDoux needed eleven stitches to close the cut over his right eye. He announced he was taking a vacation from fighting, at least until June.

As the weeks passed, even Eddie Futch, Bobick's trainer, seemed anxious for the fight. "I don't see how the LeDoux people can deprive him of this big payday, the biggest he ever will get," he said.

Futch had another obligation, one that took priority over a fight with LeDoux: He was preparing Joe Frazier for a probable third fight with Muhammad Ali later in the year, and wanted Bobick at Frazier's training camp. (That October 1 epic between Ali and Frazier, the "Thrilla in Manila," culminated in one of the most intense rivalries in all of sports and is considered one the greatest battles in boxing history.)

There were other complications. The Minnesota Boxing Commission granted a one-year boxing franchise in Bloomington to Sternberg but rejected an application from LeDoux's co-managers—Daszkiewicz, Palmer, and Gunn—who were collectively calling themselves Minnesota Promotions.

When asked if a LeDoux–Duane Bobick fight was still a possibility, Palmer said, "I don't know." Daszkiewicz was blunt. "One thing is certain: We won't fight for Sternberg."

While promoters bickered, LeDoux did his fighting in the ring, beginning with a six-round technical knockout of Terry Daniels, of Bayonne, New Jersey, in Orlando in July.

"That was a scary fight," LeDoux recalled, years later. "I started blasting him in the first round and I was blasting him in the second round.

And in the third round, one of his eyes swells shut and I'm still blasting this guy. And I tie him up, and I say to the referee, 'This guy can't see.' The referee steps between us and looks at Terry and looks back at me and says, 'Box.' I'm like, 'What?'

"When the bell rang, I went over in the corner and said, 'Joe, he can't see me anymore.' And Joe says, 'You gotta knock him out. If he cuts you, or butts you, you lose. You gotta take him out of there.'" Finally, in the sixth round, a cut near Daniels's right eye forced the referee to stop the fight.

A month later, LeDoux fought to a draw with George (Scrap Iron) Johnson at the St. Paul Civic Center. At first, a split decision was given to LeDoux, triggering massive boos from the crowd that thought Johnson had won. The commission's decision to change the verdict to a draw did little to quiet disbelieving fans. LeDoux claimed later to have a staph infection that night. He said he was so sick that his weight dropped from 220 pounds to 207 a week after that bout.

It was the second blemish on LeDoux's record—he was now 14–1–1—and this was an opponent who would suffer a technical knockout against Duane Bobick at the Met Center in November. A severe cut over Johnson's right eye ended that fight. Both fighters needed stitches when it was over. "We bumped heads," Johnson said. "I hit him with a right hand," said Bobick.

Regardless, Johnson wasn't impressed. "I think LeDoux will beat Bobick if they fight because LeDoux hits harder."

LeDoux, meanwhile, won every round in a unanimous decision over Brian O'Melia at the State Fairgrounds in September.

Then came a drama that could have been scripted for reality TV.

When it was announced in mid-November that LeDoux might fight Ron Stander, the "Omaha Butcher," in Minneapolis in early December, LeDoux's managers expressed surprise. Promoter Ron Peterson announced that Stander already had agreed to the fight. Peterson went on to say that he had Stander's manager, Bill Cooley, talk to Daszkiewicz, and Papa Joe seemed interested. "Isn't that the way to start negotiations?" Peterson asked. He quickly added, "It happens that Daszkiewicz and I aren't speaking."

Dick Gunn, the respected lawyer, seemed puzzled by it all. "We haven't even talked to Peterson about it," said Gunn, LeDoux's co-manager.

"We are committed to fight for Ben Sternberg at the Met Center if he can find a suitable opponent."

LeDoux's team wanted Jimmy Ellis, the former champ who won the World Boxing Association heavyweight title in 1968 after Ali was stripped of the title for refusing to enter the military.

Stander, with a 30–7–2 record, was hardly a former world champion. His claim to fame may have been lasting five rounds with then-champion Frazier. A powerful fighter, Stander's conditioning had been questioned until he signed with Cooley, the Minneapolis manager, who demanded he train seriously.

LeDoux's camp agreed to the fight, and the verbal sparring between both sides continued. Gunn and Daszkiewicz wanted a larger ring than the seventeen-by-eighteen-foot ring proposed, so LeDoux could move around. They suggested a twenty-square-foot ring that could be transported from Crosby. Stander's team called it "a strange request," wondered if the Crosby ring had sentimental value to LeDoux, and warned that this match had all the makings of a "back-alley brawl."

At a Monday press conference at the Seventh Street Gym in Minneapolis, two days before LeDoux's December 10 bout with Stander, a "Blood Donors Wanted" sign hung on the podium. LeDoux arrived first, sat quietly in the front of the room, and began cracking his knuckles when Stander entered the room.

Daszkiewicz was asked why LeDoux, ranked nineteenth among heavyweights by *Boxing Illustrated*, hadn't fought since September, while Stander had three fights over the same period. "Let me answer that, Joe," LeDoux said. "Stander lost to Rodney Bobick. I fought in April and destroyed him. That ought to answer that, right?"

Crushing a cup in his hands, Stander growled, "I am confident. I'm not going to lose another fight. My hands feel like sledge hammers."

For a promoter like Sternberg, the verbal sparring packed a potential financial wallop. The livelier the verbal barbs, the more interest in the fight. "A war, a war," said Sternberg. "This is more than a war. It's bad blood between these camps. They've argued about the size of the ring, the weight of the gloves and the referees."

LeDoux called it "a good matchup."

When Stander fought then-heavyweight champion Frazier in 1972, Stander suffered cuts around both eyes and on the bridge of his nose. It was Stander who decided he had had enough after the fourth round. The fight was such a mismatch that Stander's wife, Darlene, commented to the national media, "You don't enter a Volkswagen in the Indianapolis 500."

LeDoux sensed that something special was about to happen. For the first time in his career, LeDoux was becoming a boxer, not just a puncher. His left jab kept foes off balance. Against Rodney Bobick, he realized how effective pounding a body can be. "I've discarded whatever was left of my amateur notions. I'm a pro now."

When LeDoux and Stander finally fought, LeDoux admitted, "I'm rusty. I haven't fought in three months."

Daszkiewicz also appeared concerned minutes before the fight. He was checking his bag, looking for smelling salts and gauze when he asked LeDoux if he had seen the ice bag. "It's in my pocket," LeDoux said.

"Stander's in shape for this one," Papa Joe said. He began stuffing ice into the bag.

It didn't matter. LeDoux opened up a cut above Stander's left eye in the second round. LeDoux scored with a quick left hook in the fourth. He staggered Stander with three rights in the fifth. A savage right hook followed by a left uppercut had Stander spinning in the sixth. Stander connected with a hard left in the ninth round, but the unanimous decision ultimately went to LeDoux, who had only respect for Stander.

"I hope me and Ron meet again," LeDoux said. "I could use a man like him to help me. He's tough. A couple of times, I saw his big left coming and I said, 'Oh, Lord, LeDoux, duck, he'll kill you.'"

But LeDoux had bigger dreams waiting. It had been understood before the fight that the winner would face Ken Norton, the chiseled former Marine who broke Ali's jaw in 1973. Speculation was that LeDoux would be guaranteed $15,000 for the fight, which was being promoted by Don King. King, a virtual unknown two years before, had become omnipresent in the boxing world after promoting the 1974 Ali–George Foreman title fight in Zaire, the "Rumble in the Jungle."

Daszkiewicz was wasting no time. He planned to hire as a sparring partner Eddie Brooks, the Milwaukee heavyweight whose style was similar to Norton's. There were plans to go to New York, where more sparring partners awaited, and plans to fly to Las Vegas, a week before the fight. "We will be prepared," Daszkiewicz said. "LeDoux starts work Monday."

LeDoux learned on Christmas Eve that his planned bout with Norton would have to wait, as Norton had signed to fight Pedro Lovell of Argentina. Plans changed again when Lovell became ill, and LeDoux was tabbed to substitute if Lovell wasn't able to fight, but ultimately, Lovell recovered and was granted the fight.

"Be patient," King told LeDoux. "I have plans for you."

10

ONE FOR THE RECORD BOOKS

*T*he fight LeDoux wanted—the fight all of Minnesota wanted—was with Duane Bobick. Two Minnesota heavyweights with championship aspirations going toe-to-toe at the Metropolitan Sports Center in Bloomington, with state's bragging rights the cherry on top of it all. What could be better than that?

Yet at the start of the new year, Minnesota's dream fight seemed destined for New York's Madison Square Garden. It was up to LeDoux. Teddy Brenner, the Garden's president and matchmaker, offered LeDoux $10,000 to fight Bobick February 6 at the venue commonly known as the "world's most famous arena." But Daszkiewicz figured the fight could take in nearly $100,000 in receipts at the Met Center, and LeDoux would receive 25 percent.

Brenner wasn't budging. He told Daszkiewicz that he had exclusive rights to Bobick's services and that the fight had to be held at the Garden. Brenner and Bobick's managers, Joe Frazier and Eddie Futch, saw Bobick as a serious challenger to the heavyweight title.

"I'm standing pat on my refusal of the $10,000 offer," Daszkiewicz said.

Brenner told insiders that he would find another opponent for Bobick if LeDoux wasn't available.

LeDoux was not in a New York state of mind. Sandy gave birth to the couple's first child, Joshua, on January 27, and LeDoux wanted to be close to home. He announced a couple weeks later that he would headline a card at the Minneapolis Auditorium on February 7—a rare Saturday night fight show in Minneapolis. "Everything's set except opponents for us," LeDoux said of a card that would feature him as one of the headliners.

Greg Osowiecki, of Waterbury, Connecticut, was the recommended opponent for LeDoux. Osowiecki had never been knocked down in his previous twelve fights, but he was knocked out of this one before it ever began. Gunn and Daszkiewicz, LeDoux's co-managers, were unaware that Osowiecki had performed poorly in recent fights. The Connecticut boxing commission talked about suspending him, and the Minnesota Boxing Commission deemed Osowiecki an unworthy opponent, based on his record. When LeDoux's handlers learned that Osowiecki had misrepresented his record, they decided to look elsewhere.

The promoters then turned to Charlie James, a Los Angeles heavyweight who had beaten Ron Stander the previous summer. He became available when a rematch with Stander was canceled. But the musical corner stools kept revolving. LeDoux's co-managers eventually settled for Wild Bill Carson, a six-foot-two, 220-pound heavyweight out of Dumont, New Jersey.

"He comes right at you," said state boxing commissioner Erwin Dauphin. "And he is known for getting off the corner stool fast and starting the action."

The public wasn't buying it. Carson was near the end of a less than mediocre career and had lost his two previous fights. LeDoux would be the best-known opponent he would ever meet. The LeDoux–Carson fight wasn't even the card's main event. To entice Minneapolis fans, women and youths sixteen and under could attend at half price. "We feel that women are interested in boxing," Dick Gunn said.

After knocking out Carson in nine rounds, LeDoux took on Larry Middleton, the most experienced fighter he had faced. Middleton, of Baltimore, had knocked out Joe Bugner and faced top heavyweights in Ron Lyle and Jerry Quarry, each of whom gained split decisions over him. More recently, Middleton had lost a unanimous decision to Duane Bobick at Madison Square Garden. "I've had trouble getting fights," the 215-pound Middleton said. "The Bobick fight was my first in eight months. It was what I needed to get sharp."

Although Middleton appeared to be just another palooka staggering toward the end of his career, LeDoux saw this fight as a potential springboard. "It's time for me to make a strong move," he said. "It's time to find out whether I'm ready to meet the best."

The Middleton fight presented more questions than answers. Le-

Doux thought he dominated the action, saying, "I made the fight. I went to him and I think I did some damage. The right hands I landed on him will take Duane Bobick out."

Not everyone agreed. The Minneapolis Auditorium crowd actually booed the ten-round decision that gave the fight to LeDoux. Judge LeRoy Benson scored it 98–95, and Judge George Reiter favored LeDoux, 97–96. Referee Wally Holm called it even, at 96–96. Dick Cullum, the veteran boxing writer for the *Minneapolis Tribune,* scored the fight in Middleton's favor, 98–96. "It was a good heavyweight fight," Cullum wrote. "Both men gave their best and punishment was obvious on both sides."

LeDoux said his eardrum was shattered. Middleton nearly lost an eye.

Finally, on March 31, the preliminaries ended. LeDoux became the first to sign on for a bout against Bobick, a fight that had been discussed since the previous April. Yet promoter Ben Sternberg hardly sounded like a man who was halfway home.

LeDoux made demands for a ring larger than the one in permanent use at the Met Center. He also wanted the right to name the referee. "But these terms are not in the contract," Sternberg said. "And they won't be."

Sternberg was promising a "blockbuster card," but there was a major problem: Bobick hadn't signed, and publicly his manager remained pessimistic about the fight ever happening. "The time has passed for this fight," Futch had said previously when he was in Minneapolis. "Duane has been moving up. We've left this fight behind. We won't go back to fight the likes of LeDoux."

The grandstanding from the Bobick camp lasted all of five days— when the undefeated White Hope saw green.

On April 5, after a year of verbal barbs that threatened to score a technical knockout of the only bout that seemed to matter to Minnesota fight fans, LeDoux and Bobick agreed to a ten-rounder on April 22, 1976, at the Metropolitan Sports Center. Both boxers were expected to earn personal bests of $20,000-plus from a gate predicted to reach $100,000—big money for a nontitle fight in those days, and a potential record gate in Minnesota.

"I may as well tell you that I knew all the while I had to sign," Futch said. "Duane has been pushing me into it. He can't wait to get at LeDoux." LeDoux countered: "I know I can take Bobick's best punch and I don't think he can take mine."

A victory against Bobick would literally open the doors to new arenas for LeDoux. Two top promoters would be watching: Don King told Sternberg that he would be in the winner's dressing room with a contract to fight either Dino Denis or Larry Holmes, both undefeated. Mike Malitz, the head of Top Rank, already had Bobick under contract to fight European champ Bunny Johnson in Munich on May 24, part of a card featuring Muhammad Ali. "If LeDoux wins decisively, and certainly if he scores a knockout, we'd have to substitute him for Bobick against Johnson," Malitz said.

LeDoux was maturing not only as a fighter during this time but also as a person—or so it seemed. Becoming a parent may have been the life-changing event that made him refocus his priorities and lessened the frequency of LeDoux's boxing-related tantrums, according to friends.

He also put more consideration into how his boxing career affected Sandy. "Like most women, she doesn't enjoy boxing," he said. "It's no fun for her to see me come home after a fight with a broken eardrum, one eye cut, the other closed and watch me be sick for a week and urinate blood."

LeDoux was even beginning to look like a grown-up. After he defeated Rodney Bobick the previous April, Papa Joe told him, "Scott, you got enough money now. Go buy yourself a suit." And he did. Decades later, Chuck Daszkiewicz recalled LeDoux showing up in a three-piece blue suit, nearly bursting the vest buttons with pride. "Things really started to take off for him then," Daszkiewicz remembered. "He was very stubborn. He was like a spoiled little kid then. If he didn't get his way, he would stomp and shout. He'd be the easiest guy to rattle."

Years later, lifelong friend Diane Resch—one of the few people who knew that LeDoux had been molested when he was five—wondered how much the emotional scarring of that horrific event pushed her buddy toward tantrums. But Chuck Daszkiewicz and the others in LeDoux's corner knew nothing about that life-changing childhood trauma. Daszkiewicz just knew that this guy he goaded when they sparred "started to tame down, started to learn discipline, started to put things together."

LeDoux would pull out all the stops for his date with Bobick. He brought in Eddie Brooks as a sparring partner and summoned Ron Stander. A week before the Bobick fight, LeDoux went a total of ten rounds against three sparring partners: Tom Van Hoof, Lou Hokanson, and Brooks. Van Hoof was certain that LeDoux was ready: "I've worked many rounds with LeDoux, but today he hit me the hardest right hand I've ever taken from him."

Others weren't convinced. LeDoux appeared vulnerable to Brooks's right hand, they said.

On to the fight. Let the verbal sparring begin. LeDoux: "I can punch harder than Bobick and I can take a punch better. I've seen him staggered. No one has ever seen me staggered."

Bobick countered: "You are going to see a smart matador against a dumb bull Thursday, and I'm the matador. I'm tired of hearing about good fighters going into the Twin Cities and beating LeDoux but losing decisions to him. Scrap Iron Johnson beat him and only got a draw. Larry Middleton beat him and lost the decision. That kind of officiating is bad for boxing. I intend to take the decisions out of the official's hands. He is boasting that he will stop me in five or six rounds, but I intend to turn that around, and maybe it won't take me that long.

"I expect him to try to make a long-range fight and hope to get lucky with his right hand and maybe get me tired. But I won't get tired. I plan to stay on top of him and work on his body, watching for him to make a mistake. It may be a rough fight for a little while, but he'll make the mistake sooner or later. He usually makes it sooner."

LeDoux: "He has always portrayed himself as an All-American boy, but I know better. I have known Bobick for a long time and I've always known he is arrogant."

Sternberg was salivating. Bobick, the betting favorite, was 34–0. LeDoux was 18–1–1. Tickets priced at $5, $7.50, $10, and $15 were being sold at Dayton's department stores, the Met Center, the Kahler Motel in downtown Minneapolis, and the Seventh Street Gym—and they were selling briskly enough that Sternberg had visions of a $100,000 gate. The previous Minnesota record gate for boxing was the $69,642 that came in the night LeDoux beat Rodney Bobick and Duane defeated Raul Gorosito.

LeDoux got things rolling at the prefight press conference, arriving first and asking, "Where is the prima donna?"

Bobick, who said he had gone home to Bowlus the night before so his mother could give him his first haircut since Christmas, arrived ten minutes later. He held a camera. "I want to get a picture of Scott LeDoux, before and after," he said.

LeDoux was not amused.

"I believe I have the heart, courage and intelligence to defeat Bobick," LeDoux said. "I believe I have the power to win by a knockout. Bobick can be hit and hurt."

As the state-record crowd of 13,789 filed into the Met Center for the Thursday night grudge match, the bad blood between the two combatants boiled over behind closed doors. The scene seemed right out of a twenty-first-century pro wrestling script. LeDoux got in the first jab by switching the dressing-room signs on the unsuspecting Bobick because, LeDoux said, "I've had this one the last seven fights."

Bobick's camp more than evened the score by doing something that LeDoux, years later, described as "very disgusting, and I'll leave it at that." Two people close to LeDoux—one of whom was there—would only say that a shoe box was left for LeDoux but would not divulge the contents, at least not for the record. For good measure, the Bobick camp also delivered a sympathy card to LeDoux, signed "Duane."

The crowd, which included former vice president Hubert Humphrey, paid a Minnesota gate record of $113,725. They got their money's worth. Bobick won a clear ten-round decision. Yet, it was LeDoux's power, stamina, and—yes—courage that captured the crowd's imagination and hearts. He remained strong to the end, with the final three rounds his best.

Bobick, clearly the more skilled of the combatants, rarely missed when he took aim at LeDoux. But LeDoux stood calmly, taking every one of Bobick's best shots, as if to ask, "Is that the best you've got?" Even when LeDoux swung and missed, he generated the kind of oohs and aahs baseball fans often exuded when a slugger like the Twins' Harmon Killebrew would swing for the fences.

"That LeDoux is a tough son of a buck," said Joe Frazier, Bobick's manager. Frazier, dressed to the nines in a cream-colored suit and flowered shirt and dripping in chains and other jewelry, went on: "Duane Bobick is a strong puncher and he couldn't knock this guy out. I thought his (LeDoux's) legs were gone, but he kept coming."

Under a headline that read, "Top crowd hails LeDoux," veteran *Minneapolis Star* boxing writer Bill Hengen began his report by nearly ignoring the fight's winner. "The most outstanding part of the heavyweight fights was not what Bobick did to win the unanimous decision, but the courage displayed by LeDoux for 30 minutes," Hengen wrote. "And at the end, the 27-year-old loser—left eye completely closed, right cheekbones so swollen an X-ray is necessary, and spitting blood—rightfully accepted his share of the standing ovation at the Metropolitan Sports Center."

There was plenty of great theater to go along with a sporting event teeming with enough emotion to get any fan's blood percolating. The fight began with LeDoux vaulting into the ring like a professional wrestler, pointing at Bobick, and shouting, "I'll get you, you . . ." Twice in the early rounds, LeDoux was warned by referee Mert Herrick for throwing low blows. Bobick complained about LeDoux's errant elbows and thumbs.

"He's a tough man," Bobick said afterwards, "but it was not a tough fight for me mentally because he stood right in front of me. All I had to do was hit him. But he wouldn't go down."

LeDoux called it "losing a battle, not a war. I think I proved myself as a fighter and I'd like to fight him again, or anyone.

"Bobick is a sharp puncher, but not devastating," LeDoux went on. "He telegraphs some punches. He won. But probably the biggest surprise to each of us was the fact it went all 10."

And the financial winner of the fight? Bobick's handlers demanded a $20,000 guarantee against 20 percent of the gate receipts. That came to $22,740. It was his largest payday since becoming a professional.

LeDoux's corner took a gamble. Instead of demanding an exact guaranteed amount, they took a straight guarantee of 27.5 percent of the gate. Although he lost the decision, LeDoux was the night's big financial winner. He took in $31,267—a good $8,500 more than Bobick.

"I knew he'd be tough to knock down, but I never realized he'd be that tough," Bobick said. "I'm ready to fight him anytime Eddie [trainer Eddie Futch] gives me the word."

LeDoux echoed that sentiment. "What I don't like about Bobick is that he thinks he's something special, not a regular guy. . . . He fought a smart fight. He did some things I've never seen him do before. But I do know this much: Duane has all the moves, but he can't crack an egg.

"I'm ready to fight him any time we can get together. Next time I'll be better prepared."

11

A FOREMAN GRILLING

*P*addy Flood, a fight manager who was associated with Don King in the 1970s, once described young heavyweights to *Sports Illustrated*'s Mark Kram as "unpredictable as some 3-year-old horses—and they eat a lot more.

"They can break your heart," Flood told *Sports Illustrated*. "They can frustrate you to pieces, and you have to have the patience of a saint. You never know what's comin' next. One punch and it can be all over.

"With a big, young heavyweight, he begins to get noticed after five fights," Flood continued in an interview published May 31, 1976. "Their egos build real fast, so fast that they start talkin' before their talent is in bloom."

Against Bobick, LeDoux's ego took a massive hit. He said he stood over a dressing-room sink and cried after the fight. Further, despite the greatest payday of his blossoming career, "we were a young family and we were broke." Chuck Daszkiewicz said that LeDoux was his own worst enemy when it came to finances, lavishing himself with expensive toys, like a motorcycle and Triumph Spitfire.

LeDoux had just lost a decision to an undefeated heavyweight. But when he was offered a chance to make $22,000 by fighting another, he jumped at it.

John (Dino) Denis, a fifth-year professional, was born in Trieste, a seaport in northeast Italy, and raised in Attleboro, Massachusetts. At six foot three and 210 pounds and with no losses and only one draw against twenty-seven victories, Denis was considered the best heavyweight to come out of New England since Rocky Marciano, the undefeated all-fury-no-finesse Brockton Blockbuster, who won forty-three of his forty-nine fights by knockouts. Denis's manager, Al Braverman, marveled at the way his twenty-three-year-old fighter paid attention to instruction. "The only thing we got to teach him is not to lose his cool," Braverman said.

Half of his fights ended in knockouts. *The Ring* magazine had him ranked tenth in the world in 1976. But a month before meeting LeDoux, Denis told *Sports Illustrated* that he was still waiting for his body to fill out, and that he was still "a year or so away."

The fight—fought at the North Providence Arena in Rhode Island, practically Denis's backyard—was televised nationally and served as a coming-out party for both fighters. LeDoux dropped the unanimous ten-round decision but finished impressively. He caught Denis with several hard overhand rights, but Denis hit LeDoux almost at will in the early rounds with his left jab.

"I think I would have won the fight if I had won the 10th," LeDoux said afterwards. "But I didn't fight a good tenth round. I should have jabbed more, as my corner had instructed me. I was up for this fight and thought I fought a good fight, but I guess Denis was up higher than I was."

LeDoux won the first and fourth rounds. He opened up a large cut over Denis's left eye in the second round, and a cut under his right eye in the fourth. Denis, the hometown favorite, with the crowd strongly behind him, blasted LeDoux with shots to the left eye and chin.

Years later, in a bit of revisionist history, LeDoux claimed he was robbed. "Big time," LeDoux said. "I beat him up really bad. Here's the interesting thing: I cut him over both eyes, busted up his nose, busted up his ribs and, when the fight was over, on the judges' scorecards, I did not win a single round!

"Wait a minute! Who was hitting him then? Somebody better take a look at the referee, 'cause somebody busted this kid up."

But even through battered, puffy eyes, LeDoux could see the bottom line. "Up until two years ago, I was a truck driver and if I was still driving a truck, I'd be making $15,000," he said.

Despite two consecutive losses, LeDoux was about to become a former truck driver on the fast track to stardom. And the wallflower who not so quietly planned to be his escort to the land of dreams was the man tossing thunderbolts at a sport that was already up to its Everlast gloves in controversy—the suddenly legendary Don King.

The architect behind the Rumble in the Jungle and Thrilla in Manila was quickly assembling a stable of Hall of Fame–caliber talent, promoting fights featuring Muhammad Ali, Joe Frazier, and George Foreman, and he would later include in his stable of box-office bonanzas Larry Holmes, Mike Tyson, and Evander Holyfield as well—heavyweight champions all. With hair that stood erect, King looked as if he had stuck his finger in a light socket, but it was his oratory ability that was pure electricity. "My hair is like an aura from God," King once said. "It is like Samson's hair. But forget the hair. Ask me about my genius."

When it came to promoting—boxers, fights, himself—King rarely had to be asked or prodded. Others may not have understood him, but King knew exactly who he was. "They tell me to be cool, Jack, not to make waves," he said. "I am the wave."

King's journey is well chronicled: An illegal bookmaker, he was charged with killing men in separate incidents thirteen years apart. One was determined to be justifiable homicide after King shot in the back a man who tried to rob one of King's gambling houses. Then, in 1966, King was convicted of second-degree murder after stomping to death an employee who owed him $600. That conviction was reduced to non-negligent manslaughter. King served three years and eleven months in prison. He would later be pardoned for the crime, in 1983, by Ohio governor Jim Rhodes.

In 1974, he took the boxing world by a storm with his pairing of Ali and then-champion Foreman in Africa and by staging the epic third battle between Ali and Frazier in the Philippines. Both bouts reached legendary status overnight. Decades later, boxing fans still talk about the Ali–Frazier slugfest.

The great ones rarely let the facts get in the way of a good promotion, and King was without peer. Like a preacher whose voice keeps rising as pulses thump feverishly, King was always the main attraction before the combatants entered the ring. OK, so maybe LeDoux never ate rusty nails for breakfast, chased bears in northern Minnesota, or took law courses at the University of Minnesota in 1976, as King suggested. It sounded good, and if it got the public's attention, the flamboyant King knew it might sell tickets.

Equally fascinating was LeDoux's proposed opponent: Foreman.

Television viewers who recall Foreman as a lovable, God-fearing pitchman for hamburger grills bearing his name (the "Lean Mean Fat

Reducing Grilling Machine") should watch video of his 1973 championship fight against Joe Frazier. Foreman, an Olympic gold medalist and winner of all thirty-seven of his professional fights, was facing in Frazier, a heavyweight champion whose vicious left hooks dismantled the great Ali in 1971, in the first of their three epic battles. Frazier was a beast, but he was no match for the six-foot-three Foreman, who said his greatest fear before the fight was knocking Frazier down and then paying the price for awakening a sleeping giant.

But once the fight was under way, the greatest fears of many fans were that Frazier might get off the canvas for more. Broadcaster Howard Cosell's call in the first round is legendary: "Down goes Frazier, down goes Frazier, down goes Frazier." Foreman, who was four inches taller than the champ, decked Frazier three times in the first round. He so overwhelmed the previously unbeaten champion that in the second round Foreman reportedly told Frazier's trainer, Yancey Durham, "Stop it or I'm going to kill him." Referee Arthur Mercante did just that with one minute, thirty-five seconds left in the second round.

Even more stunning were the events that took place in the ring the following year. In his second title defense, Foreman buckled the knees of the great Ken Norton, who didn't make it through the second round. Foreman seemed invincible.

Until he took on Ali in Zaire. The former champ, a decided underdog, allowed Foreman to tattoo his body but not his head. He tagged Foreman's face several times and then leaned back as Foreman flailed away, often missing badly and exerting himself to the point of near exhaustion by the seventh round. Along with his rope-a-dope strategy, Ali taunted Foreman throughout and then knocked him down in the eighth with a right to the jaw.

No longer champion, Foreman began a comeback by brutally eliminating Ron Lyle in five rounds. Before Foreman's rematch with Frazier on June 15, 1976, Smoking Joe's manager, Eddie Futch, predicted things would be much different the second time around. "Frazier won't get nailed early next time," Futch said. "After the fourth round, we won't have any trouble."

Foreman took Frazier out in the fifth round.

Next up: LeDoux.

"Scott insisted on the fight," said co-manager Daszkiewicz. "We didn't push him. We only yielded to his insistence."

CBS was thrilled with the charismatic LeDoux's performance against Denis and couldn't wait to air another of his fights. LeDoux wanted the fight in Minnesota, of course, but Foreman wanted it elsewhere. King, who was promoting the package, settled on Utica, New York, a city of sixty thousand and the halfway point between Albany and Syracuse.

"It's not going to be a great pay day for LeDoux, but the national recognition makes it worthwhile," Daszkiewicz said. "And if he should beat the former champion, well, who knows? Maybe Muhammad Ali?"

After agreeing to three fights against Norton only to have Norton pull out each time, LeDoux was antsy to fight a big-time opponent. Further, by this point, LeDoux increasingly was calling the shots. Publicly, he claimed that he didn't care about the money. "If I can get the wins, they can have the money. I don't like to lose," he said before the Foreman fight. Privately, however, he talked about splitting managerial duties with Daszkiewicz and divorcing himself from the team that had backed him financially since early in his pro career. That would be fine with Gunn, who let Palmer buy out his share of LeDoux, and the more promoters like King became involved with LeDoux's career, the less appealing the already seamy world of professional boxing became for Palmer. "See, Don King still runs boxing," Palmer said in 2010. "There's a sordid side of boxing. I pretty much had had it with all the politics of the sport."

LeDoux wasn't living on another planet. The Ali fight aside, Foreman's power, size, and aggression matched that of the greatest boxers of the century. LeDoux knew what the odds makers in Vegas were thinking.

"If you don't believe in yourself you'd better get a new job," LeDoux said. "I realize that I've got to fight a good fight against Foreman. But why not Foreman? You don't learn anything, you don't gain anything by fighting someone below you. You've got to step forward.

"When you go in the ring against George Foreman, you don't want to go out and stick your head out and say, 'Take your best shot,'" LeDoux said. "It'll be up there in orbit.

"The key to the fight will be to box him well enough to stay in the fight through five rounds. After five rounds, then I could make a move. Everybody knows that for five rounds he's an animal, but after that he starts fading.

"I think in the later rounds I can take him out when he's tired. You're not going to take him out with one punch."

Foreman saw the fight as little more than a tune-up. "By fighting Le-Doux, I'm keeping the tools greased all the time, so when a [title] shot comes along, I'll be ready," he said.

Utica Mayor Edward Hanna couldn't even remember LeDoux's name just days before the bout. He was talking about how the fight with Foreman would give the economically depressed city a boost when he referred to LeDoux as "the other guy . . . what's his name."

LeDoux took the slight in stride. "I know the crowd will be for Foreman," he said. "I mean, who is Scott LeDoux? They've never heard of me before. They probably expect me to come out there in boots and a pick axe."

Some of the central New York media seemed more interested in interviewing Sandy LeDoux than her husband. In an interview with the *Utica Daily Press*, she talked about the family dog, about her husband's sensitive side, about being ignored by a public consumed by her athletic husband. "Most people think this is a life of glamor, but it's far from that," she said. "Not that it's bad . . . but some women can't accept it all.

"Our dog has had his name in the paper more than I have."

The media was falling in love with her. Sandy was the one person who could bring sunshine to a place like Utica, where like most of central New York, the sun sets in October and doesn't reappear until early May. Her husband wasn't quite the orator that King was, but LeDoux knew how to grab the public's attention—and he was quickly becoming a media darling because of it.

"If you gave George Foreman a piece of bubble gum and told him to walk, he'd have a hard time," LeDoux said four days before the fight.

LeDoux, justifiably the underdog, had become annoyed with the media that didn't give him a chance. He lambasted the *St. Paul Pioneer Press*'s Don Riley, telling the veteran columnist, "Bull! Riley! Bull! I know a damn lot more about this than you do. It's no execution. Do I look like a lamb? . . . I've got some surprises, for you and Foreman.

"Marie Antoinette? How was her job?"

LeDoux didn't stop there. He said Foreman didn't train hard enough, "doesn't know how to box," and that "it's going to be my fight after the fifth round."

King loved the rhetoric. "He really believes he's going to win," King said.

Looking back, Denny Nelson, the referee who worked many of Le-Doux's fights in Minnesota, understood LeDoux's confidence. "Scott was always a rough and tumble kind of kid," Nelson said. "He always had heart and desired to fight. Never backed down from anybody." Nelson told a story of how Foreman said that when he got into the ring with Frazier the first time, his knees were knocking. "It takes a lot of nerve, a lot of guts to walk up those steps," Nelson said.

If LeDoux needed a reminder of where he stood on boxing's totem pole, the Utica mayor gave Foreman the key to the city two days before the fight. Almost as an afterthought, Mayor Hanna had one of his aides give LeDoux—the guy whose name he couldn't remember—a similar key.

Many experts thought the key to LeDoux's chances against Foreman was survival.

LeDoux didn't survive.

Foreman battered LeDoux, knocking him out two minutes and fifty-eight seconds into the third round.

Lou Hokanson, who fought LeDoux as an amateur in 1973 and then became his sparring partner, was in LeDoux's corner in Utica when Le-Doux sat down after the first round.

"Hey, Lou," said a bleary-eyed LeDoux.

"Yeah, Scott," Hokanson replied.

"Hey, Lou," LeDoux repeated.

"I'm right here, Scott," his friend responded, trying to get LeDoux to focus.

"Hey, Lou," LeDoux said for a third time. "Is my forehead still in the front of my face? Because after he hit me, I can't feel it anymore."

A left-right combination left LeDoux wobbly in the second round. His nose was bleeding. In the third round, Foreman pummeled LeDoux with lefts and rights. Foreman threw an uppercut—and LeDoux went down. He had never been knocked off his feet before.

"The very first round I had bleeding out of his nose," LeDoux recalled years later. "I hit him with a left jab and some good right jabs to the body.

"In the second round, I was doing OK, but then he blasted me with a right hand. I mean, there's no disaster when you get hit by a guy like George Foreman. Who hasn't he hit that he hasn't taken out, except Ali? I don't know of anybody else." As Ron Lyle, a future opponent of LeDoux's, once noted, "When George Foreman hit you, it felt like the house fell on you."

After the fight, Foreman admitted that he had been worried by Le-Doux's prematch confidence. "He was loud-mouthing me," Foreman said. "He called me a fool. He was mean to me. So I expected him to come right at me. But instead, he started counter-punching me a lot. He did a real good job of it.

"He was extremely smart. He didn't go for any of my stuff. I had a tough time with this guy. He had my nose bleeding. I couldn't believe it. I think he can beat a lot of guys who can't punch as hard as I can."

For his effort against Foreman, LeDoux was paid approximately $25,000.

"It's been a good year," he said, "and better than driving a truck."

12

A HAIR-RAISING FIX

$\mathcal{F}$ ive months after the Foreman fight, LeDoux was strolling the
streets of Montreal, Canada, to attend a fight featuring Minneapolis super welterweight Rafael Rodriguez, when he was approached by
Paddy Flood, the boxing manager associated with Don King.

"Word on the street is you're gonna lose," LeDoux remembered Flood
telling him that day in January 1977.

"Who you kidding?" LeDoux said with a laugh. "I'll murder this guy,"
he said of his next opponent, rising heavyweight Johnny Boudreaux.

"Word on the street is you're gonna lose," Flood repeated, according
to LeDoux.

Thus began the wild tale of a bout that for many fight fans would de-
fine LeDoux's career.

LeDoux needed to make a comeback statement, something far greater than his second round–knockout victory over Junior Bentley in the
Minneapolis Auditorium the previous November, three months after the
Foreman defeat. Fight fans were still talking about LeDoux's three consecutive defeats to Bobick, Denis, and Foreman—fighters who had a combined record of 105–1–1, with the lone loss being Foreman's defeat to Ali.
Once an up-and-comer himself, LeDoux was on the verge of becoming an
afterthought, a never-was, his fights destined to be found on the inside
pages of the sports section, in tiny print, next to the pro hockey standings.

"You gotta start fighting some lesser opponents, get some wins back,"
Daszkiewicz told LeDoux.

Enter Don King.

It was King who contacted the LeDoux camp and set up the fight
with Denis in Providence. The promoter promised him a good fight in an

overlooked venue, saying Providence "could be the mecca of boxing." He probably said the same about Utica.

"He was a big man, a wild guy and I think the act was 60 percent of what he did, because he knew he had to perform to be a promoter," Le-Doux said. "He was very smart. To me, he was the best promoter I ever saw. He could come in and sell a fight to dogs. He was just phenomenal.

"Ben Sternberg was tremendously honest, a very nice man. But Bob Arum and Don King got the big fights. I had a family to raise. I quit the trucking company, but I was still working construction. I was a cable finder, you know, find the cables so they don't dig them up.

"I needed something big."

And King was planning something big—a nationally televised tournament that would determine a new American heavyweight champion. "We will show that boxing belongs, that the undesirable elements long associated with it are no more," King told *Sports Illustrated* in January 1977. "Some things die hard. People don't know what they're talking about when they talk of fixes and gangsterism inside boxing. That's a holdover from years and years ago.

"What about baseball and basketball and football and horse racing? The scandals in those sports have been outrageous and on a larger scale. Yet they come back bigger than ever. Why? Because of television, of the concerted efforts and promotion behind them.

"That's what we intend to do with boxing: unify it and point it in a new direction."

King's plan to unify boxing stemmed from a division between him and Ali. King came into prominence via his professional marriage to Ali, but when Ali moved to promoter Bob Arum, King's greatest rival, King scrambled to find something other than Foreman's comeback on which to rest his reputation, future, and fortune. Flood, a former boxer himself with an honorable reputation, urged King to promote a tournament that might capture the public's imagination—as did the recently ordained powerhouse 1976 U.S. Olympic team that featured gold medalists Sugar Ray Leonard, brothers Leon and Michael Spinks, Howard Davis, and Leo Randolph. "If you're going to be remembered at all, you'll be remembered because of this tournament, not because of Ali," Flood told King.

The tournament, coming on the heels of the success of the Montreal Olympics and the first *Rocky* movie, would crown undisputed American champions in several weight classes. That the current heavyweight champ, Ali, was from Louisville and still the face of American boxing didn't phase tournament organizers. "Any kind of title is worth something," said Al Braverman, a former fighter who joined forces with King in 1975. Braverman, who negotiated contracts for King-promoted fights, coordinated the 1977 tournament along with fellow boxing manager Flood. "An American title? Well, that's clout if you have it."

King needed financial muscle and credibility to make the tournament work.

The Ring magazine, the self-proclaimed "Bible of Boxing," offered an image of legitimacy—even though the magazine's circulation had been in free fall for more than a decade. In many boxing circles, however, *The Ring*'s reputation for ranking fighters was still the gospel. Once King got the support of *The Ring*—after promising the magazine $70,000 for its rankings—as well as support from the New York State athletic commissioner, James A. Farley Jr., ABC invested $1.5 million in the tournament, promising to carry some of the fights on prime-time network TV. The heavyweights would receive $15,000 for eight-round quarterfinal matches, and $30,000 in the semifinals, and the winner would earn $135,000 with the runner-up taking home $45,000.

If it all sounded too good to be true, the list of heavyweight participants, scheduled to fight at the U.S. Naval Base in Annapolis, Maryland, had some boxing experts scratching their heads. The heavyweight entrants were Larry Holmes, Dino Denis, Tom Prater, Leroy Jones, Boudreaux, and LeDoux, with Jeff Merritt and Kevin Isaac as alternates. Missing were Ron Lyle, Ken Norton, and Foreman—three of boxing's biggest heavyweight names at the time.

"Al Braverman was the matchmaker, and he called us in November and signed us for the tournament," LeDoux said. "The contract called for three fights, assuming you got past the first two. It was a great deal for a fighter like me and I needed it."

"Promoter Don King has promised us a title fight if we win, so it's a chance worth taking," Daszkiewicz said of the February 13 bout against the eighth-ranked Boudreaux.

Boudreaux and LeDoux had three common ring opponents: Both outpointed Brian O'Melia. Both beat Terry Daniels, LeDoux by a knockout. LeDoux lost to Cookie Wallace by technical knockout, after a Wallace head butt opened a cut above LeDoux's eye; Boudreaux beat Wallace by decision.

King appeared to have the tournament package of his dreams. He wanted more. No, he didn't ask for more money. In fact, he wanted everyone to know that he was only being reimbursed for production costs and was happy with the arrangement. But King had something worth much more—the enticement of network TV exposure for fighters hoping to participate in his tournament. In return for the privilege of participating, he wanted participants to sign exclusive contracts with him for future fights.

Marvelous Marvin Hagler, who later became middleweight champion, refused to sign with King and was omitted from the tournament.

Then there was LeDoux, still an outsider. He and Daszkiewicz agreed to the tournament but didn't sign over LeDoux's future to King. After the tournament, LeDoux said King had ties to eleven of the twenty-four fighters who competed. Flood, who told LeDoux he was going to lose when the two met in Montreal just weeks before the Boudreaux fight, was a King associate who controlled six of the fighters. Five others were controlled by Chris Cline, another King associate, according to LeDoux.

"We are up against the odds," Daszkiewicz said. "We have a couple of young fighters in our camp who are better than the people in this tournament in the lower weight classes. But they couldn't get in because they're not owned by the right people.

"We didn't find out until we got here that most of the fighters are owned by the same people. If we had known that, we wouldn't have entered the tournament."

Just who were some of these fighters? Many of the participants were hardly the great challengers tournament officials purported them to be. One middleweight, a Texas policeman named Ike Fluellen, was ranked tenth by The Ring magazine. He had been inactive recently, but after signing a deal with a manager with ties to King, Fluellen was suddenly credited with two phantom victories in Mexico. A month later, The Ring ranked him number three.

Just before the tournament commenced, eleven of its fighters were found to have had records that were believed to have been falsified by The Ring. The magazine blamed the mistakes and inflated rankings on clerical errors and on unsubstantiated records provided by managers.

Again, this was long before the Internet, social media, and the watchdog journalism of today.

The unusual venues for the tournament also raised a few eyebrows. Among them were a U.S. Navy aircraft carrier, the U.S. Naval Academy, and the Ohio prison where King had served nearly four years for manslaughter. All were outside the jurisdiction of state boxing commissions.

But nobody blew a whistle. Until the LeDoux–Boudreaux fight.

"LeDoux was supposed to be a stepping-stone for Boudreaux—and Scott just beat the hell out of him," recalled Jerry Blackledge, who had met LeDoux two years before, when they drove trucks for rival Twin Cities companies. Blackledge was in LeDoux's corner in Annapolis.

LeDoux flattened Boudreaux early for the fight's only knockdown and appeared to dominate the eight-round bout. Flood, acting as advisor to Boudreaux, said he almost stopped the fight because of an injury to Boudreaux's right foot.

"I was thinking I did everything right in the fight," LeDoux told the media after the bout. "I was the aggressor. I was body punching—the lost art of boxing. And my jabs were good.

"There was no doubt in my mind. It was one of my best fights and if I wasn't doing something in the ring, Boudreaux would just move around.

"Howard Cosell was there and he says to me, 'As soon as they announce the decision, come down here at ringside because I want to interview you.'

"My God, I said to myself, this is the big time."

Then the decision was given to Boudreaux.

When LeDoux heard Boudreaux's name, he thought the public-address announcer was asking fans to give Boudreaux a hand. Then he realized that Boudreaux had won. To paraphrase the Associated Press report, LeDoux "went berserk." He watched Boudreaux about to be interviewed by Cosell and decided "that wasn't going to happen . . . Boudreaux wasn't going to be on television."

Daszkiewicz shouted at King, then fell. According to LeDoux, "Boudreaux and his people started kicking Joe."

"Boy, that was a hornet's nest," Daszkiewicz said. He protested that many of the fighters were "owned" by King's organization. "I started to get bumped around, and so I crawled under the press table," Daszkiewicz said.

LeDoux watched in disbelief. "That's when I went crazy," he said.

LeDoux went over the ropes, above Cosell, and shouted, "Come on, Howard. Do what you say you do. Tell it like it is. You know I won this fight.

"Then Boudreaux turned around and made a face at me. I kicked at him and missed. Boudreaux saw my foot coming, and he jumped out of the way, and he got tangled in the wires down there."

Those wires extended to the headset Cosell was wearing. Boudreaux jumped back, jerking the headphones off Cosell.

And Cosell's toupee went flying with the headset.

"You could see the toupee flying and Howard's head as clear as can be on tape," LeDoux said years later. "There wasn't much taping equipment around [in 1977], and Howard was able to put a halt to anyone getting copies from ABC."

(Before the scene with Cosell became a YouTube favorite on the Internet, someone from Minnesota sent LeDoux a tape of the hair-raising incident. "When I'm feeling down, I play that tape," LeDoux said. "It always gives me a good laugh to see Howard's wig go flying.")

Cosell's hairpiece had become unglued. And so would the United States Boxing Championships.

LeDoux claimed he went after Boudreaux because Boudreaux called him a chump. Now, it was LeDoux making all the noise. "Fix, fix," he shouted before doing an interview with Cosell.

Roone Arledge, president of ABC Sports, watched in disbelief as the entire horror show played out. This is how he described the fiasco in his memoir, *Roone*:

"I was watching from home as a fighter named Scott LeDoux pummeled the bejeezus out of an unfortunate named Johnny Boudreaux. But to my astonishment, and that of Howard and George Foreman, and seemingly everyone else in the arena, the unanimous verdict of the judges went to Boudreaux.

"LeDoux thereupon cried, 'Fix,' and dropkicked Boudreaux as he was being interviewed by Howard. In the process, Howard's toupee was knocked sideways. Moments later, 'The American Sportsman' went on. That's when it was scheduled to start. And I grabbed for the Roone phone.

"'Goddamn, you can't just go off the air on something like that!' I shouted at Chet Forte, who was producing. 'The name of ABC Sports is on this thing. Get the kid back and let Howard interview him!'"

The chaos continued in the fighters' dressing rooms.

"I made a fool of myself," LeDoux said. "I tried to apologize to that clown in there, but he wouldn't let me. I apologized to the fans. If you're going to fight, leave it in the ring."

Boudreaux, who had his foot soaking in ice after the fight, said that if he called LeDoux any names, "it was during the fight and then I can call him anything I want."

In his dressing room, LeDoux was asked to sign a legal document that the promoters were asking all the participants to sign, a pledge of allegiance to the tournament of sorts. He refused. LeDoux was told he would not be paid the $15,000 the promoters promised.

"Scott then really shouted," Daszkiewicz said. "He said he signed for a fight; he fought a fight, and he wouldn't leave until he was paid."

King thrived on the controversy and all the publicity it initially brought, at least publicly. "As a boxing fan, I would have voted for LeDoux," he said two days after the fight. "But I am not a boxing official."

Each of the three officials who scored the fight gave it to Boudreaux. Referee Joe Bunsa scored it three rounds for Boudreaux, two for LeDoux, and three even. Judge Harold Valan gave five rounds to Boudreaux and three to LeDoux. Judge Carol Polis scored it four for Boudreaux, three for LeDoux, and one even. More than three decades later, Polis said she was sure she scored the fight properly. She said that LeDoux connected with more punches but said many of those punches were "ineffective."

Appointed the first female professional boxing judge in the United States in 1973 by Pennsylvania governor Milton Shapp, Polis said she judged twenty-seven title fights. She appeared on the TV quiz shows *What's My Line?* and *To Tell the Truth.* She did one fight at Philadelphia's legendary Blue Horizon. "My daughter was about to give birth," she recalled. "I went from one bloody arena to another."

The LeDoux–Boudreaux fight is one she never forgot. "It was an honor for me to work that tournament," she said. "It was a great idea that Don King had. I was excited to go to the Admiral's dinner [at the Naval Academy]. Everything was good.

"It was a unanimous decision. Anybody who would try to get to us . . . they don't know us. It just wasn't going to happen.

"I remember [LeDoux being] a very cocky guy, very arrogant," she said. "It makes me feel sad to say that. But he was unbelievably obnoxious. Fighters don't act like that. It was a unanimous decision."

(At least one former champion, not involved in the tournament, thought the decision was absurd. "The decision was the worst," said Ken Norton. "They had eight referees and judges on the list. . . . All five qualified officials that weren't used had LeDoux winning when they were interviewed.")

After a heated verbal exchange involving LeDoux, Daszkiewicz, and members of the tournament's promotion team, LeDoux was paid.

For King, it was just another day at the office. He was convinced that LeDoux and Daszkiewicz were "so impassioned after the fight" because the tournament was important to them and they wanted to remain in it. "I think controversy enhances the tournament," King said.

ABC, which put up $1.5 million in purses for the tournament in six weight divisions, wasn't as certain. "Any challenge to the integrity of the tournament casts a heavy shadow on the promotion as a whole," Arledge said.

LeDoux was still breathing fire as he left his dressing room. Then it hit him: Fighting Boudreaux was one thing, but now he was taking on the boxing establishment. "Who knows what happens when you get in a hassle with people who run boxing?" LeDoux said after the debacle. "I felt I was the winner 6–1 in rounds going into the last round. I had Boudreaux bleeding early and I'm sure my body attack broke some of his ribs. And I knocked him down in the second round."

"I'm not afraid to stand up to boxing," LeDoux said. "I blast it when I have to."

Outside the arena, LeDoux and Daszkiewicz were told that there was a limousine waiting to take them back to their hotel. "No way we're getting in that limo," Papa Joe told LeDoux and the others in his corner.

The group crammed into another vehicle—as many as seven of them piled into a two-door Pontiac LeMans, recalled Chuck Daszkiewicz—and arrived at their hotel to discover that their bags had been packed and brought down to the front door. LeDoux never learned how or why the bags were taken out of their rooms, and he didn't care.

"We've already had a bomb threat," a hotel official told LeDoux's party. Chuck Daszkiewicz remembered the man telling them, "You guys gotta get out of here. We don't want you here. Everything's taken care of. We've paid off your rooms. Please, please leave."

They were more than willing to comply. A cab was already waiting.

"We wanted to get to the airport and out of Maryland as fast as possible," he said.

"The connecting flight to Chicago was unbelievable, with people telling me they saw me on TV and that I was robbed," LeDoux said. "I felt like a celebrity, on top of the world."

He signed autographs. Joe Daszkiewicz cringed until his son, Chuck, told him, "Dad, are you kidding me? This is the biggest thing ever to happen to the sport. You'll have so many fights.

"Who stands up to Don King?"

Then LeDoux called Sandy. Through tears, she told him that she had received three threatening phone calls. One caller, LeDoux said, told her, "Tell your husband to keep his mouth shut or he's gonna be dead." LeDoux said he was later told that there was a contract on him. The threat was never verified, but it got LeDoux's attention. He said he "thought about getting another dog to team with my old English sheep dog for house protection. Then one day my wife and I sat down and talked about it." They decided not to listen to "the voices of doom."

When someone from CBS's news department called, though, LeDoux was all ears. He was asked if he would be willing to be interviewed. "Ask me one question," he told the network. "Ask me, 'Are you afraid of Don King?'" He was told, "Oh, we'd love to ask that."

LeDoux said he was flown to New York for the interview, and the question was asked. His answer: "No. Because if anything ever happens to me, they'll know where to look."

But LeDoux was scared, mostly for his wife and young son. "Sure I felt some fear," he said. "Wouldn't you? I even began remembering some of those old movies and what happened to a fighter who went against the establishment."

Two days after LeDoux's questionable loss to Boudreaux, he was offered a ten-round headliner with Pedro Soto at Madison Square Garden on March 2. LeDoux jumped at the opportunity. "I've always wanted to fight in Madison Square Garden," he said. "Your first fight in the Garden is called a shooting match. You win that and they use you again. I want to win a shooting match."

Later that week, however, the Maryland State Athletic Commission said it would hold a hearing to determine if LeDoux and Daszkiewicz should be disciplined for their part in the ringside scuffle.

The Boudreaux melee may have been in the record books, but it was hardly over, and apparently it wasn't going away anytime soon. LeDoux, who had become something of a media darling thanks to his candor and availability, was ready to take advantage of his sudden thrust into the limelight when he reached New York.

King and ABC could have their U.S. tournament. The Garden was ready to crown the March 2 winners "American" champions.

Using his right-handed power while keeping Soto off balance with left jabs, LeDoux came back strong in the later rounds to win a split decision. LeDoux bloodied Soto's face, may have broken his nose, and buckled Soto's knees in the ninth round. Still, his victory came by split decision and was anything but overwhelming. Judge Artie Aidala had scored the fight a decisive 7–3 for Soto. The Associated Press scored it 6–4 for Soto. Soto was a Garden favorite. When he lost the decision, a near-riot ensued.

"Yes, it was a little disturbance, all right," said the Garden's Teddy Brenner.

No matter. It was a win, and in his column after the fight, legendary *New York Times* columnist Red Smith referred to LeDoux as one of the "American" champions.

It was just a month removed from the Boudreaux debacle, and LeDoux was told that a fight with Ali in Korea later in the year was possible. Garden matchmaker Brenner wanted LeDoux for future bouts. Even LeDoux's Minnesota rival Duane Bobick was literally in his corner cheering him on against Soto.

"The publicity from the fight against Boudreaux was a big help," LeDoux said, who earned $10,000 for beating Soto. "All across the country they said I was robbed. And a lot of nice things happened in the Garden."

Then reality hit the heavy bag, in the form of a subpoena. LeDoux was called to testify before a federal grand jury in Baltimore.

Because the fights had taken place at the U.S. Naval Academy, any crimes committed fell under federal jurisdiction. The FBI, which reportedly was brought in for the investigation, had plenty of leads to work with. There was LeDoux's claim that he was told weeks before his fight that he couldn't win. New reports surfaced, claiming that at least one fighter in the tournament paid $3,300 in alleged kickbacks to participate in elimination bouts.

Jervis Finney, the U.S. attorney for Maryland, refused to confirm or deny the investigation was taking place. The FBI also refused to comment. Sandy LeDoux told a reporter that her husband "doesn't want to say anything about it. We'd prefer you say nothing about it."

King and his associates had plenty to say to the media.

"Nobody has done anything wrong," Braverman said. He called LeDoux's charges "the crying squeals of a loser. There's nothing to investigate. It's all ridiculous." King called LeDoux's claims "ludicrous" and said he welcomed a federal grand jury investigation. "I know I will be exonerated and it will give the tournament more credibility," King said.

Dan Rather's CBS report—the one for which LeDoux was interviewed—aired on April 12, 1977. Rather used footage from the LeDoux–Boudreaux fight, but his report was a full-scale lambasting of professional boxing's current sorry state. In it, Rather even went after CBS, his own network, for controlling fighters.

More affidavits and allegations were surfacing. Fluellen, the Houston cop, was not the only tournament participant accused of being in The Ring magazine–reported phantom fights. The Ring credited lightweight Pat Dolan with four phony 1975 wins in New York and New Jersey. Featherweight Hilbert Stevenson was credited with five fake wins in 1976. Junior middleweight Anthony House was credited with a total of seven phony fights. Junior middleweight Mel Dennis was listed as scoring two phony knockouts in Argentina. Four other fighters—Greg Coverson, Vonzell Johnson, Floyd Mayweather, and Richard Rozelle—were given a total of eleven phony wins.

(There was more. Sports Illustrated reported that the 1975 edition of The Ring Record Book listed a phony Congelese heavyweight named Muhammed Wee Wee. He was credited with a knockout of Tommy Farr in London in 1974. If that had happened, Farr, who retired in 1953, would have been sixty-one years old.)

LeDoux remembered accompanying his Minneapolis attorney, Stephen Grossman, to Baltimore for a Tuesday hearing with the grand jury, but the rest was a blur. "They might as well blindfold you," he said. "To this day, I don't know where it was that I testified. I remember them ushering us through a back door and asking me to tell my story. Other than that, I'm not sure who it was I talked to.

"To be honest, for a while, I wasn't sure if I was in Philadelphia or Baltimore. That's how secretive the feds were."

Grossman recalled receiving vouchers and having to fly at "crazy" times. The FBI picked up him and LeDoux at the airport, brought them through the back door of a building, and then into a lower level. When it was time for LeDoux to testify, he and Grossman were brought upstairs. When finished, they were escorted out of the building, through the front door.

"Now, they give us to the press," Grossman said. "Chris Schenkel stuck a mike in my face. I think I said, 'Hi, Mom.'"

Fight judge Carol Polis said that the FBI began investigating her two days after she returned from the tournament in Annapolis. She said her bank account was subpoenaed. Polis kept a diary of every fight. She was prepared to tell the grand jury that "you can throw 500 to 800 punches in a round. If they are not effective, they don't count."

Polis, a diminutive woman who stood a hair over five feet, said she was asked by a commissioner, "Have you ever been approached?" "I gave him the Groucho Marx eyebrows," she said.

While the grand jury hearings and FBI investigation were taking place, King sprang into action. Braverman and Flood, the consultants connected to several boxers in the tournament, were suspended by King. "I agreed to pay Al and Paddy $20,000 each for their advice on the tournament," King said. "Whatever their fighters made in the tournament, they had a rightful share to, but I told them not to bother anybody else."

Ironically, LeDoux also had ties to Braverman. He allegedly collected a $1,500 booker's fee from LeDoux while Flood worked Boudreaux's corner. Braverman helped arrange, for a fee, LeDoux's bouts with Foreman and Denis, both King promotions.

"People talk about kickbacks," King said. "But it would have been easier to put up smaller purses for the boxers and keep the difference."

As the latest revelations surfaced, ABC canceled bouts scheduled for Miami, stopped the tournament, and hired a special investigator.

LeDoux was ready to move on—hoping for a rematch with Duane Bobick. "How can I learn something if I don't fight the best fighters?" LeDoux asked. "A bum can't teach me anything. I never duck a fight. I'd fight Ali right now, today. Maybe I've made a mistake with that philosophy and I don't recommend the course for every fighter. For me, it's the best way."

But, first, he would have to contend with the Maryland State Athletic Commission.

13

A SUSPENSION,
A MISSING MOUTHPIECE, A REMATCH

*F*our months after the Boudreaux debacle, and two months after ABC canceled the remainder of the United States Boxing Championships, LeDoux said he still heard the "voices of doom." Middleweight Marvin Hagler would later say that he was blacklisted for refusing to hire King associates Flood or Braverman to manage his career. LeDoux feared he could suffer a similar fate, or worse—whatever that was.

"I was told that I could be in bad trouble, that a fighter has to be out of his mind to go against the people who were promoting the show," LeDoux said while working out at a local gym in the spring of 1977. "It was even suggested that I might be physically harmed.

"I regretted the kick and apologized," LeDoux said. "But it turned out I must have been right about other things because of the reaction nationally."

"I'd run into Don King and he'd flash that big smile at me, a smile that said, 'I'll get you,'" LeDoux said years later. "Ali was still the most powerful man in boxing. But Don King could make or break your career."

Five losses and the uncertainty of possible action by the Maryland State Athletic Commission notwithstanding, LeDoux felt he was just coming into his prime and hoped to fight his way into contender status. For the first time, he convinced anyone who would listen that he had taken control of his destiny. He bought out Arnie Palmer—he said for $50,000, although Palmer didn't recall it costing LeDoux that much—and now he and Daszkiewicz, still working from a handshake deal, would call the shots that would make or break his career.

"I plan to fight for maybe four more years and I plan to have something to show for it," LeDoux said. "When I was beginning, I had only $15 to buy my wife a Christmas present. That will never happen again."

LeDoux said he had confined his worrying to his June 23 main event against Tommy Prater in Minnesota at the Met Center. He said he had wanted to fight Prater two years before. Now, they would meet with identical 20–5–1 records. Amazingly, he was looking beyond Prater before their Thursday night brawl took place. "I feel I'm boxing better than ever. I know Prater is a good fighter. He never quits," LeDoux said, spewing the usual ticket-selling prefight spiel.

Then he kept talking, as if a victory over Prater was a foregone conclusion. Who would he fight next? "It might be Duane Bobick in July," he said, and as always in boxing, there was more. "I want to fight Boudreaux here [in Minnesota]. And I'd like a chance to even up the decision I lost to Dino Denis."

LeDoux cranked up the bravado at the requisite prefight media circus. "That's Tommy Prater?" LeDoux said, throwing the first jab as the 210-pound Prater entered the news conference. "I thought that was a middleweight.

"No offense, Tommy," LeDoux said to Prater, whose previous defeat was to future heavyweight champion Larry Holmes, "but I've fought George Foreman, Larry Middleton, Dino Denis, and Duane Bobick in my last fights and this one with you is gonna be a picnic. Who have you fought? You've fought nobody!"

Prater's response: "Scott LeDoux, I consider him an amateur. As far as boxing is concerned, LeDoux has been on television a few times but he has been forgotten. I told some boxing people in Miami that I was coming up here to fight Scott LeDoux and they said, 'Who's he?' So he hasn't impressed anyone.

"The only guy he fought who was any good was George Foreman. I can't say Dino Denis and Johnny Boudreaux are tough fighters."

The fight itself wasn't nearly as entertaining. The 2,200 who attended saw the 227-pound LeDoux punish Prater for six rounds. Prater's mouth bled in the second round. LeDoux's overhand right in the fourth left the Indianapolis boxer rubber legged. Prater claimed he was ready to come out for the seventh round but couldn't because his corner men misplaced his mouthpiece.

"They lost my mouthpiece! My corner lost my mouthpiece!" Prater said. "Yeah, he hurt me, but I got freshened up back in the corner. I could have come back out, but then I didn't have no mouthpiece."

"He was ready to go?" LeDoux said incredulously. "Tell that to the doctor who checks his ribs out. Hey, how did he look at the end of the sixth round? Did he look fresh and ready to go?"

At the time, amateur boxing rules stated that a fighter had to have his mouthpiece to begin a round, but there was no such rule in professional boxing. Referee Mert Herrick called LeDoux the winner by technical knockout in the seventh round.

"For a change, I fought a smart fight," LeDoux said. "That's the best job I've ever done, picking a guy apart and taking my time. Prater was crying from some of my body shots."

LeDoux, always the entertainer, said he was more concerned that Prater had spewed blood all over his brand-new, bright-blue trunks. Prater, refusing to credit LeDoux, insisted that his spitting blood was the result of a training injury sustained ten days before.

Of his soiled trunks, LeDoux said, "He must have known they were new trunks. I kept thinking my wife is gonna kill me."

LeDoux also managed to grab the ring microphone to challenge Duane Bobick to a rematch. Bobick, sensing a victory and another big payday, was equally eager. Both fighters signed to meet July 28, 1977, at the Met Center, pending approval of the Minnesota Boxing Commission.

One problem: The Minnesota authority was well aware that the first LeDoux–Bobick match had garnered state boxing record attendance and gate figures fifteen months before, but ratifying the fight also risked embarrassment and legal ramifications because on July 7, just three weeks before the Bobick fight, LeDoux was suspended by the Maryland commission. All the state commissions controlling boxing were members of the World Boxing Association and honored each other's edicts, said promoter Ben Sternberg.

LeDoux called his six-month suspension "unwarranted," but that was hardly good enough for Sternberg, who worried about having too little time to promote the fight.

LeDoux and Daszkiewicz had no alternative: They challenged the Maryland suspension—even though the Maryland authorities made it clear that the decision to suspend LeDoux came, in part, because of his failure to attend a June 16 hearing for unsportsmanlike conduct follow-ing the disputed loss to Boudreaux. Daszkiewicz was suspended for three months.

"We didn't go down there [to the hearing], because there was no rea-son for us to go," Daszkiewicz said. "We never fought under the Maryland commission sanction. We answered their letter informing us of the formal hearing and told them that. We fought at a federal government facility. They informed Scott they wanted him to come as a witness, not as a foe.

"We're agreeing we were ungentlemanly, but all the other accusa-tions they made were wrong. The federal grand jury just went along with what we said, that the tournament was a phony, with false records, and with fighters selected or owned by Don King Productions. They weren't chosen on their merits.

"And the members of the Maryland commission were used strictly as clerks, with no jurisdiction over the tournament and nothing to say about sanctioning the matches, the weights, the records or anything. They filled out applications, that's all."

The tournament's executive committee was comprised of New York-ers, including tournament commissioner James A. Farley, who resigned under pressure.

"What happened," Daszkiewicz said, "is that [Chester] O'Sullivan, from the Maryland Boxing Commission, was just appointed president of the WBA [World Boxing Association]. And he's trying to show that he's got the power of the WBA to spank us for not coming to the Maryland hearing.

"Now, it'll be interesting to see how the WBA members react. The WBA and the WBC [World Boxing Council] both condemned that tour-nament. We honestly and truthfully feel that the Minnesota board will go along with us in rejecting Maryland's decision because that tourna-ment was not a just tournament.

"If other states back us up, we won't bother appealing the decision. We just won't ever plan to fight in Maryland again, and we probably wouldn't anyway. If the other states don't support us, we'll appeal it, and we might end up with a heck of a lawsuit.

"We're standing up to be counted and now it'll be interesting to see if other WBA members stand up behind us."

Two days later, Sternberg said that he received signed contracts before the Maryland State Athletic Commission had notified the Minnesota Boxing Commission of the LeDoux suspension. "I feel my signed contracts should supersede any action taken by the Maryland commission," Sternberg said. "When I called the Minnesota commission, they hadn't heard a thing from Maryland. So I contend the fight should go on."

Three days later, on July 12, the Minnesota Boxing Commission met at the Kahler Inn in Rochester, verified that it had not heard from the Maryland authorities or the WBA in a timely fashion of Maryland's action, and voted to let the fight go on as scheduled. Minnesota Boxing Commission chairman Richard Plunkett appointed a committee to decide whether another hearing should be held after the LeDoux–Bobick fight and to then consider the suspensions.

"I've got one fight that I wanted—with Bobick—for July 28," said LeDoux, who attended the Minnesota hearing, "but I'm sort of left hanging for a livelihood in boxing by that Maryland suspension of six months until it expires December 15."

Although one commissioner, Robert Thompson, said the board was "ducking the issue" by not making an immediate decision, the board's verdict was good enough for Sternberg, who planned to keep the Bobick–LeDoux battle as the main event of his five-bout card.

Meanwhile, there was a fight to promote, but unlike the first Bobick–LeDoux fight, this one was going to be a much tougher sell. The novelty of two rising Minnesota heavyweights no longer existed. LeDoux had five losses, including the loss to Bobick, and Bobick was no longer undefeated.

On May 10, Bobick—a perfect 38–0 with thirty-two knockouts—stepped into the ring with Ken Norton, the chiseled ex-Marine who once stripped Ali of his crown while breaking the Great One's jaw. Bobick was ranked number five, but many scoffed at his elevated status. Don Riley of the *St. Paul Pioneer Press* said Bobick achieved his lofty ranking "by beating old ladies, round-heeled has-beens and clowns moonlighting in the Shrine Circus." Others had never forgotten Bobick's failure to win Olympic gold in Munich in 1972. Norton, attempting a comeback that might ultimately include another title shot, wondered aloud why he would step into the Madison Square Garden ring with a fighter that had never beaten anyone of merit.

(There were 250,000 reasons, actually. The night's purse was $250,000. Bobick said he pocketed $58,000 after taxes.)

"If Bobick and his people want to fight me, I guess they don't think much of me," Norton said. "I'm insulted."

Bobick didn't do much for his own mystique with comments like these: "I'm just like those old time trappers. They weren't as interested in hunting the game as they were in seeing what was ahead over the next hill. That's me," and "I'm a fair boxer, a fair puncher, but I put it together and it works."

Nothing worked that night in New York against Norton.

"I'm always a slow starter," Bobick said. "I guess I started even slower than usual."

It was over before it started. The fight lasted fifty-eight seconds. Norton surprised Bobick with an overhand right to the head, a left and right to the body, and then a right uppercut that caught Bobick's throat. As Bobick staggered toward his corner, Norton continued the assault, hitting the twenty-six-year-old from Bowlus in the head with more overhand rights. Bobick fell, took a nine-count, and somehow managed to stagger to his feet. Referee Petey Delia grabbed him and said, "The fight is over, son."

Sports Illustrated dubbed him "America's great white hopeless." For the kid from rural Minnesota, who used to hide in the pea patch behind the house, there no longer was any place to hide. For decades, he would be asked about being a human punching bag for fifty-eight seconds.

"They'll probably just remember him for that Norton fight," said Marvis Frazier, Joe Frazier's son. "I don't care about how much good you do in the world, or what you do, but people always remember the bad thing, the dirt."

Indeed, when Bobick was asked ten years later how he would be remembered as a boxer, he replied tersely, "The Norton fight."

Three weeks after the Norton fight, Bobick learned that his brother, Rodney, was killed in an auto accident. "I lost the fight with Norton and then I lost my brother and drained into emptiness," Bobick said. "I couldn't get over the fact that he was dead."

The road toward a comeback to reality began with Bobick's next fight, against archrival LeDoux. The Bobick camp, predictably, was predicting victory. "More likely an easier time," said Bobick's co-manager and trainer Eddie Futch, who predicted a knockout. "A 38–1 record is pretty good. If we beat LeDoux, we'll have a good start toward our new climb. He's no mere trial horse, you know. He's a pretty good fighter. We respect him as an opponent. The victory, which we expect, will win us national recognition."

When asked what happened to Bobick against Norton, Futch opened his personal silver linings playbook: "If he had survived that first round and been careful for a couple rounds, it might have been a different fight."

LeDoux was a glass-half-full equal when explaining why this fight with Bobick would be different than the first. "When I lost to Bobick last year, I didn't know what to expect," LeDoux said. "He had had twice as many fights as I had had and he was undefeated. I wasn't sure of myself.

"I spent too much time showing that I could take his punches, which I did, and didn't try to charge aggressively. Now I feel that I can take charge.

"I'm twice the fighter I was a year ago."

He wasn't done. When promoting a fight, a boxer is never done.

"Bobick can't hit hard enough to keep me from banging at his body."

"Bobick knows he has to beat me to stay in business. After being knocked out by Ken Norton, he'll be apprehensive and too careful. The pressure is on him this time."

"I throw the same kind of hard right that Norton stopped Bobick with."

Daszkiewicz thought emotion played a vital part in Bobick's clear-cut ten-round decision the first time around: A messenger delivered a card of condolences to LeDoux's dressing room, rattling LeDoux. And two guys came into the room and attempted to carry out a bench LeDoux was sitting on. "Believe me, there was almost a fight before the fight," Daszkiewicz said.

This time, emotion again played a part. Two days before the fight, the Maryland State Athletic Commission announced it had no quarrel with LeDoux fighting Bobick, because the fight was signed before Maryland suspended LeDoux. The Maryland board said it expected LeDoux's six-month suspension to start after the match.

And what of Bobick?

The rivalry between the two Minnesota heavyweights was real enough—even though Bobick had been in LeDoux's corner at the Pedro Soto fight and decades later would refer to LeDoux as his "friend." (LeDoux never said the same of Bobick, at least not publicly.) But Bobick had incentive beyond trying to resurrect his reputation, which took such a national beating after the Norton fight that he was even parodied on *Saturday Night Live*. Bobick never forgot that LeDoux beat his brother,

Rodney (whom LeDoux, years later, always referred to as "a good guy"). "Before the fight I walked into his dressing room and said, 'You don't beat up my brother,'" Bobick said. "That set the tone."

The fight, witnessed by a crowd of 9,122, was more one-sided than the first. LeDoux staggered into the eighth round, when Bobick's right to LeDoux's jaw dropped the Fighting Frenchman for an eight-count. LeDoux didn't stay vertical for very long. Bobick knocked LeDoux down with another right. LeDoux again rose to his feet, but referee Wally Holm stopped the fight, calling it a technical knockout.

Bobick said he was confident of the victory by the fourth round.

"I thought that I fought a good fight, my kind of fight, but Duane had it all together," LeDoux said. "Things worked out for him. I couldn't stay out of the corners. The small ring, which I thought would work for me, just didn't give me enough room to stay away from the ropes."

Bobick predicted that there would not be another rematch. "Fight him again?" Bobick asked, repeating a question. "I don't think so. I've given him two pretty bad beatings. I don't think Scott LeDoux will want to fight me again."

At least they knew that a third Bobick–LeDoux bout could be held in Minnesota. The Minnesota Board of Boxing announced six days after the fight that it would not hold a hearing to consider LeDoux's six-month suspension or the three-month suspension Daszkiewicz received from the Maryland State Athletic Commission. In other words, LeDoux could fight in Minnesota.

His next fight, though, would take place in Las Vegas, and against a most unlikely opponent: Leon Spinks, an Olympic gold medal winner as a light heavyweight, was now a professional heavyweight, fighting at 194 pounds. He won each of his five professional fights leading to the LeDoux match.

"We know what we're getting into," Daszkiewicz said of the Spinks fight, "and it's not for the money. It's for a shot at national prominence.

"We look at the fight with our eyes wide open. We know CBS and promoter Bob Arum are pushing Spinks as the next heavyweight champion and they figure if Bobick can beat LeDoux, so can Spinks. But he's young and inexperienced and we know Scott is durable, strong and tough.

"Spinks comes out like a tiger and Scott just might catch him or he might walk into a punch. We think they may be pushing Spinks too fast. This fight could project Scott right back into the heavyweight picture."

But a loss against an unproven pro like Spinks could be devastating to LeDoux's career.

It was a Las Vegas gamble LeDoux was willing to take.

14

"TO BE SOMEBODY"

*L*eDoux was in bed with the flu on October 3, 1977, the day Daszkiewicz called, telling him "they want you to fight this kid, Spinks."

"I'm sicker than a dog and I said, 'Make the match. There's not a guy
200 pounds yet that I can't whip,'" LeDoux recalled telling his trainer.
"'I'll be there.'"

"But you're sick," Daszkiewicz reminded him.

"I'll be at the gym tonight," LeDoux told him.

And he was.

For LeDoux, this was more than a shot at national prominence. Even
in the strange world of boxing, where you never know what kind of spec-
imen might crawl into the ring, or which back alleys led him there, one
would be hard pressed to find two fighters with less in common.

LeDoux, a freight salesman who had become a media darling always
ready with a quick verbal jab, was still being depicted by many in the national press as a country bumpkin, a farm boy with ties to Paul Bunyan.
He was still searching for ways to get off the milking stool and climb that
elusive pedestal.

Spinks, an Olympic hero during a year-long, feel-good bicentenni-
al celebration, already had reached the top through his performance in
Montreal. The oldest of seven kids from a St. Louis housing project, his
slum-to-stardom story, as *Time* magazine called it, came with several
painful detours. Spinks learned to fight on the streets, where local thugs
christened him "Messover," because he was easy to mess over. He was
mugged for small change. He didn't earn that famous, toothless smile
by playing hockey. His parents split when he was kid. His mother taught
Bible classes at home and waited for her welfare check. His father once

beat Leon while the child was suspended from a nail. Leon would "never amount to anything," his dad told him.

"That became my thing," Spinks said. "To be somebody."

In his later years, Spinks would be hit by a series of demoralizing one-two combinations to his pride and overall well-being. Nearly broke in 2006, he was working weekends as a janitor for the minimum wage of $5.15 an hour at a YMCA in Columbus, Nebraska, in a town where Buffalo Bill held the first dress rehearsal for his Wild West show. On weekdays, he worked as a janitor at a local McDonald's. "I like it," he said. "I like doin' what I'm doin'. I'm still breathin', still makin' money and I have people 'round who look out for me."

The man who traded in his bright-red Everlast gloves for orange Rubbermaid gloves walked with a slight limp. Dementia, arthritis, and bad relationships had taken their toll on the ex-Marine. He was arrested for cocaine possession (months after the LeDoux fight). On his bad days, the missing teeth and dementia made communication difficult. "Everybody loves to steal them," he once said of the lower and upper incisors he lost when head butted in the Marines. "They love my smile so much they steal my teeth. Sometimes I leave them in the hotel. One time they were stolen by a maid or somebody who got a key to my room. People do some crazy stuff. I got mugged in Detroit once and I was trying to bite the guy and they came out and he stole them. It's so damn weird, people taking my teeth."

LeDoux didn't care about Spinks's missing teeth when the two met at the Aladdin Theater. He was more concerned with the gap in his own boxing résumé. He needed to make a big statement, and in boxing there are few stages where the lights are brighter than those in Vegas.

LeDoux resumed training at 229 pounds and weighed 224 for the fight—30 pounds more than Spinks's 194, a significant advantage for LeDoux.

"Spinks has never really been tested," Daszkiewicz said. "TV has ruined a lot of young fighters, bringing them on before they're ready."

Daszkiewicz could not have been more prophetic.

There were no knockdowns, but LeDoux hit Spinks's midsection repeatedly with lefts. Spinks countered with hard rights to LeDoux's head. Spinks threw more punches, but LeDoux easily blocked many of them with his gloves and arms.

Confusion reigned in Spinks's corner. His brother Michael ran around the ring apron, trying to encourage Spinks, while others screamed instructions from the corner and ringside. "The only one not advising Leon was Ann Landers," LeDoux quipped.

Bob Dolan, the Minneapolis attorney, who traveled worldwide to watch his buddy LeDoux fight, thought even before the fight that LeDoux had little chance of winning. "We figured he had to knock out Leon to get a draw," Dolan said.

This was how the Associated Press began its report of the fight:

"Minnesota farm boy Scott LeDoux proved to be the first roadblock in Olympic champion Leon Spinks's path toward a title shot Saturday when the two heavyweights slugged their way to a 10-round draw in a nationally televised bout."

"It was my first 10-rounder," said the disappointed Spinks. "I'm still trying to adjust myself to that pace.

"I felt I did good for my sixth fight," Spinks said. "Scott has a really good punch, but I was never really hurt."

LeDoux said he stunned Spinks at least three times but never went after him because "he's an amateur fighter and they're most dangerous when they're hurt." Decades later, LeDoux said he simply outsmarted his less experienced foe. "Leon was quicker, but I was able to use a lot of the tools I had learned along the way," LeDoux recalled. "I would reach in. My left hand grabbed his left elbow. I'd pull him, let go, and hit him with a kidney shot. He never figured it out. He kept getting over to my right side, and I'd hit him with an elbow and then a hook. Keep his head up and smack him, hit him with the left hook, and he still couldn't figure it out.

"In the middle of the fight, he hit me in the cup once, so I hit him in the cup three times. He said, 'Are you gonna cheat to win?' And I said, 'Leon, we're not fighting for a trophy. We're fighting for money.'"

"He's not a hard KO puncher who will explode on a real heavyweight," LeDoux said after the fight. "He'll sting you, but he's not a heavyweight stinger."

LeDoux's observations would become fascinating when revisited four months later, after Spinks's eighth professional match—a title bout against heavyweight champ Ali.

LeDoux said later that he was convinced that Spinks's February 15, 1978, fight with Ali had been scheduled before his October 22, 1977, bout with Spinks—and that, LeDoux surmised, was the reason their fight ended in a draw.

"Well, he did get a draw," said LeDoux's friend Dolan. "Quite frankly, that was a pretty close fight. Leon had already signed to fight Ali, so it was a foregone conclusion that Leon was not going to lose. And I didn't think he'd ever get a shot at the title after that."

Arnie Palmer, LeDoux's former manager, was more succinct. "An outrageous fix," he called it.

LeDoux just wanted to move on. He was proud of his nationally televised performance. And he said it was impossible to be angry with Spinks.

"To have a ten-round draw, and you know you've won the fight, with a gold medalist is pretty doggone good," LeDoux recalled.

"After a night of talking trash to me, he came into my dressing room after the fight. He gave me a hug and said, 'You're a tough son of a bitch. I love you brother.'

"It's the only time that's ever happened. I've only gone to one dressing room my whole career. That was Dino Denis. I went there an hour and a half after the fight and he was still layin' on the floor, all beat up.

"How can you not love Leon Spinks?"

Two days later, spokesmen for Ali announced that the champ would be meeting LeDoux in five weeks in Chicago for a five-round exhibition match, to be held for charity. The exhibition would be just that—an exhibition that would not affect either boxer's record. But for LeDoux, this was, possibly, the opportunity of a lifetime. Ali no longer floated like a butterfly, but Ali was Ali, the champion by whom all others were measured. A good showing by LeDoux could even lead to a title fight. It surely would get him matches against boxing's upper echelon.

Incredibly, Daszkiewicz said the fight was off unless Ali agreed to forgo protective headgear and heavy gloves and fight under "championship conditions."

"I'm sure they can find somebody else," Daszkiewicz said.

15

THE GREATEST?

*W*ho snubs Muhammad Ali?

Daszkiewicz and LeDoux actually did. Then the bluster cleared, and they realized the opportunity they had squandered. LeDoux couldn't wait to sign.

One day after declining to meet the champ for a five-round exhibition to benefit the Chicago Children's Institute for Developmental Disabilities, newspapers nationwide ran photos of LeDoux and Ali playfully exchanging punches under the headline "Ali, LeDoux to meet in ring." In the photo, LeDoux, looking dapper in a three-piece suit, is also sporting a slight cut at the bridge of his nose and discoloration under his left eye, remnants of the Spinks bout in Las Vegas just three days before.

LeDoux and Daszkiewicz ultimately relented to Ali's camp, agreeing that heavy gloves and headgear would be worn, but LeDoux confided later that those were minor details. This exhibition didn't just happen overnight, he said. It had been bandied about from almost the moment the Spinks fight had been set. Further, the negotiations for this charitable exhibition had much more at stake than arguing over gloves and headgear. "We told Ali we would only box with him if he would sign us for a title fight within six months," LeDoux said years later. "We had a signed contract.

"For me, it was unbelievable. To be in the ring with Ali... I can still see myself as a teenager, standing on a chair, excited, listening to that Philco radio and hearing the round-by-round reports of Ali and Sonny Liston. Unbelievable! Unbelievable to think I could have ascended to that level."

If Ali and LeDoux did sign a contract for a title fight in six months, only the inner circles of the two camps knew about it. No date or venue was set. Ali already was signed to fight Spinks on February 15, 1978, in Las Vegas.

During a Chicago TV program, Ali told LeDoux that if LeDoux looked good in the December 5 exhibition, he would give LeDoux a title shot.

What would happen if LeDoux knocked the thirty-six-year-old Ali down during the exhibition at the Chicago Auditorium Theatre? "Don't be silly," said Daszkiewicz. "If that would happen, we would be up there in the ring screaming that the title is ours. Nobody is saying that is going to happen. But wouldn't it be something if it did?"

For LeDoux, the iron-ore miner's son, and Daszkiewicz, who toiled for years in mildew-scented gymnasiums training pugs and palookas, this was a chance to dream. And their fantasies were every bit as magical as those of the children they hoped this exhibition would benefit.

Daszkiewicz talked about a surprise move that LeDoux might try if Ali covered up his head and let him bang away. LeDoux talked about his boxing style and how it could confuse Ali.

Dreams.

"Listen, Scott is not going in that ring to play around," Daszkiewicz told reporters. "He is going to fight. We think if we smack Ali around a little, he might be intimidated into a fight. If Ali clowns around while the other guy is going all out, well . . .

"Whatever the outcome, Ali has a lot more to lose in this than Scott does. If we put on a good show—and we plan to put on a good show—it should open up all sorts of horizons for Scott. Just the other day I got a call from Joe Frazier's agent asking about a fight. I told him if the money was right we would take one."

LeDoux had everything to gain and nothing to lose going up against the greatest and most compelling athlete of his generation and, arguably, of all time. "It's a freebie," LeDoux said. "If this goes well, it could make me a lot of money. A title shot. If it doesn't, it was worth a try.

"I think that I have the style to give Ali a rough time," LeDoux said. "I'm confusing by nature, not by design. I'm rough and I'm awkward. He's not the Ali of old. If he were, Scott LeDoux would have said, 'Thanks, but no thanks.' Scott LeDoux would have gotten caught in a buzz saw."

For all the comedy and bravado of the prefight theatrics and the potential savagery of the ring, this was the start of a cordial relationship between LeDoux and Ali that lasted years after each hung up their Everlast gloves for the final time. Ali later hosted LeDoux and Daszkiewicz at his California mansion, where they watched movies together. It wasn't like they shared social circles. In fact, many years after their respective retirements, a clean-shaven LeDoux approached Ali, who was sitting at a table in a restaurant. LeDoux's size caught Ali's attention, but the champ couldn't place him. Then LeDoux said, "No mustache," and Ali immediately broke into that famous smile and said, "Scott LeDoux! Sit down."

"He always had fun with me," LeDoux said. "Every time he'd see me, he'd start talking trash, then give me a hug and say, 'I love you brother.' Or he'd make that face, you know the one where he bites his lower lip."

One day before the exhibition, Ali was snapping his fingers, playfully shadowing Daszkiewicz, when the champ spotted LeDoux's wife. "How did he get you?" the champ asked Sandy LeDoux. "He got me when I was young," she said with a laugh.

However, the scene before the exhibition match in Chicago was one lacking the hugs and playful jabs. It was vintage Ali, boxing's greatest salesman this side of Don King.

"This guy's out to get a reputation," Ali said. "And I'm going to give him his chance. I'm overweight and out of shape." To make his point, Ali then lifted his sweatshirt and revealed a paunch that hung over his sweat pants. "You know why I'm doing all this? Because that's how I'm going to whup Scott LeDoux. I'm going to whup him with all this extra weight. He wants to be like the guys who got Wyatt Earp and Doc Holliday. But I believe I'm that great that I can fight him even if I'm not in shape."

If there was any question about who the event's star was, the advertising poster said it all: "A Night at the Theatre with Muhammad Ali." Below that headline was a photo of Ali wearing a black tie, ruffled shirt, and carnation. Below the picture read the words "Vs. Scott LeDoux, the challenger."

The day before the exhibition, LeDoux strolled into the Windy City gymnasium, expecting the place to be empty. It wasn't. Ali was there. "What are you doing here?" Ali asked LeDoux. "What you doin' in this gym when I'm working out? You don't belong here."

LeDoux was ready to play along. "What do you mean you're working out?" he yelled to Ali. "All I see you doin' is talkin'. Do something and quit talkin', Ali. You're waddling around like a man 55 years old who weighs 260 pounds."

Ali gave LeDoux the kind of glare he usually saved for weigh-ins. Then he stepped toward him. "Listen sucker. I'm warning you. When you come to that Auditorium Theatre you'd better be in shape. I'm promisin' you right now. I'm gonna knock you out."

LeDoux loved it. Now, it was his turn. "Ali, you sure look old and fat. I don't even think you'll last three rounds."

LeDoux's team quickly ushered him out of the gym, but he couldn't stop talking about Ali. "He's not as big as I thought," LeDoux said from his hotel room. "I guess you always think Ali's bigger because he's the champion . . . But I'm just as big as he is. Maybe even a little bit bigger."

"Look, I've been training hard now for ten years. . . . I've never made enough money at it to quit my job with the trucking company, either. So if something good comes out of this exhibition, then it will be a case of a guy who worked hard to make his break."

"Can you win?" he was asked.

"Aren't we all little boys at heart?" LeDoux replied. "Don't we all dream?"

There were no losers at the charitable exhibition. Ali wore headgear, LeDoux did not. Ali taunted LeDoux throughout. LeDoux simply responded with his fists. Ali even asked the audience if they wanted LeDoux to fall . . . and then continued to spar.

LeDoux held his own, but when he left Chicago, he had reason to worry. Ali appeared vulnerable.

"In the first round, I hit him right in the chin," LeDoux recalled years later. "That should never have happened. I would never have been able to hit Ali in his prime. You could see he didn't care.

"I had him bleeding from the nose and mouth after two rounds. How could that happen? He was really puffy and wasn't exactly floating like a butterfly. I had big gloves on, but I could still hit Ali at will.

"I'd just fought Leon a few weeks before and I remember telling Papa Joe that we might be in trouble, that if Ali doesn't take his training seriously, Leon could wear him out.

"I told Papa Joe, 'I think Leon's going to beat him.'"

Spinks, a ten-to-one underdog, outlasted Ali in fifteen rounds, winning a split decision and with it, the heavyweight crown. That fight in Las Vegas was considered one of the greatest upsets ever, in any sport. It was the first time Ali had lost his title in the ring.

The crowd booed when the split decision was announced.

Imagine how LeDoux felt.

"When Ali lost to Leon, I lost my title shot," he said, years later. "Ali didn't care anymore. He was just fighting for money. And any chance I had for the title went out the window. You have no idea how disappointed I was."

Ali shrugged it off. "Do you know if I beat him [Spinks] the first time I wouldn't of got no credit for it," Ali told *New York* magazine. "He only had seven fights . . . the kid was nothing. . . . So I'm glad he won. It's a perfect scene. You couldn't write a better movie than this. This is it. Just what I need. Competition. Fighting odds. Can the old champ regain his title for a third time? Think of it. A third time. Do or die. And you know what makes me laugh? He's the same guy. Only difference is he got eight fights now."

Ali wanted a rematch with Spinks, but so did LeDoux. "I'll fight heavy-weight champion Leon Spinks in my back yard for nothing," LeDoux said after watching Spinks best Ali on television. "I've fought 'em both. And I'd like a rematch with Spinks because I beat him over ten rounds at Las Vegas October 22."

Daszkiewicz said he would demand a rematch with the new champ. "They're talking about LeDoux for Joe Frazier's comeback at Met Center April 16, but they can stick that match in their ear. We're not signed for it. We want Spinks.

"Scott fought 'em both and I liked the kid over Ali. It was obvious to me when we fought the champ, Ali, that he was shot. And Scott had Spinks hurt five times. That's why we want him again."

But Spinks wanted a rematch with Ali. That's where the money was. In their second fight—the Battle of New Orleans—Ali regained his title. Part of it anyway. The World Boxing Council stripped Spinks of his title for dodging Ken Norton, the top contender, but Spinks knew he could make hundreds of thousands more by giving Ali the rematch.

Once again, the WBC and the WBA would recognize different champions.

LeDoux's opportunities didn't double. He would never fight Ali again. He would never get his rematch with Spinks—not that it mattered anymore. In fact, LeDoux wondered when he would fight again. Period.

LeDoux's last official fight was against Spinks on October 22, 1977. Despite credible showings against Ali and Spinks, LeDoux, who was trying to support a young family, would not fight again for eleven months—an eternity for a fighter in his prime.

16

ALWAYS KING

*T*he proposed fight between LeDoux and ex-champ Joe Frazier had all the makings of a perfect storm. Frazier was one of the greats, and his three epic battles with Ali were legendary. And as Duane Bobick's manager, Frazier had already established an adversarial relationship with LeDoux. No matter how badly he was beaten in surrendering his title to George Foreman, Frazier's proposed comeback would command plenty of space at the top of the nation's sports pages. He hadn't fought since his second loss to Foreman, on June 15, 1976.

It seemed too good—and maybe too far-fetched—to be true, but LeDoux and Daszkiewicz were eager to listen. At least, they were at first.

In early February 1978, a Frazier–LeDoux fight was proposed for April 16, in Minnesota at the Met Center. The match was to be nationally televised by NBC and jointly promoted by Madison Square Garden and Minnesota's Ben Sternberg. Madison Square Garden wanted the fight, but the Garden was to be occupied by the Ringling Bros. Circus at the time. In this case, the Ringling Bros. show was the circus that got prioritized.

Frazier was reportedly offered $225,000 for the fight. He was asking for $300,000 but could be had for $275,000. LeDoux was told he would be paid $50,000.

The fight was not an automatic for the Met Center. The Twins also played in Bloomington, at nearby Metropolitan Stadium, and had a scheduled Sunday doubleheader with the Seattle Mariners that afternoon. Sternberg said he planned to contact Twins owner Calvin Griffith and would ask him to move up the starting time for the first game, giving fans a chance to attend that game and then run over to see Frazier–

LeDoux. But Griffith, a baseball dinosaur who could pinch pennies with the best of them, had a well-earned reputation as a stubborn negotiator. There were other financial considerations for Sternberg to ponder, and he was worried about competition from other promoters.

"I think it could attract a gate of at least $150,000," Sternberg said. "When LeDoux fought Duane Bobick we had a state record $114,786, and prices would be higher for LeDoux–Frazier. Still, it would take a heck of a crowd just to break even."

LeDoux called the opportunity to fight Frazier a "once in a lifetime" chance.

Daszkiewicz expressed excitement, but, really, what else could he say? "It's a natural," he said.

What came out of his mouth next, though, was stark reality. "We have the feeling that the way things are now, we'll never get a chance to fight Ken Norton," he said. "Scott is only 29 and really at the peak of his career. This would be another big chance for him."

Then Spinks beat Ali, and LeDoux and Daszkiewicz were clamoring for a Spinks rematch. That wouldn't happen. The supposedly signed LeDoux–Ali title bout was dead. Frazier reconsidered his comeback. Promoter Bob Arum, who promised to get LeDoux fights after LeDoux's valiant showing against Spinks, all but disappeared.

"We tried to match him in a number of other fights, but we never could," Arum said. "We tried to book LeDoux in competitive fights, but whenever we mentioned an opponent to Daszkiewicz that looked as if he could give LeDoux a good fight, Daszkiewicz asked for astronomical numbers. I was willing to pay well, but not numbers where I would have to take a loss. [Don] King isn't that fussy."

The Garden's Teddy Brenner also disappeared from LeDoux's life. LeDoux also had concerns at home. His son, Josh, now two years old, was taking medicine three times a day to repress seizures. Sandy was pregnant and expecting in late September. And LeDoux hadn't fought in months.

It wasn't a lack of skill or charisma that kept him out of the ring. Nor was it his reputation with the Maryland State Athletic Commission. It was Don King. LeDoux's cry of "fix" and the ensuing grand jury investigation amounted to a mere flesh wound for King. In fact, it may have prompted a public-relations bonanza.

King was a master self-promoter, and thanks in part to LeDoux, his name and electric hair were everywhere. By slapping Braverman's and Flood's wrists, he was acknowledging mistakes while passing the buck at the same time. He had *The Ring* magazine to blame for falsifying fighters' records in his United States Boxing Championships. Even with his carnival barker's delivery, King couldn't buy this kind of publicity. King didn't have to sell snake oil. By circling the wagons, LeDoux and Daszkiewicz brought the boxing world to the tip of his jewel-studded walking stick.

On April 19, LeDoux did what he needed to save his boxing career: He signed an exclusive pact with King in New York.

"It's a chance to get some big fights and for him to get back to work," Daszkiewicz said. "Scott is at his boxing prime, but he has got to stay active.

"King divorced himself from the U.S. Boxing Championships and has come clean," Daszkiewicz said. "It's not a case of, 'If you can't beat 'em, join 'em.' King has got to be the No. 1 promoter in the world and he holds all the trump cards. Where does a guy go when he wants to be the heavyweight champion of the world? To Don King. He's got almost every rated fighter."

LeDoux wasn't fussy, saying he would take on all comers. "Why else would I have fought some of the fights I've fought lately?" LeDoux asked.

LeDoux was promised three fights a year "at good money," Daszkiewicz said. King hoped to begin with a televised match against Earnie Shavers.

"We have high hopes for LeDoux's future against such fighters as Shavers, Alfredo Evangelista, Larry Holmes or Ken Norton," King said.

King made LeDoux wait. For another five months. When LeDoux finally entered the ring in the first of a series of elimination bouts for the World Boxing Council's heavyweight championship, in Miami Beach's Convention Hall on September 26, it wasn't against Norton, Holmes, or Shavers. It was against up-and-comer Bill Sharkey.

Sharkey had an 18–2 record but was only five feet eleven and 200 pounds. "I've seen Sharkey fight," LeDoux told King. "He isn't much of a fighter. Sure, I'll go to Florida."

Moments after agreeing to the Sharkey fight, LeDoux thought to himself, "I wonder what's gonna happen to me down in Miami."

LeDoux couldn't help but think back to the chance meeting he had with Johnny Flood, Paddy Flood's brother, just months before. "He says, 'You did the right thing when you stood up to Don King, you know,'" LeDoux remembered.

He said Flood brought up the Boudreaux fight. "You got screwed in that fight," LeDoux said Flood told him. "Johnny Flood's the guy who told me there was a contract on me."

LeDoux quickly shifted gears and began thinking of the immediate task ahead of him, his date with Sharkey. Thinking about his relationship with King added to LeDoux's usual prefight jitters in his dressing room—until he was told, "Five minutes to go."

LeDoux said he left any rust from months of nonactivity in his dressing room. He fought with the same confidence—and size advantage—he had exhibited against Spinks. "I pounded this guy for ten rounds," he recalled. "Cut him over both eyes. Beat the crap out of him. And I get a . . . draw? I looked over at Don King and he's got that big smile on his face. And all I could say to him was, 'OK.'"

Sharkey was lightly regarded, but amazingly, LeDoux was soon ranked tenth among world heavyweights, ahead of Duane Bobick, who, of course, beat LeDoux twice.

"The WBC ratings are a farce," Arum said. "Everyone knows that Jose Sulaiman [president of the WBC] and King have a nefarious relationship. If it suited King's purposes, he'd have you rated in the top ten."

Bob Busse, a Texas boxing commissioner who headed the WBC's ratings committee, tried to explain the ratings dilemma: "Since the WBC is located in Mexico, we have a lot of trouble trying to collect information about boxers. We don't have all the records. Any rating is going to say that LeDoux is a better fighter than Bobick. Anybody in the top 20 in the world has beaten somebody that beat the guy above them."

Three days after the Sharkey fight, Sandy gave birth to a healthy baby girl, Molly. LeDoux was ecstatic—and immediately back on the road.

This time it was Winnipeg, where he knocked out Sylvester Wilder of Cleveland in the second round. Wilder left Winnipeg with a 4–33 record, having lost twenty-six straight. The local promoter, Tom "Tex" Burns, reportedly made a hasty exit through the back door before the fight was over. "Wilder's sole aim was to go into the tank as quickly as possible," wrote Hal Sigurdson of the *Winnipeg Free Press*.

LeDoux had actually gone to Winnipeg to fight Verbie Garland, a little-known fighter from Toledo, Ohio, who won a total of four times in seven-plus years as a professional. A week before the fight, LeDoux was told by one of King's associates that Garland had backed out. Burns replaced Garland with Wilder.

"The guy was a stiff," LeDoux said. "But what was I supposed to do? It's like stealing when they offer you a thousand bucks to fight someone like that."

Daszkiewicz was skeptical about Wilder before the fight. "I said to Burns, 'How can the commissioner approve something like that?' He said, 'Don't worry about the commissioner. The commissioner is in charge of some local charity and I'll give him a hundred dollars.' He begged me to take the fight. He said I'd break him if I didn't go through with it."

Daszkiewicz shrugged off the critics. "A guy like Bobick has 40 bums on his record and no one says a word."

A month later, on November 10, 1978, LeDoux was fighting in Caesars Palace, in Las Vegas. He was supposed to fight Jimmy Young, another fighter in King's stable. Young was ranked second worldwide—even though he had not fought in fourteen months. But King couldn't get the two fighters to agree to a contract.

So LeDoux's Vegas opponent was listed as 228-pound James Brown, whom *Sports Illustrated* described as "an overblown middleweight." But Brown's real name was James Bannon—and the perceived switching of identities and confusion over records prompted questions about the opponents King was signing to fight LeDoux, and about LeDoux's sudden rise in the rankings.

Bannon's record was listed as no wins, two losses before meeting LeDoux.

Sort of.

His manager, Don White, explained that Bannon spent four or five years as a middleweight, then grew into a heavyweight, so Bannon and White "just wiped that slate clean." When asked what Bannon's record was as a middleweight, White said, "He probably won about 10 and lost about 10." He then said Bannon's record as a heavyweight before meeting LeDoux was 9–2, even though a friend said, "He's never won a fight, but he almost won one."

LeDoux knocked out Brown in the second round. Almost immediately, King had LeDoux signed to fight in Omaha, Nebraska, on December

15—against an opponent to be named later. That opponent, Joe Donatto, had won only three of eight fights and was knocked out in the third round.

LeDoux couldn't find a decent opponent to fight, but that didn't stop a Twin Cities group from asking him to help coach fighters. That group was the National Hockey League's Minnesota North Stars.

"We've got all the equipment—heavy bag, weights, but they're no good if used improperly," said Stars general manager Lou Nanne. "The other day, St. Louis defenseman Steve Durbano broke his hand punching the heavy bag. LeDoux offered to work with some of our players."

At least two Stars players, forward Al MacAdam and defenseman Greg Smith, said they were interested in talking to LeDoux.

"The idea of working on the heavy bag is not how hard you can hit it, but speed and quickness," LeDoux explained. "I don't think you're going to knock out anybody punching off skates, but you want quickness—bing, bing, bing.

"That's what my manager tells me in the ring—get off first. Come out punching, and I know when I'm punching, the other guy is usually taking and he's losing. I've never fought on skates, but the principle is the same."

LeDoux was killing time—and it was killing him.

He nearly had another chance to fight on national TV. Bill Sharkey was supposed to fight South African Kallie Knoetze in Miami on CBS. But LeDoux was contacted in early January of 1979 after the U.S. State Department revoked Knoetze's entry visa. The State Department said Knoetze, who knocked out Duane Bobick in February 1978, was ineligible for a visitor's visa on the grounds of a specific conviction for obstruction of justice. Adding pressure to revoke the visa was a Chicago-based organization, headed by Rev. Jessie Jackson.

LeDoux, who tended bar to earn extra cash, was being tabbed as a substitute for Knoetze. LeDoux was interested in meeting Sharkey again until CBS canceled the TV contract.

"They're going to stage a minor-league card now and we're not interested," Daszkiewicz said. "We'll look elsewhere for fights." Daszkiewicz had heard enough. He had Minneapolis attorney Richard Ince write to King, telling the promoter that LeDoux was now a free agent who would arrange his own fights.

LeDoux said his three-month contract with King had to get him a fight against a Top 10 fighter, or the contract would void itself.

"We could have lived with the contract so long as he lived up to his end of it," Daszkiewicz said of King. "He was supposed to promote fights by certain dates, and if we gave him notice, that would be the end of it. All we ever got from him were Sharkey and Brown."

Said LeDoux: "We'll just have to yell and scream until they give us a fight. It's the guys who yell the loudest who are getting the fights."

LeDoux then signed to fight six-foot-nine, 242-pound Jim Beattie at the Met Center on February 20.

"It's been a long year for me," LeDoux said. "I want to fight and I can't get a match. They talk about white fighters being such a rare commodity. . . . Every time I get a promise for a fight it falls through. You know how much I made my last fight? Six hundred and fifty dollars. It's not only embarrassing, it's dangerous. You could get beat by a lucky punch or cut over the eye and it's over."

Daszkiewicz insisted that Beattie post a $2,500 performance bond. "How do we know Beattie will show up?" Daszkiewicz asked.

"I'm an old man, all washed up," said Beattie, thirty-six. "He has to beat me. He wants to fight for the title, after all. All I want to do is have some fun, have a little action."

"Poor Scott LeDoux," Beattie said. "He's tough, he's rugged, he can knock you out with either hand. But unfortunately, he wasn't trained in the finer points of boxing and if he has another encounter with the likes of George Foreman, he could be hurt seriously."

Poor Jim Beattie. Referee Mert Herrick stopped the fight in the third round.

Beattie had been given a standing eight-count after a LeDoux right in the first round. A LeDoux left dropped him for an eight-count in the third before a right-left combination sent him down for the last time.

"It was so unfair," Beattie said. "I'm fine. I wasn't wobbly. I said to Herrick, 'You can't be doing this to me. Be professional.'"

"I didn't want to stop it," Herrick said. "But when you look down at the man on the floor and he doesn't even see you, it's time."

For the first time in months, LeDoux was seeing the boxing world in a new light. He had won four straight and was unbeaten in his last six fights.

"If I was ever going to make my run toward a title shot," he said, "this was it."

17

SIX MONTHS TO LIVE

*L*eDoux had won four straight fights but had not battled a big-name opponent since his draw with Leon Spinks in October 1977. Now, it was 1979, and LeDoux wondered if he might ever get a shot at a well-known foe and the big payday that could transform his career. He had been seeking a match with Ken Norton for years. Beat the former champion who broke Ali's jaw and the rest of the boxing world will consider you a legitimate contender, he said. But each time LeDoux versus Norton seemed inevitable, a negotiations snag killed the fight.

When LeDoux and Daszkiewicz went to Las Vegas to see Norton take on Earnie Shavers, they did so with the understanding that LeDoux would fight Norton in May. LeDoux wasn't thinking about fighting Shavers, whom he had never met, but who would later become a true friend, a man LeDoux highly respected away from boxing. What LeDoux and Daszkiewicz seemed to overlook was that Shavers could be pretty impressive in the ring, too. Shavers had a reputation as one of the hardest punchers of his era. Ali said getting hit by Shavers was like "getting hit by a truck." And Shavers had recently beaten Norton, in a split decision. A Norton win against Shavers was about as reliable as those *Ring* magazine records of boxers nobody had ever seen.

At the prefight weigh-in, Shavers told Norton, "I'm going to destroy you." Norton, his best days apparently behind, told Shavers, "Earnie, we can make a lot of money." To which Shavers replied, "Ken, I'm the only one going to remember that."

Norton didn't make it through the second round.

With Norton suddenly no longer a viable option, LeDoux's plan B was to take on Ron Lyle in Las Vegas or New York on May 12. Nobody gave serious consideration to holding the fight in the Twin Cities, because May 12, after all, was the start of the walleye season.

The nationally televised fight in Vegas was promoted by Don King, who held contractual rights to unbeaten Larry Holmes, the World Boxing Council's version of heavyweight champion.

LeDoux was looking beyond dollar signs when he agreed to a fight orchestrated by the ostentatious King. The fight, LeDoux said, would not pay him much. "I would give what I'm getting to charity, but it wouldn't help them," he said.

King promised that if LeDoux could beat Lyle, "his hopes for a title shot will be fulfilled. I'll give the white boy a chance."

LeDoux, now 25–6–3, was eager to grab it. "I'm going to be awfully hungry to get some of that money that's out there," LeDoux said. "We're going to come in hungry, and Lyle's got to pay for that. They tell me he's a tough guy. He better be."

Lyle (37–5–2) lost a title shot against Ali in eleven rounds in 1975. Four years later, he was making a different sort of comeback. Just five months before his fight against LeDoux, Lyle was acquitted on second-degree murder charges involving the shooting death of a former roadwork aide, Vern Clark, in Lyle's suburban Denver home.

Lyle, the youngest of nineteen children, grew up in the Denver projects, hanging around street corners, where trouble inevitably found him. When someone chased him with a pipe, he borrowed a gun "just to scare the guy." A fatal shot was fired, and Lyle was convicted of second-degree murder. He was sentenced to fifteen to twenty-five years in the Colorado State Penitentiary.

Prison recreation director Clifford Mattax tried to nurture the six-foot-three, 216-pound Lyle, a sensational all-around athlete, but Lyle would have none of it. "Man, you're a screw and I'm a convict," he told Mattax.

When an inmate stabbed Lyle in the stomach with a knife and Lyle lost thirty-five pints of blood and nearly died twice, there was Mattax at his bedside after Lyle underwent seven hours of surgery. "It was the turning point of my life," Lyle told *Sports Illustrated* in 1972. "Mattax was white and he wore a badge, but he really cared. He believed in me and my ability. Right then I decided to be a success."

Lyle was paroled after nearly eight years of prison. His notable fights included a dismantling of Shavers and an epic, losing battle against George Foreman. But after his acquittal, in December 1978, for Clark's death, Lyle's career was all but over. At a press conference before the Le-Doux fight, Lyle, thirty-seven, said he would be ready for a title shot "in seven or eight months after a few major fights."

"I want to be world champion not because of what I can reap, but because of my dream," Lyle said. "Every man has a dream, and he believes if he works hard, if he sweats and toils in the fields, he can realize that dream. I have slaved in the fields and I want my dream to be fulfilled."

LeDoux came from a totally different world, but his dream was no different. LeDoux accepted a meager payday from King, thinking of possibilities, not his bank account.

"Once the ice is broken and you get a major fight and with it a promise that if you win you might get a fight with the champion, you're suddenly part of the big time," Daszkiewicz said. "We think right now LeDoux is in a position to prove that he belongs.

"Once, all he talked about was how much money he might get for a fight. Now he doesn't talk money; now he says, 'If we produce, money will follow.'"

LeDoux could not have been more focused. He was told by a hotel guest, "Frank wants to meet you."

"Frank who?" he asked.

"Frank Sinatra."

"I told the guy, 'I have to go to bed,'" he recalled. "It would have taken just five minutes, and I've regretted it ever since. But I went to bed."

"There's no question this is my most important fight," LeDoux said. "This is the first time we've ever been told that if we win the fight, there will be a title fight. I'd better do it now."

The weigh-in included the usual shenanigans. LeDoux told Lyle, "Just get used to being second, because I'm weighing in first."

Lyle shoved LeDoux, who shoved back before their respective handlers separated the two. Soon King was interjecting his unique pearls of wisdom, and the conversation turned to race. King said LeDoux was "the only visible white hope out there today." LeDoux countered by saying that white fighters in heavier weight divisions had to conquer racial discrimination as well as their opponents.

"What does a white guy have to do to get a title shot?" he asked earlier in the week. "Why do we have to keep passing tests? You tell me a white fighter isn't on the short end of the stick. For this Saturday, after I pay my manager, sparring partner and taxes, if I make $10,000 I'll be very happy. [He was reportedly to be paid $25,000 before expenses.] I can make more money at home fighting bums."

Lyle was to receive $125,000.

The thirty-year-old LeDoux loved his chances. He had been running six miles a day, was in great shape, and was confident enough to say, "I don't think I have to fight my best fight to win. I just have to fight a good fight. But I'd like to fight my best fight to show people I'm as good as I say I am."

It was not his best fight, but most of the reporters who covered it said LeDoux fought well enough to win.

But he didn't win.

Lyle, who was embraced in the ring by King before the decision was announced, won by the narrowest of margins, a split decision in a fight that heavyweight champion Larry Holmes, a ringside spectator, called "dead even."

"I thought I won the early rounds, lost some middle rounds and then won the final rounds," LeDoux said afterwards. "It's over, the decision has been made, there's not too much to say."

Judge Harold Buck scored it 45–44, Lyle. Judge Chuck Minker gave the fight to LeDoux by an identical score. Judge Art Lurie scored it 46–45, Lyle.

LeDoux thought he had won the fight early. He knocked Lyle down in the third round with a left hook and then a right to Lyle's chin. Lyle was given a standing eight-count. "I thought they were going to stop the fight," LeDoux said.

He also thought the fight would be stopped after four low blows by Lyle. "I think points should be taken away, and if they would have done that, I'd be the winner," he said. "I'm not crying, though. That's not my style. I'm just telling you the way it is."

For LeDoux, his seventh loss was another case of so close, yet . . . In his estimation—and in the minds of many impartial observers—he had beaten Lyle, Johnny Boudreaux, Leon Spinks, Dino Denis, and Bill Sharkey, and Cookie Wallace probably should have been disqualified for his head butt. The record book shows them all as losses or draws. His record was still a respectable 25–7–3.

"[Lyle] deserves another shot," LeDoux said when it was over, sounding as if he had been on the other side of the split decision. "If he wants a rematch, he's got it."

"I just destroyed Lyle with that punch," LeDoux said, years later, of the fight's only knockdown. "He was a mess when I got done with him. He was hurting."

LeDoux didn't fare so well, either.

"I'm back in my hotel room after the fight, hurtin', sitting on the toilet, crying," he said. "One of our guys is taking my shoes off. My wife, Sandy, is there. Joe Daszkiewicz is there, and he sees something red in the urine when I get up, and he says, 'What is that, Scottie?'

"Sandy looks at him and says, 'It's blood, Joe. It's been coming for the last three fights.'

"The Lyle fight. It was the bottom of the barrel and the top of the hill. On the plane coming back, I was crying again. Sandy looks up at me and says, 'What's wrong?'"

LeDoux hated having to explain himself. He never dodged an opponent. He never dodged the media. And he never dodged the questions of well-wishers and close friends who wanted to know—again—what happened. How could he have lost?

He drove to the King of Clubs, a northeast Minneapolis bar, when he returned home.

"So who died?" somebody asked him.

"Scottie, you don't have to go in there," a friend told him.

"Yes, I do," LeDoux said.

He urinated blood for eleven days after the Lyle fight. "One more day of that and we're going to the Mayo Clinic," Sandy told him.

They would visit the Mayo Clinic in Rochester, Minnesota, soon enough—but not before LeDoux and his buddies went on a fishing excursion to Lake Vermilion, in northeastern Minnesota, before Memorial Day. Upon returning, he noticed a bandage on Sandy's leg.

"What's that all about?" he asked her.

She had noticed a mole on her leg, while in Las Vegas, and said she couldn't shave the area. "You know I had a mole," she told him. "It changed colors while we were out there."

Sandy had never been a sunbather, but she had sat by the outdoor pool at their Las Vegas hotel. That was why the color change, LeDoux thought. That had to be it.

"You were perfectly healthy," LeDoux said. "What are they gonna do?"

"A biopsy," she told him. "They'll let me know Tuesday."

Waiting in an empty dressing room to hear the words "Five minutes to go" was excruciating for LeDoux. But the only man ever to go toe-to-toe in the ring with eleven heavyweight champions suddenly had met his match. Five minutes? He couldn't wait five seconds, much less a full weekend, till Tuesday.

He fretted for days. When Tuesday finally arrived, he called his wife's doctor over and over for the entire day. Finally, he got the answer that he didn't want and couldn't understand.

"Melanoma," the doctor said. "Your wife has melanoma."

"What does that mean?" LeDoux asked.

"It means we need to move as quickly as we can," the doctor told him.

LeDoux asked, "What's the prognosis?"

The doctor did not hesitate. "She might make six months," he said.

18

COLD, HARD CASH

$\mathcal{W}$atching a professional boxing match isn't much different than watching a vicious hit during a football game or seeing a hockey fight. Nobody wants to see permanent injury, but the sight of blood can get a spectator's adrenaline going. Then, when the game ends, the spectators leave. But the victims' pain endures.

With the exception of the Boudreaux loss, the mercurial LeDoux tried to harness his emotions in the ring. Before each fight, he was a wreck. After each fight, he had Sandy.

"He's an emotional guy," said LeDoux's close friend Bob Dolan, a Minneapolis attorney, who traveled the world to watch his buddy chase a dream. "Fortunately, Sandy was kind of the stabilizing influence. He'd get excited when he'd win—although not crazy excited like football players do now when they make a tackle and act like they just found the cure for the common cold. And when he lost a fight he didn't think he should lose, he'd get very emotional, sometimes cry and always hang his head.

"And Sandy would immediately put everything in perspective. After every fight she'd say, 'Here's another one they can't take away from us. Another adventure. They can't take this one away from us.'"

Sandy could always lighten her husband's mood. Before hopping into bed, she once pressed her palms together as if she was about to plunge into the water and then dived with childlike glee onto the mattress. At a press conference, when she was asked about her husband's heritage, Sandy explained that LeDoux knew only four sentences in French "and they all get his face slapped."

She was loyal and supportive. The media loved her.

"What's it like with Scott when he has a big fight?" a reporter asked. Never missing a beat, Sandy responded, "When he comes home, he still has to take the garbage out."

Throughout LeDoux's ring career, his wife was incredibly protective. "I don't worry about him physically," she said. "The cuts and black eyes heal. I worry about his feelings. His feelings are hurt if he loses or looks bad."

"It's bad enough losing," Sandy said. "But to get up in the morning hurt and read that you're just a club fighter or journeyman . . . That hurts."

LeDoux knew how lucky he was. "If you start getting depressed, she takes you right out of it," he said.

Now, Scott and Sandy LeDoux were about to embark on a life-and-death journey that they would have forgone in a heartbeat. After nearly ten years of marriage, they were still very much in love. He adored her. Everybody did. And she treated his moodiness and stubborn nature with a laugh. He was on the cusp of making big money, or so they thought. He took her everywhere, and sportswriters sometimes seemed more attracted to Sandy than to Scott. He lavished her with a Datsun 280Z, a nifty little sports car that Scott barely could squeeze into but drove anyway. He also rode his motorcycle. They had a nice suburban home in Andover, twenty-five miles north of Minneapolis. When Scott was feeling like a big shot and Sandy told him to take out the garbage, well, he took out the garbage.

Molly was seven months old, and Josh was three when Sandy was diagnosed. Doc and Mickey smothered their grandchildren with love and, in Josh's case, Mickey's baked goods.

It was as close as it gets to Norman Rockwell's America—with an occasional case of blood in the urine to remind them of how hard they worked to get to this point. The battles that LeDoux had faced in the ring paled in comparison to what he now faced.

After speaking to Sandy's doctor, LeDoux took his wife into their bedroom, told her the news, and did his best to hold back tears. He was the tough guy's tough guy, but Sandy was the strong one. Now, he had to match her strength. For her sake.

He told her that the doctor wanted to consult with colleagues, would come up with a plan, and get back to them in a day or two. That was Tuesday night. LeDoux called again on Wednesday—several times—and, finally, the doctor told the couple to meet with him at the hospital in Coon Rapids.

"I talked to two doctors," LeDoux said, his fists clenched and the veins popping in his neck as he told the story years later. "One of them says there's a treatment where they're gonna shoot this dye and medication into her leg and you stop the melanoma that way. Or, he says, they could amputate the leg. Or take the back of the leg and remove a chunk of it, right on her calf. Or they were talking about dishing out the melanoma, see how that works."

But, they kept telling LeDoux, "We haven't made a decision."

"The next day, Thursday, they called me and said they still hadn't come to a decision," LeDoux said, his gruff voice becoming a slow growl. "They wanted to know what choice we'd like to make.

"If we were in the ring, I would have beaten the snot out of them right then and there. I said, 'What decision would I make? I'm a fighter. I'm not a doctor. If I was a doctor, I'd have it done already. But I'm not a doctor and we need your help. Please! Isn't there anything you can do? You guys gotta get off the dime and make a decision.'"

LeDoux was told that the physicians in Coon Rapids could not agree on a procedure. On Friday morning, at six o'clock, Scott and Sandy received an unexpected wake-up call. They had a 2:30 p.m. appointment scheduled at the Mayo Clinic in Rochester, Minnesota, about a two-hour's drive from their home. Mickey came to stay with Molly, and, with Josh in tow, Sandy and Scott embarked on the longest road trip of their lives.

The surgeons went into attack mode right away. Melanoma moves quickly, and the doctors wanted to extract whatever they could find. They surgically removed a portion of flesh near Sandy's calf. They then removed lymph nodes in Sandy's upper leg and found no cancer. The doctors were comfortable in knowing they had gotten any obvious cancer, but they couldn't promise that more cancer would not surface in Sandy's bloodstream. "We don't know where it is, or where it might be," the surgeons told Sandy.

Scott and Sandy left Rochester and the Mayo Clinic for the Twin Cities, saying very little at the start of the drive. "We were scared to death," Scott said.

They got another scare, forcing them to head right back to Rochester after only twenty miles. Josh had a seizure and needed immediate treatment. Thankfully, they were heading back to one of the best medical campuses in the world. Physicians prescribed medication, which Josh took three times daily. It was his last epileptic seizure.

More good medical news awaited. They were relieved—no, ecstatic—when the Mayo Clinic called to say that tests revealed no more cancer. And they were overwhelmed by the showing of support they received—much of it from strangers they would never meet.

The boxing fraternity is as close-knit as any that can be found in professional sports. Only in the ring can two huge, brutally strong men bash away at each other round after round, until both are about to drop from exhaustion. And when it's over? Leon Spinks hugs Scott LeDoux. Ron Lyle does the same. Duane Bobick, LeDoux's greatest rival, travels to New York to be in LeDoux's corner and, years after both retire, calls LeDoux his "friend."

The first boxer to contact Sandy was one she and Scott had never met—Earnie Shavers. He sent a letter to Sandy while she was in the hospital, told her he was praying for her and the LeDoux family, and asked if there was anything he could do. Scott and Sandy finally met Shavers three years later and had him over to their house.

"Earnie Shavers was the fiercest puncher I'd ever seen, but you'll never meet a sweeter man," LeDoux said.

"We started hearing from lots of guys—guys that, if you listened to all the prefight buildups, you'd think they couldn't stand me. It's all show, you know, well, a lot of it.

"They talk about tough guys pouring their hearts out in the ring. Well, I can tell you that it happens outside the ring. These guys are brutes, but they could not have been nicer when they found out about Sandy."

Further medical tests proved negative. No physician would dare say that Sandy was cancer free, and there were warnings about recurrences. Still, for the moment, there was reason for hope, reason to continue seeking dreams.

"I was scared," LeDoux admitted. "I wasn't drinking a lot, but I was a binge drinker during that time. When I didn't have a fight, I might go out a couple nights and get hammered."

His next fight would be one he had sought for more than two years—against Norton, who was seeking a comeback after being dismantled by

Shavers. This time, LeDoux would not have to rely on Don King to meet a "name" contender.

Bob Arum and Teddy Brenner were no longer the only promoters on the national scene challenging King. The latest entrant was Muhammad Ali Professional Sports, Inc., better known as MAPS. Ali had virtually nothing to do with the organization—other than accepting $500,000 for promotional appearances and the right to use his name. It began as a California-based outfit that promoted track meets and would evolve into a monster virtually overnight, lavishing outrageously huge cash payments to well-known boxers in an attempt to quietly overtake King's growing legions in the increasingly competitive and often lucrative world of professional boxing. MAPS promoted a couple of minor fights, but the LeDoux–Norton fight would be the organization's introduction to big-time boxing.

So began an incredible saga, one that makes some of the sleaziest undertakings in boxing's oft sordid history look like Sunday school lessons. Little did LeDoux and Daszkiewicz know that they were about to become pawns in what prosecutor Dean Allison called the biggest sports and bank scandal in U.S. history.

The key figure in MAPS was Harold J. Smith. But long before he became Harold Smith, he was Ross Fields. Fields had a real connection to the track circuit, having run on the winning Intercollegiate Association of Amateur Athletes of America indoor-mile team for American University in Washington, D.C., in the 1960s. Fields dropped out of college, operated a discotheque in Washington, and then promoted closed-circuit boxing shows. He left Washington, leaving a trail of bad checks that landed his name on 1976 FBI posters. In those days, he used aliases like Gerald Fidelman and Gerald Tishman, interesting aliases, at the time, for a black man to use.

He found the name Harold Smith on the birth certificate of a white man who lived in North Carolina. The six-foot-two Fields grew a beard, gained fifty pounds, and introduced himself to Ali as Harold J. Smith. Wanted man Ross Fields was about to become a promotional giant, as Harold Smith—doing it all without a proper license.

He had plenty of help, however. Ben Lewis and Sammie Marshall, middle managers for the Wells Fargo bank in Beverly Hills, oversaw the withdrawals of hundreds of thousands of dollars, and then, by managing computer records or erasing transactions altogether, made it appear as if they already had been repaid or they had never occurred.

But Harold Smith was after more than money. He wanted fame and the lifestyle that accompanied it. According to the book *Empire of Deceit,* written by prosecutor Allison and Bruce B. Henderson, Smith thought nothing of betting $10,000 on a single horse race or placing $25,000 on a roll of the dice in Las Vegas. He claimed to have won $250,000 betting on Roberto Duran in Duran's first boxing match with Sugar Ray Leonard. Now he was betting on Scott LeDoux and Ken Norton to take his MAPS boxing operation to a level that King and Arum might one day envy.

Smith had little trouble in getting the attention of his two featured combatants. Norton wanted to avenge the humiliation he suffered at the gloves of Shavers, and LeDoux again thought this could be his shot at the big time. NBC wanted the fight. Ken Norton was still Ken Norton.

Before meeting Smith, though, LeDoux and Daszkiewicz were introduced to Lewis and Marshall in a plot so ridiculous that no book editor or Hollywood producer would even consider it as plausible fiction.

LeDoux and Daszkiewicz were told to meet Marshall and Lewis at a Minneapolis–St. Paul airport restaurant. They still hadn't settled on a location for the fight, but Marshall had a contract waiting to be signed. Wearing dark, conservative bankers' business suits, the men sat across from LeDoux and Daszkiewicz. Pleasantries followed introductions. Then Marshall shoved a contract across the table for Daszkiewicz to study. Marshall wiped his brow repeatedly as the contract was read. According to Henderson and Allison's book, LeDoux was to receive a $15,000 advance and a total of $50,000 for fighting Norton. (Norton was to receive a $100,000 advance.)

LeDoux, however, remembered it much differently:

Lewis and Marshall handed him a brown paper bag. Inside, there was $50,000, in cash. All one-hundred-dollar bills.

"You don't have to claim it," Marshall kept telling him, LeDoux recalled. "This is cash money. This is yours. You don't have to claim it."

This, apparently, was how Smith and his cohorts operated. Smith also recruited Shavers—with $300,000 in an airline pilot's bag. Smith emptied the money on a coffee table in Shavers's hotel room—packages of fifties and one hundreds. Smith tried to stack the money packages containing

$5,000 and $10,000, but Shavers began prying each package apart. Then he counted the contents of each of them, peeling back every bill.

"Look, Earnie, it's all there, believe me, I wouldn't cheat you," Smith said.

Shavers looked up and replied, "Oh, no, Harold, I'm not worried about that. I'd just feel bad if I counted this money and you'd given me more than you were supposed to."

Shavers counted for an hour.

LeDoux and Daszkiewicz weren't as nonchalant. They signed the contract, the visitors left the paper bag, and the two couples went their separate ways.

LeDoux went into a panic. "What do we do? We just can't just go to the bank with $50,000," he said, his hands shaking.

Daszkiewicz, who was to be paid $12,500 of the total, was even more nervous. They did nothing wrong, he was certain. They had signed a contract and got an advance, as they had done a couple dozen times before. But never cash. Never $50,000 in cash. And without knowing that the money came from an illegal $250,000 withdrawal from Wells Fargo, money that was supposed to cover all expenses of the August 19 fight.

"We're gonna declare this tomorrow," Daszkiewicz told LeDoux. "You and I are going straight to the IRS, first thing in the morning, and declare it."

The government official who met with LeDoux thought he was crazy. "He wanted to know if I was joking," LeDoux said. "He told me that nobody walks around handing over paper bags with $50,000 in cash at airports. He assumed I was making this up and suggested I put the money in the bank and declare it before I paid taxes next April.

"Well, how could I walk into a bank with nearly $50,000. I could deposit some of it, but I was nervous driving around with that kind of money."

So LeDoux, after verbally declaring his earnings, did what seemed logical at the moment. He went home with $37,500 in cash, and he and Sandy wrapped much of it in tin foil and then hid it in the back of their freezer and left it there for nearly six months before depositing it in a bank. (Nearly a dozen years later, when LeDoux was moving and cleaning out the house, he found one of the tin bricks buried behind some frozen hamburger meat—nearly $1,000 in cold, hard cash.)

There was more: Smith also arranged for LeDoux to fight Mike

Weaver, for the United States Boxing Association heavyweight title. Le-Doux would be paid $150,000—although he said years later that he received $250,000. Regardless, it was his biggest payday, by far, to that point.

Smith wasn't done. He signed LeDoux for a third fight—against unbeaten Marty Monroe—and was on the verge of concocting a LeDoux–Holmes fight—even though Holmes was signed to King.

The arrangement of that fight was made in November 1979 (after LeDoux's bouts with Norton and Weaver) and was scripted straight out of a gangster drama. Daszkiewicz and LeDoux were told by Smith's associates to fly to Las Vegas immediately, without explanation. There would be a meeting at Caesars Palace the next day.

Upon arriving, Daszkiewicz walked into the casino and ran into Henry Grooms, a respected trainer from Detroit who had worked with Ali and Leon Spinks, among others.

"Papa Joe, what the hell's going on here?" Grooms asked Daszkiewicz.

"What are you talking about?" Daszkiewicz replied.

"Jesus, there's so many boxing people. What are you guys up to?"

There was a welterweight title fight in town, between Wilfred Benitez and Sugar Ray Leonard, but the number of boxing luminaries at the hotel seemed over the top.

"Who ya seen?" Papa Joe asked.

"Don King's here," Grooms told him.

"Oh, Jesus Christ," said an ashen Daszkiewicz. "Don's here?"

Sensing trouble—and from men who were experts at creating it—Daszkiewicz and LeDoux headed straight to Smith's suite. They would listen to him and leave the hotel as quickly as possible. When they got to Smith's room, they were stunned to find Smith and Marshall with Holmes and a suitcase. Smith opened the satchel, exposing more cash than LeDoux, Daszkiewicz, and, likely, Holmes had ever seen. One million dollars, according to Smith.

"Larry, this is your signing bonus, if you sign to fight Scott LeDoux," Smith told him.

Earlier that week, Smith had called Lewis at Wells Fargo and told him he needed a $250,000 cashier's check, made out to Holmes. Lewis immediately complied, not thinking about how he might cover for a quarter-of-a-million-dollar withdrawal, with no return payment to come. If they could sign Holmes, the heavyweight champ, they could control boxing. Through various payments, they allegedly promised Holmes a total of $1.5 million to fight LeDoux.

Seconds later, there was a pounding at the door, and then the door burst open. King was standing in the hallway, according to LeDoux and Chuck Daszkiewicz, who got a full report from his father. In *Empire of Deceit*, Allison tells it a bit differently, saying that Smith's hotel suite door was wide open, and when Smith walked out, there was King blocking his path.

All accounts agree that Daszkiewicz, now standing in the hallway, heard a loud commotion within the room.

"Don, I'm gonna walk you down. Get outta here," Smith told King, according to the account Joe Daszkiewicz told his son.

Papa Joe told his son that he was certain King had a gun in his pocket and told Smith, "Harold, I'll blow you away."

At that point, Daszkiewicz grabbed LeDoux and said, "Let's get the hell out of here."

They didn't go far. According to Allison's book, King yelled at Smith, punctuating his anger with a racial slur. "You tell me you need help and then you double-cross me, you son of a bitch. If it's the last thing I'll do, I'll get you out of boxing."

King then told Smith, "I'm gonna walk you down."

"I've never been so scared," recalled LeDoux. "I was sure shots were gonna be fired and we were gonna be part of it."

In spite of all the accusations and horror stories associated with King, Chuck Daszkiewicz said he and his father grew to like and respect him. In the midst of the Boudreaux grand jury investigation, Al Braverman mentioned LeDoux and Papa Joe to King and said, "They're not going to go away."

For all the headaches he may have caused LeDoux, King always returned to the one great white hope he never tired of promoting. "If you want to fight for the title," he told LeDoux a few months later, "I'll give you the title fight and I'll give it to you in Minneapolis."

Again, that conversation was months away. First, King had to deal with his champion, Holmes. "You go to your room," he ordered the champ, who did so without asking questions.

"I'll be there directly," he told King, according to LeDoux.

Smith went back to Los Angeles and turned the cashier's check, intended for Holmes, over to Lewis.

He would promote LeDoux's next three fights—Norton, Weaver, and Monroe—and he had promotional contracts with Norton, Benitez, Gerry Cooney, Michael Spinks, and the magnificent Thomas "Hitman" Hearns, who won eight world titles in six weight divisions. Yet, while surrounding himself with the day's top boxers, Smith remained cloaked in mystery.

Ali would see Smith with beautiful girls, planes, and boats and ask, "You sure everything's OK, Harold?"

"I still don't know where he gets his money," Ali said then. "I'm still wondering."

Smith would ultimately learn that the most powerful men in boxing didn't wear gloves. They wore badges. The FBI found that Smith, a.k.a. Ross Fields, had stolen $21,305,705.18 that belonged to Wells Fargo. He was convicted of fraud and aiding and abetting embezzlement—convicted on twenty-nine counts in all and sentenced to five years in prison.

He would resurface after prison. Amazingly, the man who almost stole boxing, quietly returned to the sport in the 1990s to serve as an advisor to Holmes and Hitman Hearns.

19

LUCK OF THE DRAW

*B*y mid-July 1979, the Norton–LeDoux bout was still without a venue and set date. But that didn't prevent the combatants from going toe-to-toe verbally.

"One of us is going to walk out and the other is going to be laid out," LeDoux said in late June.

At that point, LeDoux assumed the fight would be in San Diego in mid-July, and he doubted he could get a win by decision in Norton's hometown. "A knockout is the only way I can win," LeDoux said. "I'm going to try to knock him out as soon as I can."

Norton, knocked out in the first round in his March bout with Earnie Shavers, was coming back after a three-month retirement. "I can't quit with my tail between my legs," he said.

The fight, originally to be held in July, was rescheduled for August 19 after Norton's camp said he tore cartilage in his rib cage while sparring.

"Norton said he needed a couple of weeks for his ribs," a skeptical LeDoux said later. "Anybody can tell you that it takes five or six months for damaged ribs to heal properly. He was heavy, is all. He was looking 235 pounds to me and some kind of out of shape."

Daszkiewicz also was cynical. "Norton is getting $250,000 for this fight," he said. "We get $50,000 and a postponement."

The date wasn't all that would be changed. Papa Joe cornered Harold Smith and reminded him how popular LeDoux was in Minnesota. "Scott's gonna get killed," Daszkiewicz told Smith. "People in Minnesota will want to see that. It will be a bigger draw."

Of course, that's not the reasoning Smith and Marshall used in explaining the new venue. Marshall posted the $250 needed for an application to stage the fight at the Met Center in Bloomington on August 19. This is what he told the media:

"We didn't want to cancel the match. So, since we had done a little exploring about having the bout originally in [Minnesota], we welcomed the opportunity to move it to the Midwest.

"Most boxing today is either in Las Vegas or New York," Marshall said. "And if things work out," he said of the possibility of a LeDoux victory, "a championship fight here is a strong possibility."

There were potential problems with staging the fight in Minnesota. Both fighters requested a twenty-foot ring. "The only twenty-footer I can recall seeing was in the Crosby High School gym," Daszkiewicz said. "So it must be somewhere in the state." Then LeDoux raised eyebrows when he remarked that three neutral judges should be brought in because he didn't want to "put pressure on local officials' fear of what might be called a hometown decision."

For this fight, the term *hometown* took on a familiar meaning for LeDoux. He went back to the Crosby-Ironton area, back to his parents' 120-acre farm to train. A sixteen-foot training ring was erected in the hayloft of a barn. He was met there by Magic Davis, a twenty-year-old sparring partner, who, at six feet three, was as close to replicating Norton's size as possible.

For LeDoux, the farm provided more than a chance to train. It was an escape from the trauma of his wife's cancer, the craziness of negotiating with Smith and his cohorts, and the pressures of supporting a young family while chasing that elusive shot at the crown. He had old friends and neighbors who watched him train, and he returned the love with a party—a lunch and free beer. In Crosby, he distanced himself from the eleven months he couldn't get a fight and worked as a carpenter to help feed Sandy and the kids.

He didn't mention any of that when he leaned against the ring and was interviewed by the *Minneapolis Star*. Nor did LeDoux mention an old demon that he tried to bury but said he had revisited in his mind sporadically for years, but lately, more often and without explanation. "Maybe it was because Josh was getting close to being the same age," LeDoux said. "But, yeah, there were times, when I was alone that I would think about that day I was molested.

"I'd think about Roy, the guy who molested me, and wondered what I might do if I ran into him. It was a distraction that I didn't need. But I was in Crosby-Ironton and I'd drive by where it happened. And I kept telling myself, 'Don't go there. You got Norton. Just focus.'"

So he told the *Minneapolis Star* he was in Crosby because there was "no pressure, easy to keep a schedule, complete concentration." He talked about the public's perception of him finally emerging from Duane Bobick's shadow after Bobick's all-too-brief encounter with Norton. LeDoux said he never resented Bobick. "A better word would be 'jealous,'" he said. "There were years when I was jealous because he was having so many opportunities and seemed to be getting all the breaks. All he had to do was concentrate on fighting and he was fighting all over the country.

"Still, it wasn't pure resentment. He deserved the chances. Look at his background—Olympics, service and national amateur championships. Before turning pro, he had more than double the fights I have had as a pro and amateur.

"People ask me if Duane should retire. I tell them that's his decision to make. When my time comes, I alone will decide. People now want to class Bobick as a bum. They're the same type who told me after Ron Lyle was given the decision—given you have to believe, when you see promoter Don King jump into the ring and embrace Lyle—'I hope you get in shape for the Norton fight.'

"Bobick a bum? A guy who has won 48 of his 52 fights? A guy who beat me twice? No way. Bobick has been successful. No, he hasn't won a championship. Very few do."

For LeDoux, the words showed a sudden maturity that, maybe, came along with a thirtieth birthday and Sandy's cancer diagnosis. Rarely, throughout his career, did he have a gracious word to say about Bobick. He admitted emotions got the best of him in both Bobick fights, but, for a change, he acknowledged Bobick's boxing skills.

LeDoux also seemed to be rededicating himself, putting his body through a grueling schedule to get into top shape. He often boasted that he could lift 220 pounds, balanced across his shoulders, using only the muscles surrounding his neck. In Crosby, he not only hit the weights, he hit the road, running each morning from Ironton to Crosby to Deerwood—a total of 5.2 miles.

His mother, who attended his fights but rarely watched, asked how much longer he could keep this up. "I told her that after another fifteen fights I'll take a look at the situation," he said. "But if I lose two or three in a row—fights in which I know I lost—I might just quit. I don't want to finish a discredited fighter."

The last thing LeDoux was thinking about was quitting. Rarely had he been this confident. Bobick admitted that he got nervous, waiting in his dressing room alone for what seemed an eternity, before his fight with Norton. LeDoux, by contrast, sounded downright cocky. "I'm not saying I will win," LeDoux said. "I'm saying I don't see how I can lose. Basically, I don't fear anything."

Norton was far more diplomatic. He was at the LeDoux–Lyle fight and said LeDoux won. He called LeDoux's loss to Boudreaux a joke. He took LeDoux very seriously, saying it was a "must" win fight and that both fighters were out to "destroy" one another. Promoters were calling the fight the "Crucial Confrontation."

"It's good we've got a black fighter against a white in this bout," Norton said, sounding almost like a Don King. "Fans like those matches.

"Scott is a white hope. Maybe he's the only white hope now. There aren't too many white guys left in this business."

That comment invited comparisons to Bobick, who lasted all of fifty-eight seconds against Norton. "I know that he's better than Bobick," Norton said. "He's just starting to mature as a fighter. And he is a roughhouse. He doesn't quit and anytime you meet somebody who wants to make something of himself, you've got trouble. If LeDoux wins this fight, it's the whole chicken for him."

LeDoux, well aware of Norton's chiseled frame, jokingly asked Daszkiewicz if he could wear a T-shirt in the ring throughout the fight. But when the bell rang, LeDoux was ready, and with a plan.

Norton, the thirty-four-year-old ex-champion, could not have been more focused, though rarely do athletic events live up to such hype.

This one did.

No, it wasn't the Thrilla in Manila or the Rumble in the Jungle, and maybe this confrontation was crucial only to the fighters involved, but it had drama, urgency, and a controversial ending. The fight, which drew a Minnesota record gate of $131,000, had nearly all of the 8,100 patrons— mostly LeDoux fans—on their feet, screaming up to the final bell. You couldn't ask for more. Decades later, those who were there or watched the fight on TV talk about what they witnessed with the same passion the fighters showed with every blow, every grimace, every drop of sweat.

In the early rounds, it was all Norton. Lots of left hooks. Lots of jabs. "Sure, I got hit with plenty of punches, but only a couple of times did he try to throw a bomb, and then he missed," the 218-pound LeDoux said. "I can take some pretty good shots."

Even though his punches seemed to be losing their bite, Norton dominated the fight for seven rounds. But in the eighth round, the tension in the building shifted. You could see a change in LeDoux's body language. And you could see it in Norton's eyes. One of them, anyway.

LeDoux's punch caught Norton in the eye, blinding the former champ in one eye for the remainder of the fight and for nearly two hours after that, Norton would say later.

"Norton was beating him pretty good, every round," recalled referee Denny Nelson, who worked many of LeDoux's fights, including this one. "Then came the eighth. Norton wasn't prepared. And it wasn't pretty."

Norton, clearly ahead on points, seemed desperate to buy time. Before the ninth round, Norton's corner men put ice cubes in his trunks, a tactic to shock him back into the moment and also one of boxing's age-old tricks. The ice cubes spilled onto the canvas. Referee Wally Holm spent a good thirty seconds kicking them out of harm's way, giving Norton an extra half minute to regroup.

Daszkiewicz was livid. "You look at the television tape," he said. "You'll see a bucket of ice being thrown from Norton's corner. They should have been disqualified right there."

Still, LeDoux won the round.

"I was trying to set him up for a knockout," LeDoux said.

Norton was exhausted. His swollen eye prevented him from seeing clearly. He may have never seen LeDoux's right hand coming. Down he went for an eight-count. The crowd and NBC announcer Marv Alpert could no longer contain themselves. Norton struggled to his feet and pushed against the ropes before LeDoux nailed him with another flurry of punches. Norton was draped against the ropes when Holm began his count.

Then the bell sounded. The fight was over. Norton was literally saved by the bell. "He later thanked Scott for not killing him," said LeDoux's buddy Dolan.

Nelson, a judge in this fight, scored it 95–94 Norton. Holm scored it 95–94 LeDoux. And Judge Leroy Benson scored it even, 95–95.

A draw.

The decision drew an eruption of boos from the pro-LeDoux crowd.

But it was the greatest victory of LeDoux's professional career.

"I'm inviting LeDoux to watch Holmes's [title] defense against Shavers next month," King said. "Yes, I will consider Scott as an opponent for the winner. He has paid his dues and deserves a chance."

For Norton, at 40–7–1, it appeared to be the end. For LeDoux, at 25–7–4, a career was just beginning.

20

THE MONROE DOCTRINE

*W*hile the rest of the country was discovering heavyweight contender Scott LeDoux, many of his oldest and most faithful fans missed the Norton fight. A girl driving a Volkswagen rammed into a telephone pole that held the main artery for Crosby-Ironton's cable TV. Anyone who still had an old-fashioned antenna could watch the fight. Other folks drove to Brainerd to watch their native son show the rest of the world what folks from the Iron Range already knew. And some went to Andy's Bar to watch the snowy, shadowy images that the TV's rabbit ears scarcely drew from the NBC affiliate in Alexandria.

"We didn't know the town missed the fight until we got back Monday," said LeDoux's younger sister, Denise "Stormy" Thompson. "The whole town was up in arms. It's a real shame this had to happen here."

About thirty folks cheered LeDoux at the Ironton fire station, where crew members reinstalled an antenna at the station house. Others were shut out.

"I really missed a good one, huh?" said Stan Sharp, a Crosby auto mechanic.

It may have been the only negative to a glorious Sunday afternoon for LeDoux—other than the final bell sounding when he literally had Norton on the ropes.

Sammie Marshall, of MAPS, gushed about the reception his group received from the Twin Cities boxing fans and media, so much so that he said MAPS wanted to return to Minnesota, possibly with monthly shows.

Promoter Bobby Goodman was amazed by LeDoux's confidence before and after the fight. "Scott actually thought he was going to beat Norton and he almost did," Goodman said. Goodman had tremendous respect for Daszkiewicz, trainer George Glover, and LeDoux's entire team, but years later, he wondered aloud if LeDoux might have prospered more with increased sparring, "a little better training, what the other guys had."

Part of LeDoux's mystique and charm, though, was that he wasn't one of those other guys. Don King saw that back in 1975, when he began to promote LeDoux with Bunyanesque hyperbole. King invited LeDoux and Daszkiewicz to be his guests at the September 28, 1979, World Boxing Council title fight between Larry Holmes and Earnie Shavers in Las Vegas. MAPS's representatives invited LeDoux and Daszkiewicz to the United States Boxing Association title fight between Mike Weaver and Harry Terrell in Los Angeles on September 22.

So who actually held the heavyweight title? It depended on whom you asked and who was promoting which title fight. WBC champ Holmes was undefeated. USBA champ Weaver had nine losses, included a June technical knockout dealt by Holmes in June 1979. Then there was Muhammad Ali, who hadn't fought for a year since beating Leon Spinks in September 1978 to win—for a record fourth time—the World Boxing Association heavyweight title.

LeDoux had his sights set on Holmes—which is why he was delighted for a shot at Weaver in the Twin Cities. Weaver knocked out Terrell to climb to third in the heavyweight rankings. LeDoux jumped to sixth after his late-round trouncing of Norton. MAPS was heralding the November 24 LeDoux–Weaver bout at the Met Center as a fight for the U.S. heavyweight championship. The USBA was relatively new, but CBS eagerly jumped at the chance to telecast the fight.

The nation wanted to see LeDoux. Weaver wasn't bad at promoting himself. Of his nickname, Hercules, Weaver said, "I hate that name. Hercules is a myth. I ain't no myth."

Weaver, who early in his career lost to both Rodney and Duane Bobick, claimed he hit harder than Norton and was so tough "I don't permit my daughters to see my fights."

One of fifteen children, Weaver started boxing while in the Marine Corps, though not intentionally. He said he wanted to play a song on a jukebox, when he got shoved. He shoved back, the other guy swung and missed, and Weaver knocked the guy cold. The man he knocked out was heavyweight champion of the Marine Corps.

If Weaver hoped to knock out LeDoux, he would have to knock him off cloud nine first. Bob Arum called Daszkiewicz, offering LeDoux $400,000 to fight in February 1980. King also called, making the same $400,000 offer to LeDoux to fight Holmes. The Weaver fight would pay LeDoux $150,000.

"I waited," LeDoux said. "Couldn't get another fight for 11½ months. I waited for 11 months and now I can't go 11 minutes without a phone call from either Arum or King.

"I won't sit and wait. I don't want to be the token white fighter who gets a title shot. I want to earn the title shot."

The canvas ring on which boxers fight is coated with rosin, to prevent the combatants from slipping. But before Weaver and LeDoux entered the ring for the main event of a loaded card that included four other bouts (one with rising heavyweight Greg Page, another with Olympic hero Michael Spinks), someone from Weaver's group swept the canvas clean, according to LeDoux and corner men Lou Hokanson and Chuck Daszkiewicz. LeDoux said he wore leather soles. Weaver, he said, wore rubber soles.

The twelve-round championship fight was over before it began.

"I slid all over the canvas and he hit me all over the canvas," LeDoux said years later.

"That was a good fight, a good 12-round fight, but the real story there was they had screwed up the timing on the TV thing. To kill time, they had a guy go in and sweep all the rosin out of the ring. I got in there and I couldn't stand up. It was like I was on skates. Between rounds, I was begging my trainer to do something with my shoes. Take 'em off. Let me fight barefoot. I couldn't dig in at all. I couldn't throw a punch. It was terrible."

LeDoux credited Weaver, calling him a good boxer, a powerful puncher. The decision for Weaver was unanimous—even if LeDoux, bleeding all over the swept canvas, thought he won.

"There were many fights where they cheated Scott," said his old sparring partner Lou Hokanson. "The Weaver fight was one of the worst."

Two weeks later, his championship aspirations on the verge of shambles, LeDoux still believed he beat Weaver. Daszkiewicz wouldn't go that far, but he, too, sensed that his fighter's shot at the only title that mattered would eventually come. And soon. "They're gonna use up all the other talent and then turn to us," he said.

LeDoux swore he would be ready when the call came.

"You know, it's funny. Before the fight with Norton, there were people around here writing, 'LeDoux should get out.' Then, after I beat Norton, they were writing, 'Isn't it good that LeDoux stuck around.' Now, they're writing I should get out again."

The writers, he said, "keep harping on the fact that I get hit all the time. They make me out to be a buffoon. That hurts, but I think maybe they're doing me a favor. When I go out and speak, I think people expect that I'll hardly be able to talk, so I always surprise them. Compared to what they're expecting, I sound brilliant."

He recalled the words of Sammy Gallop, who trained him as an amateur in Duluth. "I asked him when I first got started, 'Can I get punchy?' He told me, 'You won't get punchy, but I guarantee you won't get any smarter.'"

LeDoux was convinced something big would happen, a career lightning bolt that would jolt his name back into the championship conversation. Daszkiewicz felt it, too. "Whenever I get down, whenever I read all the stuff about how I should get out, Joe tells me, 'When the dogs are barking at your heels, you know you're leading.'"

LeDoux planned to begin his vault as a contender against Ron Lyle, of all people—the same guy he had lost to at Caesars Palace the previous May. The fight, originally scheduled for March 15 in Denver, was moved to the St. Paul Civic Center, for March 9. But that date conflicted with the Upper Midwest Golden Gloves championships and was rejected by the Minnesota Board of Boxing. Then the board reconsidered, and the fight, to be televised nationally by CBS, was on again.

Until Lyle broke his nose while training.

Marshall of MAPS was not about to let this cash cow wander off to pasture. MAPS suggested substituting undefeated Marty Monroe for Lyle. Monroe was the guy who hurt Lyle during a workout. Daszkiewicz said no, noting that Monroe's style was completely different than that of the bigger, more aggressive Lyle, a style for which LeDoux had trained.

A day later, after indicating that his payday for the fight had grown from $100,000 to $150,000, LeDoux decided he could change his style for a fight that was ten days away.

When Monroe learned that LeDoux had twice lost to Duane Bobick, whom Monroe sparred with in Philadelphia, he concluded that he was "going to have a picnic" against LeDoux. "I'm God-sent for this mission," Monroe said. "I'm going to smoke him like a locomotive."

The MAPS group had to be secretly rooting for LeDoux. Norman Henry, MAPS's matchmaker, noted that Ali was considering a comeback, and should LeDoux beat Monroe, well . . .

"All we know is that LeDoux would be Ali's favorite opponent for his warmup fight," Henry said.

LeDoux wasn't thinking warm-up against Monroe. He needed to do something big, something spectacular. Beating an undefeated opponent on national TV was a good place to start.

Decades after he retired, the hallway in LeDoux's home was lined with framed photographs—pictures of Ali clowning with LeDoux before their exhibition, of the Norton fight, and of an eye-catching shot of LeDoux hitting Monroe with a right hand to the jaw that snapped Monroe's head back, sending what appear to be thousands of beads of sweat into the stratosphere.

"His best fight ever," said Denny Nelson, who was the referee. "National TV. Against a kid they were expecting big things from!"

LeDoux's friend Bob Dolan thought LeDoux got a break fighting Monroe, even after LeDoux prepared for Lyle. It was Lyle, Dolan recalled, who turned LeDoux's urine bloody. Monroe, even at 21–0–1, was more of a jabber.

LeDoux called Monroe's punches "slaps," while referring to his own as "ramrods." Still, Monroe thought he won the fight.

The officials disagreed, giving LeDoux the unanimous hometown decision.

That possible "tune-up" with Ali?

"I hate that word," LeDoux said from his dressing room. "I had a fight with Ali once before, you know. Five rounds. He bled. I didn't. I don't think he considers me a tune-up."

LeDoux was not about to back down from a challenge from Ali, or anyone else. He hoped he would receive a call from King for a fight with Holmes. He needed the fight to feed his ego, to fulfill a dream, and to pay the bills.

He had purchased a condo and apartments in Florida, spending money a little too freely for Papa Joe's tastes. LeDoux had also bought himself a new motorcycle but hadn't broken the news to Sandy yet.

He decided not to tell her about something else. He broke his hand in three places during the third round of the Monroe fight. "I knew it was broken," LeDoux said, "but I just couldn't stop hitting him." He told the media that he "injured" the hand, because admitting to a break might jeopardize scheduling fights in the immediate future.

There was discussion about fighting Ali—who talked of receiving $3 million for the bout—or an April 16 fight against Gerry Cooney in Atlantic City.

It all sounded so surreal. But sometimes when life looks like easy street, there is danger at your door. When LeDoux went home, the conversation turned to the reality he preferred not talking to the media about. Sandy, who had survived the melanoma scare, had breast cancer—completely unrelated to the cancer found on her calf. Nine days after the Monroe decision—the victory that just might turn Sandy and Scott's world around—Sandy underwent a radical mastectomy.

21

"WHAT'S AN EYE WHEN YOU'VE GIVEN YOUR HEART?"

andy's surgery was going to be as complicated as it was frightening. A muscle from her back had to be pulled toward her chest to properly implant the prosthesis on the right side. She would be cut from the middle of her back, all the way around.

LeDoux had said nothing to his wife about the hand he injured in the Monroe fight, nine days before. But as Sandy was wheeled off to surgery, she told the orderly to stop. She looked at LeDoux and told him, firmly, "When I wake up, I want to see a cast on your hand."

Taking on Ken Norton, Mike Weaver, and Marty Monroe was one thing. But LeDoux knew he had met his match in Sandy, and he knew when she meant business. He made a beeline to the emergency room. When his wife awakened from her surgery, his hand was in a cast that he could remove when in public. He wore the cast in private through April and wore larger, twenty-ounce gloves when hitting the heavy bag, to protect the hand.

"How did she know about my hand?" he asked himself.

Sandy, of course, always knew everything when it came to their family. When she was released from the hospital, she and Scott received phone calls daily from Diane and Chico Resch, the hockey goalie, who was in the middle of a Stanley Cup title run with the New York Islanders.

"I think they knew that Sandy could take care of herself," LeDoux said. "I don't think they were as confident about me."

LeDoux signed in May to fight Holmes for the WBC championship—for $250,000. So here it was: After years of having victories taken away,

151

years of using his face as his first line of defense in the ring, years of being used by promoters who were often less than ethical . . . after all of that, Scott LeDoux, the Iron Ranger who lived in a modest rambler in Anoka County, Minnesota, who worked out in his garage, whose wife orchestrated a backyard barbeque for the media . . . after all of it, Scott LeDoux was getting his shot. And it was happening during the most stressful time of his life, when his wife was well into her second battle against cancer in seven months.

"Only in America," Don King said of LeDoux's ascension. The man who smirked at LeDoux after he got only a draw with Bill Sharkey, the man who embraced Ron Lyle after his battle with LeDoux, but before a decision was even announced, was now talking about LeDoux's wonderful "personage."

"What the hell, I'm a truck driver with a clean shirt on," LeDoux said.

"When he was making a hundred dollars a fight, we'd go to the same bar we go to now," Sandy LeDoux said. "The money he made in those fights was fun money. He'd hand the bartender fifty dollars and say the drinks were on the house. Then, he'd do it again.

"The people there were our friends when all of this started and they'll be our friends when this is over."

It's no wonder that legendary *New York Daily News* sports columnist Dick Young—who could be as hard-edged as a New York City manhole cover—gushed when he wrote an entire column about Sandy. For the first time, the rest of the world got a glimpse at this love affair that began more than a decade before, in Duluth.

Of course, the media never saw Sandy as she sat on the bathroom floor next to Scott as he urinated blood. Nor did the media see Scott after a fight, sitting in an Epsom-salts bath, Sandy at the side of the tub, both of them in tears. Nobody saw the anguished look on LeDoux's face when a doctor told him his wife had melanoma. Nobody saw Sandy and Scott when they came home after the Weaver fight and four-year-old Josh ran up to his dad and said, "It's OK, Papa, I'll take care of you."

Maybe King was right when he billed the July 7 Holmes–LeDoux championship bout at the Met Center as "the American Dream." "Only in America could a guy like Scott LeDoux, who has been called a journeyman fighter, but is now reenergized, become a winner when they used to call him a loser, get a chance like this," King said—as only Don King could have said.

"We're making this fight an American dream. That's what it truly is. It's a fight built on ambition, aspiration, and hope."

King could have stopped there. But then, he wouldn't be Don King. "Being that he's white, blond and blue-eyed, it would be tremendous," King said at a June 18, 1980, press conference in Bloomington of LeDoux's possibly winning the title. "It would send boxing through the roof. Even the Eskimos in their igloos would be talking in their Eskimoese about Scott LeDoux."

The pleasantries ended there. The prefight daggers that fighters hurl at one another are part of the buildup to sell tickets and boost TV ratings. Once the fight is over, though, the talk ceases. Sometimes, after a vicious battle, fighters who have beaten the hell out of each other for ten or more rounds embrace.

But Holmes and LeDoux really disliked one another—and they let fight fans know it for years after their title match. In this case, the verbal sparring began nearly three weeks before Holmes and LeDoux stepped into the ring.

"Larry talks of his great punching ability," LeDoux said. "He really showed it against [Osvaldo] Ocasio. That guy's about four-foot-one and it took him seven rounds to knock him out."

Holmes: "You've been tending bar and driving trucks while I've been defending my title."

LeDoux: "Sure, I've tended bar and driven trucks. I do what I have to do to support my family."

Holmes: "I've driven trucks, too. Now, I own them."

LeDoux: "I don't like Larry Holmes. I never liked him. He called me white boy two years ago. I don't believe it is fair to bring a racial thing into boxing. I have never called him a racial name. At a press conference two years ago, he called Duane Bobick white boy, called me the same.

"He claims he is the people's champion. Aren't white people his people, too?"

Holmes said he was taking on LeDoux for "peanuts"—actually about $1 million. LeDoux showed his appreciation by giving Holmes a gift-wrapped dead walleye. Holmes's manager, Richie Giachetti, stapled a piece of paper to the fish and wrote LeDoux's name on it. Holmes returned the fish to LeDoux.

"I would have liked to have given him a live one," LeDoux said, "but he probably couldn't handle that, either."

LeDoux certainly seemed to handle the spotlight.

"Someone says to me, 'I don't think you can win the fight.' I reply, 'You didn't think I'd ever be here either, did you?'"

When callers phoned the LeDoux home, the message on the answering machine said: "Hello, this is Scott LeDoux, the next heavyweight champion of the world."

By fight week, LeDoux's voice wasn't so calm. At a July 3 cookout for the boxing crowd at the Registry Hotel, LeDoux yelled across the parking lot to Holmes, "Shut up, boy."

"You watch your mouth around my wife," Holmes shot back. "You be praising the ground I walk on."

LeDoux called Holmes "Don King's puppet."

The prefight linguistics were reaching new lows—which is saying something in boxing. Snippets of the prefight conversation involved race. In his autobiography, *Against the Odds*, when describing the prefight rhetoric with LeDoux, Holmes said, "the racial vibes were minimal." Comments concerning race surfaced again in 1982 before Holmes's fight against Gerry Cooney—although not from Cooney, Holmes emphasized in his book. Holmes wanted no part of making any fight a racial issue but said in his book that he was told by King that that's "what happened when a black and white fought."

The black-white discussion also weighed on LeDoux, who—publicly and privately—appeared to embrace all kinds of people, regardless of race, religion, or gender. That's what made this prefight rant so shocking:

"You know what it's like in boxing now?" LeDoux asked. "A white guy has to knock a black guy out just to get a decision. White guys aren't supposed to be hungry enough to fight.

"Hungry! I haven't seen anybody hungry in this country. Look at this state. Do you see anybody hungry? Do you ever see a skinny Indian? I've never seen one. I can say that and not get into trouble because I'm part Indian.

"Let me tell you something," LeDoux continued telling Doug Grow

(Above left) Scott and his older sister, Judy, posed in front of their wagon, circa 1952. *(Above right)* Scott LeDoux earned his reputation as a tough guy, but few were tougher than his father, Doc. *(Left)* Shirley LeDoux, known to all as "Mickey," was a devoted mother who loved to cook and often worked to supplement the family's income. "She was a beauty," said her daughter Judy.

During the height of the Vietnam era, in 1969, LeDoux left college and enlisted in the army.

(Above) A slam dunk: Sandy and Scott LeDoux were married at the Deerwood community center, December 1969. *(Left)* Sandy LeDoux.

(Above) LeDoux shared a private moment with the heavy bag. *(Left)* A promotional poster of the Fighting Frenchman.

The three musketeers: manager Papa Joe Daszkiewicz (left) and trainer George Glover were with LeDoux throughout his professional boxing career.

The eyes have it—and so does the hair of promoter extraordinaire Don King, examining LeDoux's right fist. Copyright Bettmann/Corbis/AP Images.

Scott and Sandy LeDoux, who had their share of heartache, were all smiles in LeDoux's dressing room.

George Foreman and Scott LeDoux were featured on the cover of the November 1976 issue of *The Ring* magazine.

LeDoux tried to avoid a left jab from former champion George Foreman in Utica, New York, August 14, 1976. Associated Press / copyright AP Images.

Stareway to heaven: heavyweight champion Muhammad Ali engaged in a lighthearted prefight staredown with LeDoux before their five-round exhibition in December 1977.

A puffy Muhammad Ali, wearing headgear, looked defensive against LeDoux during their Chicago exhibition. Photograph by Fred Jewell, Associated Press / copyright AP Images.

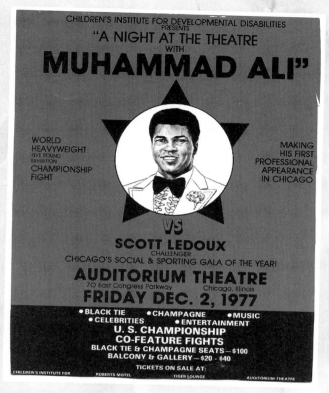

When LeDoux and Ali fought in a five-round exhibition, a poster made clear who the show's star was.

LeDoux posed with his manager, Joe Daszkiewicz, at Toots Shor's Restaurant in Manhattan after signing the contract to fight Larry Holmes for the heavyweight title in 1980. Courtesy of Chuck Daszkiewicz.

Minnesota governor Al Quie met with heavyweight champion Larry Holmes and Scott LeDoux on the steps of the state capitol before the July 7, 1980, title fight in Bloomington.

Always the center of attention, promoter Don King posed with LeDoux and Larry Holmes at Toots Shor's Restaurant in Manhattan before their title fight in 1980.

Scott LeDoux and Larry Holmes shared a cordial moment days before their title fight in 1980.

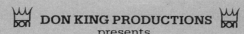

DON KING PRODUCTIONS
presents
MINNESOTA'S FIRST WORLD CHAMPIONSHIPS
MET CENTER • MONDAY EVENING, JULY 7

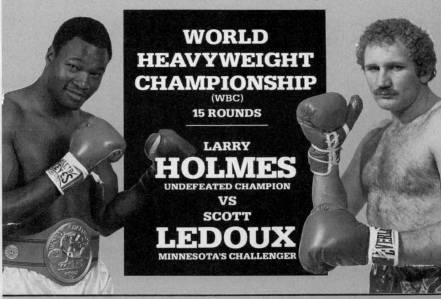

WORLD HEAVYWEIGHT CHAMPIONSHIP
(WBC)
15 ROUNDS

LARRY
HOLMES
UNDEFEATED CHAMPION
VS
SCOTT
LEDOUX
MINNESOTA'S CHALLENGER

WORLD SUPER LIGHTWEIGHT CHAMPIONSHIP
(WBC)
15 ROUNDS

SAOUL
MAMBY
CHAMPION
VS
ESTEBAN
DEJESUS
CHALLENGER

PLUS
10 ROUNDS — LIGHTHEAVYWEIGHTS
PABLO **RAMOS** CLEVELAND VS JOHNNY **TOWNSEND** MILWAUKEE

4 ROUNDS

KID **POLLACK** vs **LUSTIG** LYNN	BRIAN **BRUNETTE** vs **AVERY** ALAN	MARK **HOLMES** vs **AYERS** RON

GATES OPEN AT 5:30 PM
TICKET PRICES: $15, $25, $50, $75, $100, $200 • ALL SEATS RESERVED
ON SALE AT: ALL DAYTONS AND DONALDSONS TICKET OUTLETS AND MET CENTER BOX OFFICE
CHARGE BY PHONE On your Master Charge, Visa or Shopper Charge: Call 854-8585
Minnesota residents out of Twin Cities charge toll free 1-800-272-1836

LeDoux was listed as "Minnesota's Challenger" in his Don King–produced title fight with Larry Holmes.

Josh LeDoux's expression—and his father's swollen left eye—told the story of the championship fight with Larry Holmes.

The punch that put Scott LeDoux in contention for the heavyweight title. His victory against previously unbeaten Marty Monroe helped him earn a shot at Larry Holmes.

LeDoux embraced his son, Josh, and wife, Sandy, after beating previously undefeated Marty Monroe at the St. Paul Civic Center, March 9, 1980.

Rocky and his friends: LeDoux shared a laugh with Sylvester Stallone (the French Connection meets the Italian Stallion) as LeDoux's sparring partner Lou Hokanson looked on. Artist Leroy Neiman sat in the foreground.

LeDoux posed with Mike Tyson's other sparring partners and director Spike Lee (center) at Tyson's camp in Las Vegas.

Scott and Carol LeDoux shared a happy moment.

In the clearing stands a boxer . . . Scott LeDoux, his eye partially closed, bore the scars of his trade.

of the *Minneapolis Star*. "We never saw a welfare check in our house. My father worked. He did whatever it took. He worked in the mines and he never asked for anything. He's still up there working and all he's going to have to show for it is a gold watch. But that watch will mean something to him.

"You don't see the black man do that. You don't see the Indian do that. If you want to eat, you work. That's the way it was for my dad.

"I've never worried about what I say. I try to speak the truth."

As hurtful and inflammatory as LeDoux's words were, Holmes was in a forgiving mood the next day. "Scott just lost his composure," he said. But he again called the fight a "tune-up," adding, "Anybody who says Le-Doux has a chance is crazy."

Holmes never held back in the ring, but in this instance, he was able to harness emotions that still boiled over thirty-five years after the fight. When Holmes was asked in 2015 if he had contacted LeDoux in recent years, his answer was honest and blunt. "I wouldn't talk to him," Holmes said from his office in Easton, Pennsylvania. "He was an asshole. When it comes to racist people, they're assholes. He called me 'boy' and then he tried to make a racial issue of the fight.

"People can't help the way they were born," Holmes said. "It's God's work. We're all the same. I learned a long time ago, you don't make fun of people."

Back in 1980, rather than escalate a war of words, Holmes took the high road, acting like a champion is expected to act, telling reporters that LeDoux "lost his composure." He preferred to let his fists do the talking.

It didn't always work that way.

In an era when the media—and promoters—labeled any white fighter with a pedigree the latest "great white hope," nobody else was accusing LeDoux of being racist—not to his face and not in the media. Boxers didn't worry about being politically correct at the dawn of the 1980s. Neither was the media. Revisiting the Minneapolis newspapers of the 1970s and 1980—in which quotes liberally using the n-word surfaced time and again in the sports sections—is shocking today. But, apparently, it was not considered offensive back then.

Listen to Ali, who arrived in the Twin Cities a couple days before the big fight, talk about possibly meeting LeDoux. Remember, these two already had tangled in Chicago in 1977. LeDoux and Daszkiewicz watched movies with the champ at Ali's California mansion. Ali—like the rest of the world—adored Sandy when he met her.

"Me and LeDoux, oooh, the white dope . . . I mean hope," Ali told the *Minneapolis Tribune*'s Sid Hartman and the *Star*'s Grow. "Where is he from? South Africa?

"Oooh, LeDoux. Can you picture the redneck and the Black Muslim? Oooh, LeDoux. Some of the Black Panthers would be at ringside. That would be a rebirth of the Jack Johnson era. You are talking about big, big money. He'd get mad and call me 'nigger' a couple of times. I'd call him a honkey. We'd slap each other or something before the fight. You couldn't get that fight in a theater. The Superdome would be sold out."

Hartman offered in his column that Ali "might have been kidding."

Ali declined to pick a winner. Holmes, however, was quick to offer a sobering thought to LeDoux fans.

"This is not going to be a 'Rocky' movie," he said. "We are not discounting Scott. He's dangerous for four to five rounds. But we have been training for a 15-round fight."

The thirty-one-year-old LeDoux knew he would take a pounding—because he always took a pounding. "My head," he said, "is made of granite."

One local columnist predicted a LeDoux victory, but most others in the media suggested that Holmes would win in eight or fewer rounds.

In the Crosby-Ironton area, the locals held out hope. "He has a mean, wicked right," said LeDoux's grandmother Georgia Stangel, then seventy-eight. "If he connects, Holmes is going to hit the canvas."

Minutes before the fight, Holmes seemed certain of victory. Each fighter's team assigns one of its own to be in the opponent's corner before the fight. In this case, it was LeDoux's old sparring partner Lou Hokanson who visited with Holmes, checking the champion's wrapped hands. "He told me he would knock him out in the seventh round, that he had a plan, that he was sure of it," Hokanson said years later. "Seventh round. He was really sure about it."

Only about eight thousand people showed up for the fight, leaving half the seats in the Met Center empty. There were the usual boxing luminaries, of course: Ali, King, Howard Cosell and his hairpiece.

LeDoux was there, too—but not for long. Holmes won every round, according to the cards of each of the three officials. It was an occurrence in the sixth round, however, that ultimately led to the end of this fight and LeDoux's reign as a contender. LeDoux claimed he was thumbed in the eye in the sixth round, a tactic he said Holmes had used in previous fights. "There was instant pain and instant panic," LeDoux said. "So I dropped to my knees to gain time. I don't believe the thumbing was intentional."

The eye was checked in the sixth round and at the start of the seventh. The referee said the eye was bleeding. LeDoux said he wasn't bleeding, that he could see. He asked the referee to hold up fingers, to prove his point. "But he didn't," LeDoux said.

Dr. Jerry O'Brien, the physician who examined the eye, said the swelling he saw in the sixth round "wouldn't suggest stopping a heavyweight title fight for a swollen eye. But when the referee brought LeDoux over after stopping the fight, I could agree. The key thing was the position of the cut on the lid."

Holmes said he saw bleeding and told the referee to "stop the fight" in both the sixth and seventh rounds.

The fight was stopped in the seventh round.

When told that the ring doctor said he could have lost his eyesight, LeDoux responded, "What's an eye when you've given your heart?"

"I'm telling you," said Daszkiewicz, "we had everything going our way. All they had to do was leave the fight alone and it's going to be OK. Hey, I'm not gonna let my kid go blind.

"Everything was going according to plan."

The pro-LeDoux crowd booed. But how much of their guy's blood could they stand?

"I kicked his ass," Holmes said thirty-five years later. "He was an OK fighter. But he kept his hands down, giving you his head. You can't give your head. I knew he did that. I knew the fight would be a cakewalk."

A disconsolate LeDoux faced the media but had few answers. "We'll keep on knocking on the door," he said, his record now 26–9–4. "Back to fighting the best again. Soon as the eye heals.

"Fighting is my business. My wife, Sandy, and my family understand that, too."

Two hours later, LeDoux went to the King of Clubs in northeast Minneapolis, like he did after many of his fights in Minnesota, to once again face friends and well-wishers, to explain what had happened. No explanation was necessary. They had seen the fight in Bloomington or heard blow-by-blow descriptions of what had happened. There were hundreds of them, and they spilled into the lobby, where an auxiliary bar was hastily set up. "LeDoux! LeDoux!" they shouted, lining up to shake LeDoux's hand. By their reaction, you would have thought he had won something.

Maybe he had.

"Getting that far is an accomplishment in itself," said Rog Nafstad, a former King of Clubs owner.

"If the fight had gone on longer, it would have been a whole different fight," said Tom Daszkiewicz, another of Papa Joe's sons. "And then they didn't give him a chance. What a farce!"

It was early Tuesday morning when LeDoux finally arrived at his Andover home. He was greeted by Sandy and a very tired Josh. As LeDoux walked through the doorway, carrying the four-year-old boy, Josh looked at his dad and asked, "Papa, did you bring home the belt?"

LeDoux fought back tears.

"No, Joshy," he said. "I didn't bring home the belt."

22

LAST ROUNDS

*T*he reflexes usually go first. The healing process suddenly takes forever. The drive that separates the good athlete from the average and the champions from the occasionally great wanes, until it can no longer be willed to meet the daily grind of professional sports. Father Time always wins. We watch Mickey Mantle completely broken down in his final spring training camp, or a Hall of Fame franchise player like Harmon Killebrew, LeDoux's good friend, released by the Minnesota Twins to finish his career in a Kansas City Royals uniform, literally unable to hit his weight in his final season.

"If you're a professional athlete and you stick around long enough, it's gonna happen," LeDoux said. "It's not pretty, but what can you do?"

LeDoux could see it in the ring, where the shear physical punishment and advanced age had gotten the better of Ken Norton, Joe Frazier, and, yes, Muhammad Ali. For LeDoux, a highly emotional brute of a man who was consumed by his wife's health problems, the beginning of the end of his boxing career came the moment Holmes thumbed him in the eye.

He kept active but not necessarily in the ring. LeDoux played hockey on the Anoka Senior B amateur team. He wasn't about to call the North Stars or any other National Hockey League team and ask for a job as an enforcer. "There's no future in it for me just like there isn't any future in boxing for them," he said of his Anoka teammates. He acknowledged that the two sports had something in common. "I'd be disappointed with a team if they didn't ever get mad enough to fight."

LeDoux didn't fight again until the following April, when he took on Reggie Fleming, whom he quickly knocked out. Fleming was no title contender. It was the second of fifteen consecutive losses Fleming would endure before calling it a career. Fleming's final overall record was four wins, seventeen losses. He was knocked out fifteen times.

From a title fight with Larry Holmes to Reggie Fleming—in a matter of months.

Next up was Arnold Sam, who won six times and lost twenty-eight during a thirteen-year career of which only Sam's family can likely remember details. LeDoux hammered him but could not knock Sam out. LeDoux won a unanimous decision and expressed satisfaction after defeating his undersized opponent. "The only thing that's sore is my hands," LeDoux said. "They're killing me. I hit him with some shots, but he wouldn't go down. I hit him with an uppercut in the third round and broke the skin across the bridge of his nose. When he straightened up, the guy just grinned at me. From then on, I was just in there to go the distance. Joe said there was no sense in me going goofy and breaking my hands."

That LeDoux could admit that he was just in there to go the distance speaks volumes of where his career was headed. It wasn't that long before, when he fought Marty Monroe, that LeDoux kept slugging away after breaking his hand in three places.

If LeDoux wondered where—or if—he fit into boxing's hierarchy, he had to wonder about the places in which he was fighting. He used to fight in Las Vegas, Madison Square Garden, and the Met Center. The Sam fight was in Gillette, Wyoming.

The summer of 1981 was ending but maybe not LeDoux's career. There were still rumblings about one more shot at glory—possibly against Greg Page, the rising star who won preliminary fights in Minnesota while LeDoux fought in the main event.

There was discussion also about a fight with the retired Joe Frazier, one of the most feared champions of a golden era, who was seeing the curtain drop. Frazier and LeDoux had exchanged pleasantries years before, when Frazier managed LeDoux's archrival Duane Bobick.

Frazier, thirty-seven, hadn't fought in five years.

"I wasn't Joe's first choice," LeDoux said. "He wanted to fight John Tate, but they couldn't get together on money. I think I was Joe's third choice, so they don't think I'm easy.

"From what I hear, Joe's been working out every day in the gym since he retired. Maybe he's got it, maybe he doesn't, but if he's half as tough as he was at 32, then he's still tougher than most heavyweights."

At that point, you had to wonder if LeDoux was talking about Joe Frazier or Scott LeDoux.

"Boxers can't quit," he continued. "They can't quit the competition. It ain't the money, because when you start out, there isn't any money, except at the top. It's got to be the competition, the fun and the excitement of competition."

LeDoux said that he actually signed a contract to fight Frazier but that years later he had read in Frazier's biography that Smokin' Joe's family talked him out of a bout with LeDoux. Five years after Foreman knocked him out in five rounds, Frazier made an aborted comeback against Floyd "Jumbo" Cummings in Chicago. They fought to a draw. Frazier went back into retirement. Cummings then lost his next five fights and also called it a career.

LeDoux, once again, was left to ponder what might have been. "It would have been a great fight, and it would have helped straighten out my nose, because he had a great left hook," LeDoux said. "Joe was a warrior."

LeDoux would get another chance to prove he was one, too.

Greg Page was from Louisville, and the comparisons to another Louisville native, Ali, were inevitable—and highly unfair. Page recently had won the vacant United States Boxing Association title, beating Stan Ward, and then successfully defended his title against Marty Monroe and George Chaplin. In December 1984, he would win the World Boxing Association title in a controversial match against Gerrie Coetzee, but Page retained that title for less than five months.

In the most vicious of professional sports, where even the great success stories often end in heartbreak, Page's tragic saga hits like a sucker punch to the gut. Page had apparently retired in 1993, but three years later he mounted the first in a series of comebacks. He was forty-two years old and had boxed sporadically when he took on a muscular, heavily tattooed twenty-four-year-old named Dale Crowe in a northern Kentucky nightclub. Crowe hadn't even been born when Page was dubbed "the next Ali." Granted, Page was younger than George Foreman was when Foreman reclaimed the heavyweight title at age forty-five. But Page wasn't George Foreman.

Page lasted nine rounds with Crowe, and then the tenth brought the ultimate ring disaster. Page was battered unmercifully. When the final bell sounded, Page lay on his back under the ropes. He stared straight ahead, his vacant eyes unable to focus. He had a brain bleed. There was no emergency stretcher or oxygen tank at ringside. The ringside doctor had no license to practice medicine in Kentucky. Although the fight was sanctioned by the Kentucky Athletic Commission, a lawsuit by Page charged that eight state and federal laws governing boxing safety were violated.

The left side of Page's body was paralyzed. His speech became slurred, his short-term memory shot. His brain injuries were permanent. He died eight years later at his Louisville home, after falling out of a hospital-style bed. His head got caught in the bed railings, and he choked to death. He was fifty.

Back in December 1981, life still held promise for Page—and a USBA title for LeDoux, if he could beat him.

They fought in the Bahamas—not as the main event but as a mostly overlooked undercard. The big fight of the night was between Ali and Trevor Berbick, who would later win the WBC title—and then lose it to Mike Tyson. Ali was clearly the headliner at the Queen Elizabeth Sports Centre in Nassau.

It was Ali's last fight ever.

"The promoter had a trailer for Berbick and a trailer for Ali, and all the other fighters were put in the same dressing room to prepare for their fights," recalled LeDoux's friend Bob Dolan, who was there.

"There was a great fight in the dressing room between two guys who then went into the ring and fought each other. It was absolutely crazy."

Amazingly, it wasn't LeDoux and Page who duked it out in the dressing room, although they came close the night before. LeDoux said that he was meandering about the hotel that night when he ran into Page's brother in an elevator. According to LeDoux, Dennis Page was holding a drink when he told LeDoux what his brother was going to do to him. Instead of ignoring the comment or making a snide remark of his own, LeDoux said that he grabbed the drink and poured it on his opponent's brother's head. The two men had to be separated.

LeDoux felt more threatened by his own behavior than his adversary in the elevator. "I'm supposed to be focusing on the fight—and it was a big fight for me," he said. "I probably should have been in my room, going to bed early. I think Papa Joe wanted to kill me when he found out."

Papa Joe would have to wait his turn. Page, undefeated at the time, made a mockery of the fight in every way. At one point, when LeDoux missed with a punch, Page momentarily stopped fighting and gestured toward LeDoux with his gloves. He wiggled his hips. He taunted LeDoux verbally and physically. "I acted like a damn fool," Page said years later.

Still, that night he acted like the clear-cut USBA champion in the ring. He knocked LeDoux down three times. Page rarely got into prime fighting shape, but that night he weighed 231 pounds—light for him.

"He made me so mad," LeDoux said. "Every fight, he'd been fighting 240, 250, 260, coming in like a blimp. I get him and he's what, 224 or 223?

"He was terrific. He had a great right hand. The funny story about that fight was that he knocked me down, I think it was the second or third round. He had me down on the deck and I get back up and came to the corner and said, 'Joe, what in the hell is he hitting me with?' He says, 'He's hitting you with a right hand over your jab.' I said, 'Boy, I'm glad somebody's seeing it.'

"He could have been a great fighter. He had a lot of skills. He just couldn't motivate himself to train."

The rest of the sports world was writing LeDoux's boxing obituary, but he wasn't done.

"I've never had any idea of retiring," he said after accepting a fight against Steve Sanchez in Sioux Falls, South Dakota. "This is another fight on the road again. All it takes is a couple of good wins in the heavyweight division and you are back up there.

"The payoff in Sioux Falls won't be big. I haven't been broke in a few years, so money hasn't been a problem."

But LeDoux wasn't kidding anyone, much less himself. This was Sanchez's first professional fight. He would have only one more—and he lost them both.

LeDoux knocked out Sanchez twelve seconds into the second round. "I knew early in the first round that I could take him out," LeDoux said. "But I figured I'd give the spectators at least one round.

"The promoters make the matches. I just fight 'em. I kind of wish, in a way, it had been a better fight. On the other hand, I think I can take a quick win once in a while. I've had so many wars that I didn't get paid for.

"I remember one night in Minneapolis in 1976 against Larry Middleton. What a war we had. He lost an eye. I got a broken eardrum. We each got paid $900. For about the same money, I come down here and get an easy one. I've earned it."

LeDoux, at thirty-three years old, thought that if he could continue winning he would get another shot at the title, possibly within a year. But when he signed to fight Gerrie Coetzee in Coetzee's native South Africa, he knew he wouldn't be waiting a year. A victory in Johannesburg would make LeDoux an instant contender. A loss would all but end his career.

He seemed to be preparing for it. He bought a bar—LeDoux's Corner—in tiny Dayton, a pastoral community less than twenty-five miles northwest of Minneapolis. His son, Josh, who had suffered that epileptic seizure during Scott and Sandy's trip to the Mayo Clinic in 1980, was now six and healthier than ever. Daughter Molly was four. Sandy was about to go a period of four months without surgery—her longest stretch in a couple years. She had had the surgery on her leg, the radical mastectomy, three reconstructive surgeries, and her gall bladder removed.

"Four months ago, the doctor said, 'Well, Sandy here has a 90 percent chance to live 10 years,'" LeDoux said a few months later to Daszkiewicz. "Hell, that's all you can give anybody. Right, Joe?"

"I used to ask her if she was scared. She said she used to wonder what she would look like when she was 70, wondering if she would look like her mother. Then when she got sick, she wondered if she would see 36. Now she isn't so scared."

LeDoux was the one who was scared.

"Sandy's all he talked about," said his friend Jerry Blackledge.

LeDoux said that he once asked her doctor if they should see a marriage counselor. They had been married thirteen years. LeDoux said the doctor answered, "What the hell for? You talk about it? You love her? She loves you?"

They never saw a counselor.

Instead, he took her with him to South Africa, a two-week adventure with Bob and Jeannie Dolan. A fabulous two weeks, Sandy called it, "except for maybe twenty-five minutes."

LeDoux predicted the fight would be "a real war, because neither one of us is very pretty."

Coetzee, who grew up hero-worshipping Ali, fought 192 amateur fights, winning 180 by knockout. As a pro, he knocked out Leon Spinks in the first round of their fight, flattening the former champion three times. Coetzee lost title fights to John Tate and Mike Weaver. But eighteen months after his March 27, 1982, battle with LeDoux, Coetzee would become the first boxer from Africa to win the heavyweight title, knocking out Michael Dokes.

It wasn't Coetzee that LeDoux talked about for decades after the fight, however. It was the entire South African experience. Apartheid still reigned supreme. LeDoux, Sandy, and the Dolans arrived in Johannesburg several days before the fight to allow Scott to get better acclimated to the higher altitude.

That wasn't all they needed to get used to. There were buses for white people and buses for black people. White bathrooms and black bathrooms. Same with water fountains. "This was the height of apartheid and the things we saw just shocked me," said Dolan, the Minneapolis lawyer. "It was like seeing the things I'd read about in United States history but never experienced. It was like going back to a time that you couldn't believe could still exist anywhere."

Dolan said LeDoux met with the South African boxing commissioner Stanley Chrisodoulou, who kept telling him what a great guy Coetzee was, that he was a pillar of the community and would one day be the world champion—an odd thing to tell the guy about to fight him. "To hear him talk, we thought he was Coetzee's business manager," Dolan said.

"He's telling me all the rules, right?" LeDoux began. "I'm going, 'Cool. That's fine.' When he gets all done, he looks at me and he says, 'Gerrie Coetzee is a great fighter, be heavyweight champion someday.' I said, 'Screw you. I didn't come here to lose.' And I got up and walked out. You know, commissioners don't do that. You don't sit and tell another fighter how great your fighter is. You are a neutral body.

"The next day, it's an outdoor fight and I get in the ring first and there's a big crowd and I'm loosening up and out of the corner of my eye I see the referee in the ring. I turn to acknowledge him and guess who the referee is. The same guy. Same. We don't have a shot."

A wide-eyed LeDoux found his friend Dolan in the crowd.

"It's another case in which Scott would have to knock his opponent out just to get a draw," Dolan said. "Scott looked at me and said, 'It's over.'"

It was.

Early in the bout, whenever the fighters would clinch, the referee pushed LeDoux in the chest, to have him back up, and Coetzee would attack, Dolan said, and the video, easily found on the Internet, verifies that. But Coetzee didn't need any help from the referee. He opened a gash near

LeDoux's left eye early—one that the ref checked repeatedly in the fourth round. Coetzee simply wore LeDoux down.

LeDoux didn't see it that way—although who knows what he saw given that cut.

"I'm not worried because Papa Joe is good with the cut stuff," LeDoux recalled. "So I go to the corner after the round and Joe is standing there staring at me. I said, 'What's wrong?' He said, 'When you got cut, they came and took my bag and said it was illegal.' He had nothing. All he could do was put Vaseline on it for each round."

A flurry by Coetzee at the end of the eighth sent LeDoux to the canvas and ended the fight. LeDoux said he purposely took a knee and then stood up. The referee asked, "Are you OK?"

"Screw you," LeDoux replied.

That sealed it.

Daszkiewicz asked LeDoux why he bothered to get up. "No one's ever thrown a ten [count] over me before and it wasn't going to be him," LeDoux told his manager.

LeDoux had lost more than just a fight. For the first time in his career, he was a beaten man.

"I really think that that fight probably took the wind out of me right there," he said. "It really did. That was the beginning of the end for me. I was so disillusioned by boxing and what had happened over there and by the way I was treated. It really took it out of me.

"All the other stuff I had been able to fight up against and keep going, but that just took the wind out of my sails."

There was more.

What happened after the fight was so absurd it was comical—unless you were LeDoux. Listen to LeDoux:

"I was cut really bad, and they sent this black doctor in to stitch me up," LeDoux recalled. "He took some thread out of his kit, ran it through his fingers, and then laid it on the table. Jeannie Dolan was with me, and she was a surgical nurse. She scarfed up the needle and thread and cleaned it up and threaded the needle. The bench he put it on wasn't sanitized. Then the guy asks Papa Joe if he could borrow his glasses. He puts them on, and he says, 'Oh, that's much better.'"

Twelve stitches and a few decades later, Bob Dolan described the doctor's stitch work as the "grossest thing I've ever seen." He said the doctor applied a thick, crusted ointment over the stitches, which Jeannie Dolan then spent the next two days trying to pick off of LeDoux's wound.

Disconsolate after the fight, LeDoux was completely bewildered by the treatment he received in his dressing room. Sandy just smiled at him and said, "This is another they can't take away from us."

They spent the following week in Africa, exploring jungles and watching exotic creatures. "Within hours of the fight, he was having a ball," said Dolan. "And it was because of Sandy. She knew how to change his mood instantly."

And, in his own gruff, innocent way, LeDoux had reciprocated.

"What a great life you've given me," she told him. "I've seen the world and I've seen a lot of things that are exciting and so much fun. That's what makes a great life. Other than thirty bad minutes, it's been a great two weeks."

As disgruntled as he may have been, LeDoux kept returning to the ring. He fought Gordon Racette, the Canadian and British Commonwealth heavyweight champion, in Vancouver on September 23, 1982. If anyone could one day appreciate what LeDoux was going through, it was Racette—but thirty years later. Racette, in 2015, prepared himself to become only the third professional boxer to fight in five decades. He was sixty-three years old as he trained to fight in an effort to raise money and awareness about becoming an organ donor.

When he fought LeDoux, Racette was twenty-eight and in his prime, with a 31–2 record.

According to LeDoux, this was the fight in which Racette was going to force LeDoux into retirement. To emphasize the point, before the match the promoter gave LeDoux an oversized tennis racket, so he would have something to do when he was finished with boxing.

But more than three decades later, Racette remembered things differently. "He underestimated me and told the press he'd take up tennis if he couldn't beat me," Racette said via e-mail. "I bought him a four-foot tennis racket and told him to start practicing.

"Scott may have been near the end of his career, but fighting him a couple of years after fighting for the world title is not an end to his career. Not many would fight him. He was a tough bastard that kept on coming."

It was LeDoux who looked like the younger fighter through much of the fight. After Racette floored LeDoux in the first round, LeDoux punished his foe with an assault to the body. He knocked Racette down with a right hand in the third round and had him dazed but couldn't finish Racette off.

Nor could Racette finish off LeDoux. He had LeDoux on the ropes in the seventh round but could not put him away. Listen to Racette:

"I began my fighting career as a southpaw but would only box orthodox. I changed stance during, I believe, the first or second round and he, of course, stuttered ever so slightly wondering what happened—which I took advantage of and I gave him a right hook, which knocked him down.

"I believe it was near the end the fight [seventh or eighth round] and he caught me with a right which caused me to try and find a stable floor. Ha! I found it after what seemed like a minute, but it was a few seconds."

Racette won the fight, in a split decision.

"I'm not too surprised," LeDoux said. "It's his hometown.

"I really don't know how I couldn't put him down. Not too many guys can take that kind of punishment from me."

After the fight, Racette was taken by stretcher to the hospital. "If you saw the two of them after the fight, you would have picked Scott," Daszkiewicz said. "He was unmarked. The other guy had both eyes split and was taken to the hospital for a possible broken rib."

Racette, years later, proved to be a class act in recalling the LeDoux fight. He said it was "a great fight for me. I did defeat a world class fighter, even though his camp—and all who lose—felt they were robbed. However, my wins are only as good as the opponent I defeat, and he was one of the best."

Racette, who stayed in touch with LeDoux by phone after the fight, could not attend the postfight press conference.

LeDoux wasn't there, either—not after the promoter told him to return the tennis racket. "No way," said LeDoux. "You gave it to me. I'm not giving it back."

But LeDoux was giving back in other ways. He had become friends with several recently retired Twin Cities professional athletes—Killebrew and Frank Quilici of the Twins, Bob Lurtsema of the Vikings, among others—and they encouraged him to continue and expand his charitable work, which was becoming considerable.

He worked for the Minnesota Epilepsy League, greeting guests at a fund-raising reception. He visited schools. Anything to do with helping kids attracted him.

He even gave a recipe for "Scott LeDoux's Gourmet Cheesecake" to the *Minneapolis Star.* (The keys to the recipe were the raspberry sauce topping, dry curd cottage cheese, and a homemade graham-cracker crust.)

And he still fought. He knocked out Marlo Malino, in West Fargo, North Dakota; it was Malino's first and last fight as a professional boxer. He knocked out Steve Ward, also making his professional boxing debut. The follow-up to the Ward fight may have been more draining for LeDoux than the action in the ring. The promoter claimed he didn't have enough money to pay the fighters. Dolan, the lawyer, said he made sure LeDoux was paid fully before boarding the plane and leaving Gillette, Wyoming. He said when word leaked that LeDoux was compensated, others connected to the fight chased the promoter, hoping they, too, might get paid.

In Edmonton, LeDoux knocked out Larry Ware, who would finish his career with an unimpressive professional record of 8–13. LeDoux then won a decision over Ken Arlt, who lost seven of his final eight professional fights, including this one.

The four straight wins and commendable showing against Racette paid dividends. They were enough to earn LeDoux a shot at British champion Frank Bruno in London.

LeDoux was excited about going to London but not so much about the fight. Whether it was all the pounding, or fretting over Sandy's health, or worrying about Josh's battle with epilepsy, LeDoux found it increasingly difficult to concentrate on boxing. "When I go out, I'll go out quietly," he said a month before the Bruno fight.

The outcome of the Bruno fight was predictable. Bruno was huge, at six feet four and 224 pounds, and he could punch. Like so many other young boxers who fought LeDoux, Bruno went on to greatness. It took him less than two minutes to dispose of Coetzee in 1986. Bruno was the European champion, and he won the World Boxing Council's version of the heavyweight crown before losing to Mike Tyson, in Bruno's final fight.

But on May 3, 1983, at Wembley Stadium, thirty-four-year-old Scott LeDoux represented the biggest test of young Bruno's career. Bruno trained for a week with former heavyweight champion Floyd Patterson, who told him to throw a lot of straight left jabs.

He did. And he connected. Often.

Bruno opened a cut above LeDoux's left eye early before knocking him down at the end of the first round. The second round was worse, with the gash above the eye oozing blood. It continued, with LeDoux stumbling about, until the referee stopped the fight in the third round.

"I got frequent flyer miles in the ring," LeDoux said later. "He hit me hard and I flew through the air."

The British media asked LeDoux how he might have fared against Bruno when LeDoux was getting started as a professional fighter.

"I would have killed him when I started," LeDoux said, glaring at his questioner.

"Why do you think that?" LeDoux was asked.

"Because he was five years old when I started," LeDoux said, having lost the fight but not his sense of humor.

Minutes later, in his dressing room, he looked in the mirror and saw more than a gash over his left eye. He could see every bruise, every scar, every heartache that came with fifty professional fights. "I knew I was done," he said. "Even my wife knew it. In fact, she knew it before I did."

LeDoux's left eye was split badly, leaving a scar he would have the rest of his life. He had been knocked down, and now he knew he had been beaten down. When he entered his dressing room, there was little to be said.

"You OK?" Sandy asked.

"Yeah, I'm OK," LeDoux answered.

"It's over, isn't it," she said.

"Yep," he replied. "How did you know?"

"You're not crying," she said. "I've been with you for twenty years and I have never seen you win or lose without crying."

She was right. There were no tears.

Sandy had known her husband was finished before they left for London. "You never clean out your locker," she said. "You cleaned out your locker before you left. You brought stuff home to get washed. You never do that."

After the fight, LeDoux and Daszkiewicz went back to LeDoux's hotel room and stood at the balcony. Little was said at first. Little needed to be said. Daszkiewicz knew LeDoux as well as any of his own ten children. They had shed tears through thirty-three victories, thirteen defeats, and four draws. These men, who used their fists to speak a language only they understood, braced for the conversation that every aging athlete dreads. Daszkiewicz broke the ice.

"Scott, I don't want to see you being a piece of meat for anybody," Papa Joe told him. "It's gotta be over," Daszkiewicz told his prize fighter. "You fought for a world title. You had a heck of a career. You're gonna end up getting hurt."

Through his puffed eyes, LeDoux looked at his manager, the man he had trusted all these years on a handshake deal that never needed to be questioned. This was Papa Joe, LeDoux's second father.

He knew LeDoux heard every word. But he made sure, one final time, that his message got through. He put his hand on LeDoux's shoulder and said, very softly, "I don't want you in this game anymore."

23

GAME SEVEN

*J*ust twelve days after the Bruno fight, LeDoux was in Grantsburg, Wisconsin, completing the eleventh annual 16.2-mile Syttende Mai run. Fans along the course saw Minnesota running legends Garry Bjork-lund, who won the race, and Dick Beardsley, whose duel with Alberto Salazar in the 1982 Boston Marathon provided one of the most thrilling moments in American marathon history. They saw Alan Page, the future Pro Football Hall of Famer (and Minnesota Supreme Court justice), who had earned a reputation in the Twin Cities for bringing to distance run-ning the same dedication and passion he brought leading the Minnesota Vikings to four Super Bowls.

Seeing LeDoux, particularly so soon after his grueling bout with Bru-no, stunned many spectators along the course. "Just a way of keeping in shape," he said. "And running sixteen miles is better than getting beat up."

A year later, LeDoux sponsored his own ten-mile Great River Run, using the proceeds to set up a scholarship in the name of Paula Leu, an eighteen-year-old Anoka High School graduate who had recently died of cancer. Leu "was such a fighter and she showed so much courage" in her ten-month struggle with cancer, LeDoux said.

LeDoux, who would also complete the 1983 26.2-mile Grandma's Marathon in Duluth, just six weeks after the Bruno fight, loved to run. But he couldn't run from his past, and he couldn't outrun the future.

LeDoux had lost the one safe haven he cherished—the ring. It sounds absurd to think that a man could feel secure while getting pummeled by the likes of George Foreman, Ken Norton, or Larry Holmes, but when Le-Doux stood on that canvas, none of the demons that taunted him could crawl between the ropes. There was no threat of melanoma or breast cancer attacking Sandy there. There were no worries about Josh having an epileptic seizure when LeDoux was in the ring. There were no predators waiting to prey on him, as had been the case when he was five years old. There were no ominous warnings, like the one he received in Montreal before the Boudreaux fight, or threatening phone calls, like the ones Sandy received after the debacle in Annapolis. No grand juries. No Harold Smiths. No worries about other phobias—like his unexplainable fear of cocker spaniels.

Just LeDoux and some 220-pound brute trying to beat the hell out of him.

In that environment—one in which people settle things with their fists and, maybe, later pat each other on the back while they talk about their families and lick their wounds—LeDoux felt he was safe.

He wasn't sure he could let go.

He continued to show up in the gym and in 1984, at the age of thirty-five, even initiated discussions about a comeback. He knew he was only teasing himself. During the Bruno fight, he couldn't find the skills that made him the only Minnesota heavyweight ever to be ranked in the top ten for six consecutive years. He was hit by punches he was once able to stop. Retiring wasn't a difficult decision for him.

"I'll get a job like real people," he said.

He and Sandy talked about how when Josh was a baby, she would bring him to the gym and place him in his infant's chair. Sandy said she remembered the song that the band was playing in the hotel bar in Utica, New York, in 1976, the night before Scott fought Foreman. "'Sara Smile' was playing while we danced," she recalled, remembering the Hall and Oates classic. "We had just had a nice dinner, and everything had been special. Scott leaned over to me and said, 'No matter what happens, they can't take this away from us.'" They thought so much alike that over the years each would credit the other as having said that.

They always seemed to be there for one another. If LeDoux was the hero of the *Rocky* movies—and he had conversations about the role with Sylvester Stallone, the actor who starred in and wrote the Academy Award–winning movie—then Sandy was Rocky's love interest, Adrian.

Early in LeDoux's professional career, Daszkiewicz told him, "It's not about glory. It's not about headlines. It's about money."

But Sandy knew better.

"We cried so many times together over losing," she said. "Over things that were written, over things that were said. I am one of the few people who knows how sensitive a person Scott really is.

"A lot of people didn't realize that the ego thing with fighters is just part of the game. Scott had to get where he got by yelling and screaming sometimes, getting people to pay attention to him. He spent his own money to fly to Las Vegas once to sit in on a Larry Holmes press conference, so he could stand up and say, 'When am I gonna get my chance?'"

She recalled how Scott after beating Marty Monroe, kept $5,000 in his pocket and, during dinner after the fight, suggested that he and Sandy go to Las Vegas "right now." They did—returning twenty-four hours later so Sandy could keep her appointment at the Mayo Clinic.

"I've got no regrets," LeDoux said in 1983. "I wouldn't change a thing."

Denny Nelson, the referee in several of LeDoux's fights, left many an arena having witnessed the same thing the paying customers loved about LeDoux, the people's champion: "Anybody who fought Scott LeDoux had better be in shape to go the full ten rounds because Scott put the pressure on for ten rounds. He didn't win them all, but he was sure in their face all the time. He was a tough son of a gun."

Boxing historian Bert Sugar put it this way: "He was extremely tough, a plodding fighter. He had the linebacker physicality and fought the same way."

For Sandy, there was a new fight, a deadly battle, but she appeared to be winning. She had a simple mastectomy on her other breast, had her gall bladder removed, and had two more reconstructive surgeries.

Then her fortune changed—for the better. In 1985, doctors at the Mayo Clinic told her she had only a 1 percent cancer risk. In any other situation, a person would take those odds without thinking twice. Unless, of course, that person was Scott LeDoux. He remembered the fights against Johnny Boudreaux, Dino Dennis, Ron Lyle, Leon Spinks, Gordy Racette, and Bill Sharkey—fights in which he gave extraordinary performances and in his mind couldn't possibly lose. Yet, he didn't win any of those.

"I kept thinking back to the army days, how I was on order for Vietnam, and then got married to Sandy in December of '69," he said. "We came back and two weeks later, my orders changed. It was a God thing. He realized Sandy was gonna get cancer and I was gonna take care of her.

"I always said I had fifty pro fights, and I was scared before every one of them," he said. "But that went away when they knocked and told me, 'Five minutes to go.'

"But with Sandy and the cancer, the fear never went away, no matter how slight the odds for a recurrence."

Sandy was the strong one. She once went after Jim Murray, the legendary *Los Angeles Times* sports columnist, for calling her husband a big punching bag. "I called the *Los Angeles Times*," she said. "I told them who I was and why I was calling." Murray wasn't around. Probably a good thing for him.

Scott LeDoux never backed down from anyone. Neither did Sandy. She protected her children and her husband. And she usually did it with a smile.

"Everyone talked about Sandy," said Tim Rath, who started out as LeDoux's golfing buddy and became one his closest friends. "She was such a great mom, and she was always there for Scotty."

When the discussion centered on her husband, she was as realistic as she was proud. "Scott went further than we ever thought he would go," she said of LeDoux's boxing career. "It was fun. If we had never gone that far, it wouldn't have bothered me.

"I was married before boxing and we had a good life then. I knew we could have one after boxing just the same."

For LeDoux, that life meant spending time in Dayton, at LeDoux's Corner, tending bar while wearing a warm-up suit with gold letters that read SCOTT LEDOUX, in case anyone had any doubt. He kept a black-and-white poster of one of his greatest moments—when he hit Marty Monroe in the jaw with that big right. Hanging on a wall was that big tennis racket, the one the promoter in Vancouver wanted back after the Racette fight.

In addition to running LeDoux's Corner, where Sandy often cooked hamburgers on the grill, LeDoux worked a number of jobs in the years after boxing. He drove trucks, worked on loading docks, wrestled professionally for a brief period, and worked as a referee. He wore a sport coat and tie as a salesman for Paychex, Inc., a firm that offered a payroll service for other businesses. He was a popular speaker at business seminars, where Q&A sessions invariably turned into queries about Leon Spinks or Ken Norton or Muhammad Ali. He played a lot of golf. He ran. He made appearances for charity.

One of his favorite foils at such events was former Viking Bob Lurtsema. At banquets, Benchwarmer Bob would lie on the floor and ask, "Who's this?" And without missing a beat would say, "That's LeDoux." LeDoux would get even by telling Lurtsema, "You're so old, your highlight film is a slide."

One of the stranger jobs LeDoux held was working as a greeter at a downtown Minneapolis nightclub called Juke Box Saturday Night. The club was an attention grabber with its forty-feet-high, 150-feet-long mural of King Kong in the alley and a 1957 Chevy extending above the doorway of the club, forming a canopied entrance. There were gold-plated record albums embedded in the sidewalk outside the club. The restrooms were papered with Tootsie Pop and Cracker Jack wrappers. Mannequin legs sprouted from the ceiling above one of the club bars. LeDoux, who thought he had seen it all in Las Vegas, absolutely loved it.

The mastermind behind all this, Steve Schussler, paid LeDoux $50,000 to shake people's hands as they entered the place. "People thought I was nuts to pay a bouncer $50,000, which was a ton of money in those days," Schussler said. "But I didn't want Scott LeDoux as a bouncer. His title was Prince of Fun. People couldn't wait to get in the door and shake his hand."

For Schussler, it made perfect business sense. Schussler kept a life-size Elvis Presley robot in his home. He used to shove dirt up his nose and bang his head against lockers to get psyched up for high-school football games in Queens, New York. In an era before the advent of cellular phones, Schussler climbed to the tops of telephone poles in Miami to make free long-distance calls to find a job. He tried to change the oil of a car on fire and attempted to bodysurf in a hurricane. He kept an old Good Humor ice-cream truck outside one of his warehouses in suburban St. Louis Park, Minnesota.

In Miami, Schussler had himself packaged in a crate and sent special delivery to a Miami radio station. When the station's general manager opened the crate, out popped Schussler, wearing a Superman costume, holding a salami and a lit cigar, which he didn't even smoke. Schussler greeted the stunned general manager, telling him, "I'm your new super salesman." He was hired.

Schussler later created the Rainforest Café chain by turning his suburban Minneapolis home into a living jungle—with giant turtles and birds navigating around tropical plants—and inviting prospective investors to experience his vision.

178 // GAME SEVEN

"You can imagine some of the characters I met in boxing," LeDoux said. "But nobody comes close to Steve Schussler. Gosh, we had fun."

Sometimes, too much fun. LeDoux thought little of sharing a few rounds with the customers. He said that in those days he thought nothing of drinking two pitchers of Jack Daniel's and Diet Coke himself and then getting in the car to make the thirty-mile drive home to Andover.

He said years later that he was often intoxicated behind the wheel. Yet, the one time he was pulled over, he said he had not been drinking. He was driving Sandy's 280Z and struggling to fit behind the wheel in the little sports car when Minneapolis police pulled him over by Lowry and University Avenues. He was stopped again, minutes later, in the northern suburb of Columbia Heights. An officer told LeDoux he had been weaving back and forth, and LeDoux made a wisecrack, something to the effect that you would swerve too if your legs kept bumping against the steering wheel.

"You were out of the lane," the officer said.

"It's a little car," LeDoux replied with a smile.

The officer told LeDoux to get out of the vehicle and asked him to walk a straight line. "Touch your nose," the officer demanded.

LeDoux, still a good-looking guy after having his nose wiped across his face too many times in the ring, laughed at the officer. "With this nose, I can't miss it," he said. "How much tougher is this test gonna get?"

Having passed the sobriety test, LeDoux was told to drive safely home. Minutes later he was stopped in front of the Columbia Ice Arena in Fridley. "They put the cuffs on me," LeDoux recalled. "Then they gave me a speeding ticket and released me. It was 2:30 in the morning and I had just closed the bar up. It was pretty funny.

"I wasn't worried. Now, if it had been a Friday or Saturday night, I would have had reason to worry. I was drinking a lot on weekends then, but I didn't worry about my drinking at the time."

He dodged a bullet that time. He never was arrested for drunk driving, but he later said he could have been. If it wasn't Juke Box Saturday Night, it could have been LeDoux's Corner. Or, years later, former Minnesota Viking tight end Joe Senser's bar in Bloomington. Or one of the watering holes in Anoka County.

Sandy tried to watch over him. She had stood up for him before the media, watched him pass blood, stood by him following the Frank Bruno fight, when LeDoux's eyes were so puffy that he said, "I couldn't even cry after that one."

Sandy was the tough one, all right. She talked about how her perception of life with melanoma changed over the years. "I looked at my leg and thought I was maimed for life," she said. "That was my big concern, what my leg was going to look like. What they didn't say—or we didn't understand—is that melanoma doesn't go away. It can go dormant, but it doesn't go away."

In October 1987, the Twin Cities and Minnesota Twins fans everywhere were abuzz as the state's major-league baseball team was on the verge of winning Minnesota's first major professional sports championship since the Minneapolis Lakers in 1954, six years before the team left Minnesota for Los Angeles. LeDoux got tickets to game seven, against the St. Louis Cardinals, from Twins star and future Hall of Famer Kirby Puckett.

LeDoux met Puckett at a charitable event. LeDoux was later doing work for Make-A-Wish Foundation and learned of an eight-year-old with a terminal illness at Abbott Northwestern Hospital in Minneapolis. The child told LeDoux he wanted to meet Puckett. "I can get that done," LeDoux told the boy. "You gotta get it done now," the boy's mother whispered to LeDoux.

Puckett told LeDoux he could do it in a week. No, LeDoux told him. It has to be done now. Puckett met LeDoux at the hospital the next morning, armed with a Twins uniform, pictures, and an infectious smile. The star center fielder and adoring child talked for nearly ninety minutes, with LeDoux quietly listening. Both men hugged the little boy and left the room.

The boy died two days later. LeDoux called Puckett with the news. Puckett, who told his teammates to hop on his back, that he would carry them to a championship, broke into tears, LeDoux said.

LeDoux considered Puckett "a good friend." A collector who cherished pictures taken with show business types like Robert Goulet, David Brenner, and Sylvester Stallone, LeDoux asked Puckett to autograph each of the World Series tickets he had gotten. When passing through the Metrodome gates, LeDoux showed guards the tickets and made sure they weren't torn. He was saving them, just as he saved boxing gloves from each of his fights—and sometimes had them autographed by his opponents. The World Series—as anyone who lived in Minnesota in 1987 remembers—was a feel-good party unlike any other.

On the night of the seventh game, LeDoux and Sandy had dinner with friends at Runyon's, an eatery in Minneapolis's warehouse district. "I felt terrible," Sandy said. "I suggested to Scott that I drive home, get Josh and let him go to the game. Scott said, no, I wanted to be at that game."

She felt terrible but said nothing.

Until the seventh inning.

The Twins, who had trailed early, were now leading, 3–2, and would score an insurance run to clinch the championship in what may have been the loudest game ever played in any sport.

But where LeDoux was sitting, in the second deck behind home plate, his world suddenly grew silent when his wife uttered these four words: "I have a tumor."

"What?!!"

"I have a tumor. And it's right here. I feel it. It's about this big," she said, showing enough space between her hands to fit her husband's meaty fist.

Seventh inning, seventh game, LeDoux thought. Didn't Larry Holmes thumb him in the eye in the seventh round of a fight held on the seventh day of the seventh month?

"Some of the best moments in our life, Scott's big fights, were occurring at the same time as some of our lowest, my surgeries," she said months later.

LeDoux saw things differently. "Boxing can turn you into a bum," he said. "Sandy was always with me for the fights. She never let the temptations get to me. I remember an interview in a New York newspaper when Sandy said, 'No matter how many limo rides he gets, when Scott comes home, he still has to take out the garbage.'"

The newest melanoma tumor was removed. A hysterectomy followed. Then a colostomy. Sandy and Scott were warned that a new tumor could follow.

It did.

In the fall of 1988, Sandy went to the National Cancer Institute in Washington, D.C., where she was accepted as the twenty-seventh patient to receive experimental treatment for this form of melanoma. "I'm determined to be positive about this," she said. "It's not like I'm going to

Mexico to be injected with ground-up apricot pits. I'm going to be treated by the most innovative cancer researchers in the world. They have had some success. They have melanoma patients who are still in remission two years later."

Friends like Diane and Chico Resch called every night. Scott's sister, Judy Wynn, told Scott and Sandy that she and her husband, Wayne, would watch Josh and Molly. Doc and Mickey said the kids could stay with them.

"We thought that if anyone could handle this, it was Sandy," said friend Jerry Blackledge. "We weren't so sure about Scotty."

In LeDoux's corner, there was always someone to wipe away the tears. Scott had worked for a company that was self-insured but went out of business. An $8,000 insurance check to University Hospitals bounced. Just before Thanksgiving, Schussler helped to arrange a benefit for Sandy and Scott at Juke Box Saturday Night.

"I didn't want to do this," LeDoux said. "I didn't want to be looked at as paupers, because we're not. We would get those bills paid, if not this year, next year. But I've had friends tell me, 'Sandy has many people who love her, and they want the chance to show that.'

"You know what Willie Pep said," LeDoux went on, quoting the man many fight fans consider the greatest featherweight boxer of all time: "'First the legs go, then the reflexes, then the friends.'

"We're lucky," LeDoux said. "The friends are still with us. Great friends.

"The cancer institute is our only hope. But it is exactly that—hope."

Chuck Daszkiewicz had known Sandy as long as he had known Scott. He was the one who would help her sneak into the ring after fights so she could grab her husband's boxing gloves before officials could confiscate them. Whenever he was depressed, Scott could pick himself up by watching a video of the final round of his fight with Ken Norton. When Daszkiewicz watched the end of that fight, one of the first things he would point out was Sandy making it out of the ring with the gloves.

"We had a deal," Chuck recalled. "When a fight was over, a representative from the boxing commission would confiscate your gloves right away, to make sure you didn't doctor them up.

"Scott wanted to save every pair of gloves he used to fight a champion and then he had guys autograph them—Muhammad Ali, George Foreman, Ken Norton, whoever. So, as soon as a fight got over, I'd run into the ring with a scissors and snip 'em. Sandy would be standing in a neutral corner with this big basket that looked like a purse. I'd dump 'em, she'd leave right away, and when they asked where the gloves went, I'd say they were just cut and someone took 'em.

"Sandy made a game of it. And she was good at it."

Sandy tried to find the joy in everything, even when it meant spitting in the face of the disease that was destroying her life. Most days she was "up," her husband recalled. But her wide smile and sparkling eyes were not powerful enough to postpone the inevitable.

Together, Scott and Sandy had built LeDoux's Corner into a popular neighborhood-like tavern. But it was Scott's decision alone to close the bar.

"Why?" she asked him. "We're not losing money."

"I need to spend more time with you," he told her.

He had never missed a payment, had paid every one of his bills. The day he approached the woman from whom he bought the bar and handed her the keys was as difficult as facing the crowd at the King of Clubs in northeast Minneapolis hours after the Holmes fight.

"I'm done," he told her.

"But you're not behind on payments," she said, somewhat surprised.

"I'm done," LeDoux repeated.

How many times did he beg a referee to let a fight continue after he had been cut? Not this time. He paid off his liquor bills and walked away.

This wasn't a mere business transaction. They cherished the place. One evening, LeDoux arrived at the bar to close it, after having completed a shift at Juke Box Saturday Night. Sandy was there. "Honey, I gotta strip-search you," he teased, "because everybody steals from the bar."

Sadly, more than just the bar caused him financial angst. He had no insurance. He had spent money freely—and foolishly, some friends said—on property, toys, and the good life that came with being a celebrity. Now the money was gone—gone faster than the 280Z or those beloved motorcycles could ever move.

People who didn't know him well suggested he file for bankruptcy, but that wasn't part of his makeup. Doc never asked for anything while he looked for work when there was none in the mines near Crosby. And his son couldn't either. He just couldn't.

He could sell the house to pay off a portion of the medical bills. Bob Dolan negotiated with the hospitals and came up with a payment plan that would satisfy all. LeDoux found a $400-a-month apartment he could move into with the kids.

"Why is Mama sick?" they asked him.

He never knew how to answer. He knew Josh was angry—and remained angry for years because, he said, an accountant took advantage of his father, embezzled money, and left LeDoux with a financial mess that cost the family their home. "My dad is the *Rocky* movies," Josh said. "But this isn't the ending you hope to see at the movies."

Molly was confused, and, like her brother, she was devastated. Mature beyond her years, she realized that this wasn't just her mother she was watching deteriorate. This was her dad's partner. "He married the love of his life, and she was dying," Molly said. "How heartbreaking is that?"

The kids needed answers. But when Josh and Molly asked their father a simple question, they were really asking a big kid to give them the most difficult answer one could imagine. Because for all his brute strength, determination, and heart, that's what Scott LeDoux was—a big kid. He called his wife "Mama," just like their kids did.

"There's nothing I can do," LeDoux told Josh and Molly. "We can't get her fixed. We can't take care of her. Eventually, she's gonna die." Sandy made her husband promise that he would take the kids to grief counseling at Mercy Hospital in Coon Rapids when she was gone.

Sandy wanted to make the most of the precious little time she had left. Scott and Josh spent weekends the summer of 1989 fishing at muskie tournaments while Molly and Sandy spent time together "being girls," LeDoux said. Josh christened their boat *Seymour Butt*—and that brought a smile to his dad's face.

That fall, between visits to Washington, D.C., for treatments, Sandy began seeing friends, finding time to say good-bye to each of them individually, Jerry Blackledge remembered. He recalled facing her with tears, and she offered a smile in return.

For LeDoux, one of the potentially toughest moments was to come. After he had cleaned out the house, he told Josh and Molly to walk into every room and savor the memories. The kids were still in grade school, and he was trying to present them a remembrance they could cling to for the rest of their lives.

A few years before, Sandy told her husband, "I'm worried about my kids. I don't want them to grow up and not have a mother."

Mickey, who spent a lot of time with her grandchildren, told the kids that their mother would likely not be home for Christmas, but that their parents would be sending a gift from Washington. Josh and Molly were taken to the house. As they walked through, they heard a familiar voice from their parents' bedroom.

"I'm in here," Sandy yelled.

The kids, who assumed their mother was in Washington, ran down the hall screaming. They raced into the bedroom and collapsed into their mother's arms.

It was Sandy's final gift to her family. It was more than the perfect surprise. It was the perfect good-bye, done in the precious way that only she could.

Sandy died on November 13, 1989, a Monday afternoon, at Hennepin County Medical Center in Minneapolis. She was forty-two. She and Scott had been married a month shy of twenty years. More than half of those were spent battling cancer.

Once again, LeDoux faced the media—this time, after the greatest loss of his life.

"If I had the courage and heart that she's shown, I would've had that heavyweight championship belt," he said.

24

DOWN FOR THE COUNT

*E*ven before Sandy died, Papa Joe worried about LeDoux.
"Scott, you could get a salesman's job and have some money coming in," Daszkiewicz told him more than once. When LeDoux was out of sight, Daszkiewicz would tell his son, Chuck, "The guy spends money like there's no tomorrow."

Papa Joe was amazed when LeDoux bought a condominium in Key West, Florida, not long after hitting a few big boxing paydays. LeDoux had $300,000 in the bank, when interest rates were high. When Sandy was working as a dental hygienist, Scott told her to quit her job, that she didn't have to work "for that kind of money" anymore, Chuck Daszkiewicz recalled.

"Where did it all go?" Papa Joe asked Chuck.

Even beyond LeDoux's inner circle, it became common knowledge that he was broke.

Enter the most unlikely of heroes: Mike Tyson.

Tyson was more than unbeaten when he became, in 1986, at age twenty, the youngest world heavyweight champion ever. Long before the facial tattoo and his appearance in the comedy *The Hangover*, he was among the most feared heavyweights of all time. His personal problems have been well chronicled, and he became a boorish joke when in 1997 he was disqualified for biting the ear of champion Evander Holyfield. His shocking loss to 42–1 underdog James "Buster" Douglas in Tokyo in 1990—his first loss as a professional, the one that cost him the title—is arguably the greatest upset in sports history.

Before all that, though, Tyson was a one-man wrecking crew. He knocked out Trevor Berbick in the second round in November 1986 for the World Boxing Council title and scored a technical knockout of Larry Holmes in the fourth in January 1988, and a TKO of Frank Bruno in the fifth in February 1989. His ninety-one-second annihilation of ex-champ Michael Spinks in June 1988 is simply painful to watch. In July 1989, in the fight before he met Douglas, Tyson dismantled Carl "The Truth" Williams in ninety-three seconds.

Tyson was only twenty-three when he lost the title to Douglas. On that day, the Baddest Man on the Planet was just plain bad. After losing his crown, new trainer Richie Giachetti lined up a bunch of new sparring partners for the ex-champ. Tyson wanted someone who would force him to work on his defensive tactics.

He also wanted to reach out to a fellow fighter in need. He had heard about LeDoux losing his wife and struggling financially.

LeDoux was forty-two years old and working in sales for Pilot Air Freight. He had run in Grandma's Marathon along the Lake Superior shore (with his close friend Minneapolis attorney Bob Dolan) three weeks after the Bruno fight. In 1991, he and Dolan teamed in the 520-mile Border to Border Triathlon—biking more than 400 miles from the southwest Minnesota community of Luverne to Eveleth on the Iron Range in two days, then running 52 miles to Cook, Minnesota, and, finally, canoeing to Crane Lake.

But being in extraordinary physical condition is not the same as being in boxing shape.

LeDoux said he received a call from Kansas City matchmaker Peyton Sher, who told him, "Tyson doesn't know how to train and you do. He needs to see how you train.

"I don't care how old you are. All I know is you did a 520-mile triathlon. We need Mike to get in shape. Set an example at training camp."

Training camp was in Las Vegas. LeDoux was game. And broke. He kept asking himself, "What does Mike Tyson need me for?" It was LeDoux who needed Tyson. Iron Mike promised to pay LeDoux $1,000 a week for about two months. But LeDoux said Tyson actually paid him more than $3,000 a week and kept him on the payroll for ten weeks, far longer than necessary—and LeDoux knew it.

"I think it's a great opportunity to work with champions from four different decades," LeDoux said before acknowledging that money had a little—well, no, everything—to do with it.

"I think all of us have that itch," he said. "All of us want to see what we can do, what we have left. Other old guys want to come back and work out with KO Pectate and Dusty Trunks. I figure I'll start with the guys on top and work my way down."

At first, LeDoux wasn't sure why he was in Las Vegas. Tyson didn't show up the first two weeks. So LeDoux said he spent a lot of time at a YMCA, lifting weights, doing stomach-strengthening exercises, and running—often after midnight. LeDoux also spent time sparring with the other sparring partners—none of whom he knew and several of whom he was sure had prison backgrounds. LeDoux said he was the oldest sparring partner, "I think by a couple decades."

"He's gonna knock you out," one of them told LeDoux. "He's knocked all of us out."

Tyson finally made an appearance at the YMCA the third week of LeDoux's stay. (In some reports, LeDoux said they trained at a place called Johnny Taco's Gym.) LeDoux said he placed a forty-five-pound weight on his chest and used the Roman chair, exercise equipment that targets the abdominal muscles and lower back. Tyson did the same. LeDoux lifted weights, and Tyson followed suit. LeDoux changed shoes and ran a few miles. Tyson walked the other way.

What LeDoux remembered most about working with Tyson was also what he would have preferred forgetting—sparring with Iron Mike. LeDoux was determined to be the aggressor. That didn't last long. The first time Tyson hit LeDoux, he thought he was back in Utica, New York, with George Foreman. The second time they sparred, Tyson cut LeDoux, a serious gash.

LeDoux was stunned. How could anybody—even Mike Tyson—hit that hard?

"The fellows who have worked out with Tyson tell me that if you sting him at all, he is going to keep you in there until he gets the best of it," LeDoux said. "After we traded those jabs for a round, Giachetti told me, 'Out.' Then Tyson looked at him and Giachetti said, 'One more round.'

"I took that as a compliment."

The second Tyson opened the gash, he told LeDoux, "You're cut." "That's the only thing I've heard him say," LeDoux said. "He doesn't talk. He doesn't smile. There is no humor to Mike Tyson's workouts."

The next day—a day off for LeDoux—he took a closer look at Tyson's gloves when Tyson wasn't around. Both sides of the gloves had been cut open, the stuffing removed. No wonder the other sparring partners were fighting defensively, LeDoux thought. From that point on, so did LeDoux. He feinted and moved around as much as his forty-two-year-old legs would allow.

Giachetti, the trainer, removed the stuffing from Tyson's gloves, LeDoux said. "Mike was a man's man," said LeDoux. "He wouldn't have done a thing like that. He didn't need to anyway."

He didn't need to keep LeDoux on the payroll as long as he did, either. LeDoux didn't spar with Tyson at all in those final weeks. "I'll tell you this about Mike Tyson. He's got more heart than people give him credit for," LeDoux said.

The feeling, apparently, was mutual. During a 2014 visit to the Twin Cities to promote a fight card at Target Center, Tyson confided that LeDoux stunned him with a right hand to the head. Tyson said he had so much respect for LeDoux and what he went through with Sandy that he felt compelled to keep him on the payroll after they were done sparring.

"Say what you want about Tyson, but he could not have been nicer," LeDoux recalled. "He's a smart guy. He's just a victim of his upbringing."

"And, yes, I still have both ears."

Some of his closest friends wondered what, if anything, was between those ears.

Just before Sandy died, LeDoux ballooned to 275 pounds, many of those pounds acquired at the local taverns.

Among those who worried about him were Joe and Chuck Daszkiewicz. As Chuck said, "My dad used to tell me, 'It ain't the punches that make you goofy. It's the booze.'"

Training for the Border to Border Triathlon had gotten LeDoux back down to his fighting weight. He had help. He met Lehne Nelson, a nutritionist and former manager of a weight-loss clinic, in September, two months before Sandy died. LeDoux said she was his counselor at Jenny Craig, and he only went there after Sandy voiced concern over his recent weight gain. "I wanted to see if they could use me for an ad," LeDoux said.

He said he and Nelson began dating after Sandy died and within months announced to friends that they would be married on July 7.

"July 7? Don't you know what that date is?" Chuck Daszkiewicz asked him.

The idea of LeDoux getting married just months after Sandy's death was shocking enough. But July 7? That was the date of the 1980 Holmes fight. Daszkiewicz knew that LeDoux was every bit as date conscious and superstitious as he was.

LeDoux knew what people might think. "I'll look in the mirror sometimes and I'll say to myself, 'I took care of Sandy the best I could,'" he said a month before the marriage.

"And I'll think, 'I hope people don't think badly of me for marrying again [eight months after Sandy's death].' Well, if they think bad of me, OK, but not of Lehne. She's got a lot of fine qualities, and Molly [then eleven] really needs a woman's influence."

LeDoux was right. His friends didn't think badly of him for marrying Nelson. They were too stunned to form a logical opinion. Yet one opinion seemed to prevail among his friends. "We knew it was gonna be a disaster," said Diane Resch. "Sandy died in November. I think Scott called to tell me he was getting married in January. This is a man who just lost his wife. Maybe I'm being unfair to her, but Scott's my friend. Who goes after somebody whose wife has been gone for only two or three months?"

Molly may have been the most vulnerable of everyone involved. Years later, as an adult with children of her own, Molly Lappin's memories of Nelson were warm but also confusing. Ultimately, they turned to heartache.

"Lehne was very nice to me, very affectionate, took me to do fun things," Molly said. "I've never dealt with my mom dying and I needed a mother figure in my life. I asked Lehne, 'The day you get married, can I call you Mom?'

"Looking back, the whole thing wasn't healthy. They'd have arguments. Lehne would leave and then come back. When she moved in, all my mom's things got taken out."

LeDoux's marriage to Nelson was the rare—possibly only—chapter of his life that he talked about with reluctance, if at all. He didn't acknowledge the marriage to those unaware of it. When LeDoux's sister, Judy Wynn, went through family photos, she found a beautiful picture of LeDoux and Nelson, in her wedding dress, with Josh and Molly—and almost immediately moved on to other photos.

(It apparently was not a pleasant subject for Nelson either. Attempts to reach her for this book were not acknowledged or returned.

Chuck Daszkiewicz said he ran into her in 2014, but she avoided making conversation.)

Tim Rath, LeDoux's friend, said he met Nelson a few times and called her relationship with LeDoux "a mismatch from the start." Rath said the marriage appeared "awkward," particularly when LeDoux tried to incorporate Nelson into a world of people she didn't know. Rath said one fishing trip involving Dave Casper, the Pro Football Hall of Fame tight end who starred for the Oakland Raiders, was particularly clumsy. "Scotty was pretty vulnerable," Rath said. "Scotty was expecting Sandy and that was not going to happen—and it wasn't fair to Lehne."

Years later, Molly wondered if Nelson thought there would be more to the marriage. Molly surely had to wonder what was happening. She said Nelson would take her shopping, would slip handwritten notes into Molly's bagged lunch. Molly bought Nelson a birthday present, but, she said, Nelson went to a bar and wouldn't come home that night.

One night, she wasn't there at all—and would not return. "I need you to come home," LeDoux recalled Molly telling him over the phone. "Lehne's gone." LeDoux came home to an empty house. LeDoux said he went out one day, and when he returned home, several vehicles had been to the house. The furniture was gone. The house was virtually empty. LeDoux said he cried and asked, "Where did she go? Why didn't she talk to me?"

A different version, however, was presented on Nelson's behalf to the Anoka County court. In February 1991, just seven months after their wedding, a restraining order was filed, ordering LeDoux to stay away from Nelson.

The marriage lasted maybe six or seven months. LeDoux said the marriage was annulled and declined to say much more.

"Scotty's the kind of guy who needs to be with someone," Chuck Daszkiewicz said.

LeDoux began drinking even more.

"Our life growing up was not normal," Molly said years later. "I think my dad did the best he knew how to do. But he often told me, 'You didn't come with instructions, Molly.'

"I never saw my dad with a drinking problem," she said. "My dad would go to Joe Senser's with friends. Once or twice, Josh and I said, 'If you've had too much to drink, don't drive home.'"

Still, her father's drinking had gotten her attention—and she had yet to enter her teenage years. She said her father "didn't drink all day," and she never saw any questionable behavior at any of the huge parties he held. She said their home "was a fun place for us to be."

LeDoux no longer felt like the life of the party, though. He was reaching a breaking point, and he knew it. It wasn't just losing Sandy, or losing Nelson, or losing to Larry Holmes, or simply losing his way. More and more he began dwelling on that day in Crosby, when he was molested at age five.

More than feeling violated, he felt shame, but couldn't understand why. "I was five years old, I did nothing wrong, I didn't understand what was going on," he said years later. "So why was I the one who carried this guilt?" He wanted to confront his feelings and didn't know where to turn, other than the bottle.

In 1992, after years of repeating a scenario that played unrelentingly through his head, he decided to tell his parents about what happened thirty-seven years before. Mickey expressed surprise and a mother's understanding. Doc cried for three days—and when LeDoux learned of his father's reaction, the emotional wound cut even deeper.

LeDoux did more than cry. He wanted to find the man who had shamed him. The man he knew as "Roy" came from a large Crosby family. LeDoux had gone to school with his younger sister. LeDoux said he knew he could find him.

He became obsessed. Whenever the man moved, and he seemed to move often, LeDoux found him. Years before revealing the incident to his parents, LeDoux began calling his tormentor. The first time he called the man, LeDoux hung up the second the guy said, "Hello." The next time, LeDoux responded to the man's greeting by nervously saying his name. Then LeDoux hung up again.

For several years, LeDoux tracked down the man, called, and threatened him. He never followed through. But he decided that scaring the bejeezus out of the guy was not enough. He needed to do more. He was determined. He was just waiting for somebody to knock on a door and tell him, "Five minutes to go."

He planned to call once more—and only once more—and settle things for keeps. He wasn't sure he could go through with this. What if both parties stayed on the phone? Then what?

His sudden obsession with the man who had violated him nearly four decades before was no longer LeDoux's biggest headache, and LeDoux knew it. Scott LeDoux was Scott LeDoux's biggest problem. Plain and simple.

The one-two punch of losing Sandy and then Nelson left him sullen and ornery. Sure, he lacked health insurance for his family, but that was only part of the reason the money ran out. He had blown every cent he had—and couldn't find a way to explain his financial woes to his kids.

One night, while watching TV, LeDoux stared at an infomercial about people with drinking problems. He felt as if the TV was a mirror. He reached out for help. He stopped drinking, embraced a program, and got sober in 1993. (It wasn't just the drinking. Years later, LeDoux learned that he was clinically depressed, and took the necessary medication to combat that disease.)

For the first time in years—maybe for the first time since Sandy's melanoma was initially detected—LeDoux felt that he had regained control of his life. But he still needed to cleanse himself of the demons that had haunted him since childhood.

He would track down Roy, the social deviant who said he would hurt the five-year-old LeDoux if he ever told a soul, the predator whose vile deed had triggered the childhood bullying, the disgusting excuse for a human being who lurked from every corner in LeDoux's imagination and refused to go away. The last time he tracked down Roy, the tormentor who was sixteen or seventeen years his senior, the man was living in Two Harbors, Minnesota, just north of Duluth, along the Lake Superior shore. Now, LeDoux was forty-three, and Roy was nearing sixty.

It was time.

LeDoux, trying to contain his anger and nerves, picked up the phone and dialed.

"Roy?" LeDoux said in his deep, gruff, unforgettable voice.

There was silence. LeDoux would have none of it.

"Roy?" LeDoux repeated.

This time, the man spoke. He asked one question:

"Are you coming to kill me?"

25

CRUCIAL CONFRONTATION

*L*eDoux knew exactly how he would answer. He had anticipated this moment for years. He hadn't talked to anybody about a possible confrontation. Certainly he didn't talk to Brian O'Melia, a boxer from New Jersey whom LeDoux dominated when they fought in St. Paul in 1975.

When O'Melia, a New Jersey Boxing Hall of Fame inductee, was fourteen years old and growing up in Jersey City, New Jersey, he went to a local garage looking for work and was "violated" by the owner. The man told O'Melia that he would hurt his family if he ever told his parents. O'Melia said he turned to boxing as a way to restore his dignity and channel his anger and negative attitude. Years later, while vacationing at the Jersey shore, O'Melia spotted the offender. The man didn't recognize O'Melia, but O'Melia didn't confront him to exchange pleasantries. O'Melia walked up to the man and called him by his name. Then, he said, "I whacked him."

When the police arrived, O'Melia explained why he hit the man. They let O'Melia go. Years later, the man was convicted in a high-profile sexual assault case involving New Jersey youngsters, O'Melia said.

O'Melia taught school in Jersey City for forty years before retiring to the Jersey shore. He said he had lost touch with LeDoux over the years and was saddened to learn that LeDoux also had been a victim of molestation as a child. "It's not something you talk about, although I'm glad I did," he said. "The burden was lifted off my shoulders when they put this guy in prison—although I gotta admit, I got a lot of frustration out of the way when I whacked him. I had a lot of respect for Scott LeDoux after I fought him in St. Paul. I thought he handled himself well. But when something like this [sexual assault] happens to you and you have a chance to confront the guy, no matter how long it's been, it's hard not to let your emotions get the best of you."

LeDoux was not about to whack anybody, certainly not over the phone. No, he had a plan far more powerful.

"Are you coming to kill me?" the man asked.

"No," LeDoux said. "I'm calling to forgive you."

The man was speechless. LeDoux told him that they needed to talk.

Their conversation was not a one-sided affair, not a lecture, scolding, or series of threats by LeDoux. The man told LeDoux that he had molested other children, over a period of years. He said that he had been sexually abused himself as a child, by a state legislator.

"Now the chain is broken," LeDoux told him. "I will never do anything like what you did to me, not to a child, not to anybody.

"And God help you if you ever do."

It was over. Nearly four decades of guilt, shame, and torture had seemingly come to a screeching halt—and all because of a phone conversation that took minutes. LeDoux said he felt cleansed, maybe for the first time in his adult life. It still wasn't something he talked about often or freely. He had confided in Diane Resch in high school. His sister, Judy Wynn, knew. His daughter, Molly, knew. But his son, Josh, didn't know until he learned about the incident while interviews were conducted for this book.

A change had come over LeDoux. No more drinking. No more anguish about something that happened decades before.

He began reading the Bible. LeDoux never had been religious. As a teenager, he walked three miles to church but rarely had a clue as to what was being said. In the army, when he got orders for Vietnam, he read the Bible. When the orders were changed, the Bible collected dust. He believed that Sandy's belief in God helped her through her toughest times with cancer, but that wasn't enough to get him to take Christianity seriously.

The chaos in his life after she died opened his eyes. He was asked to be a master of ceremony at a banquet and accepted without knowing what the event was for. It was for a ministry. Three young girls spoke passionately of their dedication to Christianity. LeDoux was amazed—and immediately began questioning his own direction. He said he dedicated his life to Jesus Christ that day.

At the same time, another new presence was beginning to dominate his life. Darlene Bragg was a head turner, a popular figure (in every sense) who had dated members of the Minnesota Vikings and Minnesota Twins. Known to everyone as Dolly, she attracted attention long before adulthood.

"Dolly Bragg was a pretty girl, a very kind girl, a knockout," said Frank Perpich, the Crosby, Minnesota, native who taught at White Bear Lake High School, where Dolly was a student. "She looked like a Hollywood star." LeDoux said she looked like Raquel Welch.

"She was stunning, polite, and humble," Perpich said. "I was really shocked when Scott married her." So was Chuck Daszkiewicz. When LeDoux told him he planned to marry her, Daszkiewicz responded, "Do you know her reputation?"

LeDoux told him, "Chuck, she's been around the block. I've been around the block. I think I can make it work."

But there was a history that few people knew. While in college in Moorhead, Minnesota, Dolly was raped by two men, LeDoux said. She started drinking heavily, but LeDoux said she had been a year sober when they began dating.

"As a godly man, I couldn't sleep with her," LeDoux said. "A pastor friend said, 'You gotta marry her.'"

They were married in 1993. LeDoux, who had gotten sober on April 1 of that year, said Dolly got roaring drunk on their wedding night.

The marriage was doomed from the honeymoon. Josh could not stand her. Molly called her "an awful alcoholic." Both kids moved out of the house. "She wasn't a wonderful person," Molly said. "She was drunk most of the time they were married. I've never seen anything like it."

LeDoux had either forgotten or wasn't familiar with the Al-Anon principles that remind friends and relatives of alcoholics that you didn't cause someone's alcoholism or addiction, you can't cure it, and you can't control it. Only that person can. But just as he tried to control his fate in the ring, LeDoux tried to end Dolly's dependency on alcohol by throwing her into treatment. Again and again. Minnesota is home to a great many treatment centers, and LeDoux was determined to try every last one of them to save his marriage. Years later, LeDoux did a little stammering when he tried to name every treatment facility Dolly visited. He said she entered into treatment at least a half-dozen times, maybe as many as nine. Nothing clicked.

"You could see it eating away at his insides," said Julie Galle, who worked at Joe Senser's sports bar and knew LeDoux and Dolly. "She was desperate. At one point, when she couldn't find any alcohol, she drank a bottle of mouthwash. It was so sad."

After the couple separated, LeDoux said he told Dolly's parents to "give her tough love or she'll die." Their divorce was finalized in 1996, after two years of marriage.

She died a year later, of complications due to alcohol abuse, he said.

"My dad tried; my dad was a gentleman," Molly said. "But he went through so much. We all did. I don't think my dad started life thinking, 'I'm gonna be a single father at forty.' I don't think he ever expected anything like this."

26

SOMETHING TO PROVE

*C*arol LeDoux met her future husband on an airplane. It was February 1996, and the Kansas native had recently moved to Minneapolis. She had been in Arizona, where she had another home—"to thaw out"—and was about to board a plane back to Minnesota. She had purchased her ticket long before, and when she got to the airport, she saw she had yet to get her seat assignment. It was a holiday weekend, and the plane was virtually full. So she begged. The five-feet-four, 125-pound woman got the last seat on the plane: the middle seat between two gents who may have been the biggest guys on the aircraft. Adding to her discomfort, it was nearly ninety-five degrees on the plane, she said.

One of the men sitting next to her was Scott LeDoux, who was returning to the Twin Cities after having participated in a charity baseball and golf tournament in Phoenix. She asked him if he was an athlete. He told her he was a professional boxer, which she remembered thinking was "kind of odd." "Ever fight anybody I've heard of?" she asked. After he responded, she told him, "Oh, that's nice."

The plane landed. Scott carried Carol's belongings to her car, and she remembered thinking how "sweet" he was.

She didn't hear from him again for five weeks, when he called the optical company where she worked.

"This is a voice from your past," he told her.

"What took you so long?" she responded.

They went out to dinner and had a nice time, but she wasn't necessarily looking for a relationship. She was a small-town girl from Cottonwood, Kansas, population 958, in the heart of ranching country, where everyone knew her mother's phone number, meaning she couldn't get into trouble even had she wanted. Her family background was very different from Scott's. Her parents, products of the Great Depression, not only graduated high school but both went to college—her father at the University of Chicago, her mother at Northwestern. Their marriage didn't last.

Carol went to Wichita State. She was twice divorced and said that at the time she met Scott, she didn't want to date anybody.

But he was different. For starters, he was sober, and that meant a lot to her. They had both experienced the pain of living with alcoholics, and both were working with programs to stay sober.

She was attracted to his passion for helping others. Not just his charitable work, which was considerable and growing. She listened to him rant about children who become victims of violent crimes or drug and alcohol abuse. She heard him protest about courts that let criminals off easy. Boxing was still his love, but his passion for civil justice and helping the less fortunate resonated far more than his fame with Carol.

A few months after they began dating, he asked her if she would accompany him to another charity tournament to which he had been invited. No, she told him, we're not married.

They soon would be. He proposed, getting down on one knee in the frozen-food section of the Byerlys supermarket in suburban Minnetonka.

"What are you doing?" she blurted out. "Get up!"

"She said no," LeDoux recalled, "but told me to keep asking."

They were married in August, at a home owned by Chico and Diane Resch, on Little Trout Lake in northern Minnesota.

"Scott was a very complicated human being," Carol said. "A man who was in such a brutal sport was the kindest, most generous man I've ever met. He wanted the best for others."

Instead of attempting to remove him from his past, she tried to embrace it—Sandy in particular. Carol had never met Sandy, yet admired her courage, wit, and dedication to her children. "In the face of adversity, she found a way to laugh," Carol said. "I feel privileged to have made friends with her friends."

But she knew she wasn't Sandy—and never tried to be. What these two women shared was their faith in LeDoux. Sandy didn't want her husband to be a professional boxer, but once he made that decision, she supported him because she believed in him.

Carol also saw a ton of potential in her new husband. LeDoux had drifted from job to job—from Pilot Air Freight to a sales job with Jones Trucking to another sales job, this time with Brookdale Chrysler. He took a job with Viking Sprinkler, hauling pipe, and then got into sales there for a few years.

In 1999, LeDoux was in Montana, doing charitable work that involved filming a commercial. His stand-up work was seen, by chance, by someone from ESPN. Two months later, the sports network called, had him flown to Connecticut for an interview, and he was hired in 2000 to do color commentary for boxing matches.

For five years, he worked two fights a week for ESPN2 and loved the boxing part of the job. The travel was another story. He would fly out on Sunday night or Monday morning for a Tuesday match. Sometimes he would come home Wednesday and then fly out again Thursday for a Friday bout. Not all of these fights were in familiar cities. This was before the advent of GPS, and sometimes finding a hotel was more challenging than preparing notes for the fight.

The job allowed a new audience of fight fans to meet LeDoux. It was more than his charm and wit that made him a character. In 2000, at the age of fifty-one, he visited the training camp of Lennox Lewis and sparred with the heavyweight champion, who was preparing to defend his title against David Tua.

"His arms were so long," LeDoux said of the six-feet-five Lewis, "that he didn't even have to leave his corner to hit me."

When he wasn't commenting on fights, he was working with fighters. Among those he trained was Crosby-born, thirty-three-year-old Tony Bonsante, whose motto was right out of a Warren Zevon song: "We'll sleep when we're dead."

"We both have that iron in our blood," Bonsante said. "That heart, desire, determination."

LeDoux was so determined to get the best out of Bonsante that in April 2004, LeDoux suffered a cracked rib while Bonsante whacked away at LeDoux's midsection. LeDoux was fifty-five years old.

"Guys like Tony and me, from small towns, sometimes they think they don't deserve things," LeDoux said.

He still had something to prove. But what?

In 2004, at his wife's urging, LeDoux ran for an Anoka County commissioner's seat held by a twelve-year incumbent, Dave McCauley.

LeDoux was familiar with holding public positions. He was appointed in 2001 to the Minnesota Racing Commission. He was a founding board member of Make-A-Wish in Minnesota and later served on the board of Wishes & More. He chaired the American Cancer Society's Longest Day of Golf. He was a spokesman for the Epilepsy Foundation. He was on the state boxing commission for eighteen years. He chaired the Andover Community Center project. He even found time to challenge George Foreman and Larry Holmes, both long retired, to rematches in the ring.

But running for county board was a different challenge.

"I have name recognition, and that can't hurt," he said. "I can say things and the public will listen."

He said he approached the election like a fight, planning out his training, knocking on every door possible between July 20 and Election Day. He thought that having worked in so many different fields, he had a universal appeal, understanding what the voters wanted. And he had a Don King–like slogan: "How was your commute today? This is as good as it's ever going to get, unless things change."

They wanted LeDoux. He won by five hundred votes.

"Back in the days when we'd work out together at the gym on Seventh Street and Hennepin Avenue," his friend and former professional wrestler Jesse "The Body" Ventura said years later, "I knew that one day I would be governor and you would be an Anoka County commissioner."

"Don't underestimate him," warned Dan Erhart, a fellow Anoka County board member and the board's longtime chairman. "He's a leader. He knows how to work with people. And he can open a lot of doors that others can't."

Sure, LeDoux enjoyed telling listeners that he was his freshman class president three consecutive years. During one speech, he asked if anyone in his audience had ever boxed. Three people raised their hands. "I'll speak slowly for the rest of you," LeDoux said.

Occasionally, he would look toward the ceiling, tilting his head as if gazing at imaginary birds circling above—just to get a laugh from his audience.

There were a lot of audiences. He often spoke to organizations hours before arriving at the Anoka County Government Center for morning meetings. In 2006, he estimated he made more than a hundred charitable appearances while juggling his roles as Minnesota's boxing commissioner, county commissioner, realtor, father, and husband.

"It's tough for me to say no," LeDoux said. "Making sure we help some kids is the crux of it."

In 2005, LeDoux laced up the gloves one more time—for his favorite charity. He was nearly fifty-seven years old when he sparred for six rounds with up-and-comer Raphael Butler, at Gabby's in northeast Minneapolis. The money from the event—which included the auctioning of LeDoux's gloves—went to Wishes & More, a charity that grants wishes to children fighting terminal or life-threatening conditions.

He also found it impossible to say no to the Minnesota Wild when the professional hockey team asked him to work with left wing Derek Boogaard, a six-feet-seven, 270-pound enforcer. "I taught him how to turn the shoulders and square up when he started fighting on the ice," LeDoux said.

The Boogeyman, hockey's most fearsome fighter, became one of the National Hockey League's saddest stories. He died in 2011 in Minneapolis, at the age of twenty-eight, of a drug and alcohol overdose. An examination of his brain revealed months later that Boogaard had chronic traumatic encephalopathy (CTE), a disease similar to Alzheimer's, caused by repeated blows to the head. Among the symptoms are memory loss, mood swings, and addiction. Many boxers have had CTE diagnosed.

In 2006, LeDoux found a less painful way of staying involved with boxing. Governor Tim Pawlenty appointed LeDoux executive director of the newly reformed Minnesota Boxing Commission. LeDoux had testified a dozen times before state legislative committees in an effort to revive the commission, which Ventura, the previous governor, had abolished. LeDoux was thrilled to be a part of a commission that would allow Minnesota boxers to, once again, fight in their home state. He knew what it meant for his career. "I'll be done with boxing only when they shut the lid on my coffin," he said.

Regardless of the arena, LeDoux wasn't afraid to voice his opinions. In 2007, Mille Lacs Ojibwe chief executive Melanie Benjamin said LeDoux had repeatedly called her "stupid" and greedy during an argument over boxing concerning matches the tribe staged at Grand Casino in Hinckley, Minnesota, the halfway point between the Twin Cities and Duluth.

LeDoux defended himself, saying, "I said the tribe could save money by relying on the Minnesota Boxing Commission for help in organizing the fight and told [Jim Perrault, a state boxing judge], 'It's stupid not to do this.'

"I never said the tribe is stupid. I may be a lot of things, but I'm no racist."

And he wasn't quiet. He once told a fellow Anoka County commissioner, "You're just a housewife." When a citizen complained about a proposal to lengthen the runway at the local Anoka County airport in Blaine, LeDoux shot back, "You don't like change, then go join an Amish colony."

He was the subject of a 2008 state legislative audit—when he, as executive director, and six Combative Sports commissioners accepted tickets to an event for their families. James Nobles, the state legislative auditor, chastised the accused but wrote: "No one believed they were acting unethically. No one overtly used their position to secure these tickets." It didn't amount to much, but it was another controversy LeDoux could have done without.

"Sometimes I worry that Scott is trying to do too much," said Dan O'Connor, a fight promoter from Rochester. "Yeah, Scott's got an ego, but Scott's a good man. I think after all he's been through, he's just trying to find peace."

27

FUNERAL FOR A FRIEND

*I*n 1997, a St. Paul junior welterweight, Jumping Johnny Montantes, went down in the sixth round against a fighter named James Crayton in Las Vegas. Montantes died two days later in a Las Vegas hospital. He was twenty-eight.

"In the end, there's really no one to blame," said LeDoux, who at the time was a member of Minnesota's boxing regulatory board. "As fighters, we make a choice when we walk up those three stairs to the ring. It's no different from the construction worker who chooses to work in a dangerous career. But nobody complains when a construction worker dies.

"How many people die sitting in an office chair, working 14-hour days, and die having never pushed themselves to the limit, never having pursued their dreams? How many people have had the courage to say, 'I'm not giving up, no matter what?'"

Rhetoric aside, the connection between boxing and death and the link between fighting and debilitating illness caused from head trauma were subjects LeDoux often discussed privately. He said many times that Muhammad Ali, who suffered for years from Parkinson's disease, a neurological disorder, was "a prisoner inside his own body." "Did Ali's Parkinson's come from all the pounding he took all those years?" LeDoux asked. "And what about Greg Page and Kenny Norton?"

Look at what happened to LeDoux's contemporaries.

Page died at fifty, eight years after suffering a brain bleed in his final fight. In his fifties, Leon Spinks suffered from dementia and short-term memory impairment and had difficulty maintaining balance. Joe Frazier was sixty-seven when he died of liver cancer. Norton, injured in a near-fatal car accident in 1986, was seventy when he died. Ron Lyle also was seventy when he died of complications from a stomach abscess. Larry Middleton, whom LeDoux listed among the toughest opponents he faced, died at seventy-one.

Closer to home was the sad demise of Duane Bobick. When contacted to be interviewed for this book, Bobick was gracious, called LeDoux a "friend," but quickly ended the conversation, saying, "It's not a good day for me."

Bobick last fought in 1979. The next six years were lost in a haze of drugs and alcohol. His brother, Rodney, had been drinking the day he died in a one-car accident in 1977, two years after fighting LeDoux. Duane would not suffer the same fate. He became a reborn Christian in 1986 at the nondenominational Faith, Hope and Love Fellowship in Little Falls, Minnesota. He married Debi Atkinson and seemed happy.

Years later, while toiling as a mill worker at the Hennepin Paper Company in Little Falls, both of Bobick's arms were pulled into a paper roller. His right wrist was nearly torn off. Flesh and tissue from his right arm were peeled to the bone. His right elbow was crushed. There were also injuries to his left arm but not nearly as severe. "The flesh came off my right arm like you were skinning a pig," he told the *Minneapolis Star Tribune*.

After the bleeding was slowed, it took nearly ten hours for doctors to reattach the right wrist and rebuild and transplant nerves and arteries. Bobick lost his right index finger to amputation.

"I put up a good front, but I'm a little bit scared," he said that summer. "I can't help wondering: How whole am I going to be?" The toughest challenge was yet to come.

"Boxing was big back in the '70s and there wasn't a lot of knowledge on the effects of being punched in the head over and over," Deb Bobick said. "He never knew years later he would suffer from dementia or CTE." Bobick said he wasn't sure he would have gone into boxing had he known the effect of head trauma when he started, but he didn't regret the experience or the discipline he learned from the sport.

LeDoux was a bit stubborn when discussing the effects boxing may have had on him. Carol once told him she lamented his having participated in the sport. He countered by saying that boxing made him who he was.

"I have more injuries from football than boxing, that's for doggone sure," LeDoux told the National Associations of Counties. "I have more discomfort from all the football I played in high school and college than the boxing."

He recognized his mortality. And not just from Sandy's death. In recent years, he had lost both of his parents and his longtime trainer, George Glover, all to cancer. He lost Papa Joe to Alzheimer's.

LeDoux thought he was in relatively good health. He joked that when he stepped on the scale, it said, "One at a time, please." But he was able to fulfill his commitments, often overextending himself.

"I've accomplished way more than anybody ever anticipated," he said in 2005. "That's not ego. It just means I feel good about my career. I wasn't a cheap date, and anybody who fought me knew that."

Then, one day in 2006, while driving, he said he felt dizzy. His hands bothered him; he occasionally needed help buttoning his shirt. Then it was his shoulders. He thought he had arthritis. He had already been diagnosed with two bulging discs in his back. He was given Vicodin, which slurred his speech and had people wondering if something else was wrong.

He soldiered on and won reelection to the Anoka County Board—by the largest margin of any commissioner. His slogan: "Continue the Fight."

He was about to enter the fight of his life.

Carol noticed that his hands were shrinking and asked him to see a neurologist.

In January 2009, he went public with the diagnosis—a diagnosis he had lived with since August, a month after he filed to run for county board reelection. "I'm living with ALS [amyotrophic lateral sclerosis], but I'm not going to die from it," he said. "This is my real heavyweight championship fight."

Two weeks before, he had celebrated his sixtieth birthday, a gala affair at the Bunker Hills Golf Club in Coon Rapids. He was beaming and threatened to eat half of a huge chocolate cake in one sitting, just for old time's sake. Now his ring was shrinking, and there was no defense.

LeDoux had once laced up his gloves against boxing's elite. Now, he couldn't lace his shoes. His good friend Bob Dolan said he knew something was wrong before LeDoux told him, just by watching LeDoux's hands shake. Those massive hands that knocked down Norton in 1979 had weakened so badly that LeDoux needed help opening a packet of sweetener.

He and a reporter had been meeting each Friday for lunch at a Perkins restaurant in suburban Fridley for months. LeDoux often wolfed down his food, once eating a dozen shrimp in three minutes, as a favor to the reporter who was deathly allergic to shellfish. Then one Friday, Le-Doux ordered pancakes. He took from his pocket his own fork, one with a thick handle and a wavelike forty-five-degree curve. Then he asked the reporter to cut the pancakes for him.

He was in obvious discomfort. He pressed on his once-massive triceps and said he felt nothing but bone. At home, he used a walker— sometimes. He showed up at one Anoka County Board meeting with the kind of bruise on his forehead that made you wonder if he hadn't gone another three rounds with George Foreman. He had fallen in his yard and hit his head.

Yet, when a man at the Perkins restaurant walked by and asked, "Are you Scott LeDoux?" the people's champion offered him a big smile and replied, "My face rings a bell."

When asked about ALS, also known as Lou Gehrig's disease, LeDoux sometimes joked, "I'm finally a baseball player."

But the pain that ran from his fingertips through his legs told him that ALS was no laughing matter. It is a progressive, usually fatal neurodegenerative disease that plays havoc with nerve cells in the brain and spinal cord. When ALS kills motor neurons—the cells that run from the brain to the spinal cord and from the spinal cord to the body's muscles— the body can no longer control those muscles. The average survival after diagnosis is three years, said Dr. Eric Sorenson, a Mayo Clinic specialist. "There are people who will fight till their last breath," Dr. Sorenson said, "but the fatality rate is 95 percent."

The most notable exception is Stephen Hawking, the famed British theoretical physicist. Hawkins was diagnosed at twenty-one and was not expected to see his twenty-fifth birthday. A half century later he remained vibrant, working from his specialized chair and speaking through the computer system operated by his cheek.

LeDoux wasn't thinking about Stephen Hawking when he got the diagnosis.

"Yes, I thought about suicide," he said, but only briefly. "Suicide wasn't an option for me," LeDoux said. "As my wife explained to me, 'What would I do if I left my kids before my time and left my grandchildren before my time?' So that's my goal: to fight the fight."

Antidepression drugs helped. So did conversations with Mary

Hilgenberg, whose husband, Wally, the former Vikings linebacker, had ALS and died in 2008 at age sixty-six. She convinced LeDoux to use a walker.

LeDoux said he also spoke to former Twins star Kent Hrbek, whose father, Ed, died from ALS in 1982.

At the time of LeDoux's diagnosis, the Mayo Clinic's Sorenson said it was not known whether physical punishment has a scientific connection to ALS. The disease is linked to Gehrig, the New York Yankees Hall of Fame first baseman, who died of ALS in 1941. Other athletes who have died from ALS include Hall of Fame pitcher Jim "Catfish" Hunter and 1949 heavyweight boxing champion Ezzard Charles. Former Vikings free safety Orlando Thomas was forty-two when he died of ALS in 2014.

"Some days, while I'm lying in bed, I ask, 'Why us, God?'" Carol LeDoux said.

Nothing's guaranteed, said LeDoux. Through the school of hard knocks, he learned that a pocketful of mumbles . . . well, such are promises. As he discovered after the Boudreaux fight, some things are beyond control.

"I'll fight this disease the only way I know how," he said. "You've got to look at it as a fight in the main event."

This time, nobody had to knock on the door and tell him, "Five minutes to go." He was as ready as he would ever be. He took on Foreman, Norton, Holmes, Spinks, Tyson, and Ali. He learned about courage from Sandy. Nobody had to teach him how to fight the good fight. He had already run one marathon. He was now in the race of his life, but this time, the finish line remained a mystery.

"I'll work and work and work," he said. "I've never been shy of work."

Yet, to devote his energy to fighting—surviving—ALS, LeDoux had to make major compromises. As he contemplated his inevitable resignations from the Anoka County Board and as executive director of the Minnesota Combative Sports Commission, an old worry resurfaced: How long would he have the financial resources to combat his disease?

His friends rallied the moment news of his disease became public. Chico and Diane Resch called nearly every day. So did former Vikings Joe Senser and Bob Lurtsema. Gerry Cooney, a fellow heavyweight who fought for the world title but never fought LeDoux, called to wish LeDoux well.

"He's a tough guy who was involved in the most violent of sports, but he's really just a big softie," Dolan said.

Karla Blomberg, president of Wishes & More, said LeDoux never turned down a fund-raiser, never requested a fee to attend a charity event. But his presence paid dividends. Over three decades, LeDoux personally raised millions of dollars for charitable causes, said Richie Junghans, the catering and events coordinator for Joe Senser's Sports Theater and Restaurants.

It was time to reciprocate.

"This thing with Scott," said Frank Quilici, the former Twins infielder and manager, "it's hit us all like a ton of bricks.

"Scott's just one of the guys. Harmon [Killebrew] loves him. Harmon and I talked about what's happened to Scott and it almost makes you cry. Except Scott won't let you."

Wishes & More staged a benefit roast of LeDoux, with Lurtsema, Jesse Ventura, boxing great Sugar Ray Leonard, and local media star Joe Soucheray dishing out the wisecracks—and with LeDoux, naturally, hitting right back. There was a video tribute from George Foreman.

LeDoux, who moved slowly in his walker most days, abandoned the walker and moved slowly but deliberately to the Minneapolis City Center Marriott podium—a veteran fighter refusing to let anyone know how hurt he was. He needed to be helped when he tried to stand as Soucheray took the microphone.

"Hey, Scott, just like when you were in the ring," Soucheray said, before reminding the suddenly uneasy crowd, "Hey, people, it's a roast. Come on!"

LeDoux, still the life of the party, didn't mind being a punch line when it came to a good cause.

Noted Quilici: "I told him that when he fought Foreman, Scott was the first guy who could have sold advertisements on the bottoms of his shoes."

The next benefit—in March 2010—was for LeDoux and his family. "The Main Event: The Fight for Scott LeDoux" was held at the Landmark Center in St. Paul. There was an auction and raffle, with enough autographed items to fill a hall of fame.

"I've watched this guy in amazement for twenty-five or thirty years answer the call every time a charity needed help," said Joe Senser, one of the organizers. "What he's going through just takes your breath away. We've got to do something for this guy."

But there was little anyone could do. LeDoux was confined to a wheelchair, with an oxygen tank nearby. He was exhausted. His brother-in-law,

Wayne Wynn, built a ramp at LeDoux's home in Coon Rapids to help Le-Doux get in and out more easily. But he had reached a point where there was nowhere to go. The mountain of medical bills had grown taller than LeDoux's pile of prescriptions. He refused to complain. When he grew depressed, he watched a recording of his fight against Norton, arguably his greatest moment in the ring.

(One of LeDoux's favorite stories was introducing Norton to Carol at a chance meeting. "You beat me up," Norton said in front of LeDoux's bride. "Thanks for not killing me.")

LeDoux never grew tired of watching the final two rounds of the Norton fight. He knew, however, as he struggled more for breath with each day, that the conclusion of his final fight would end on a quieter note.

Scott LeDoux died on August 11, 2011, a Thursday, at his home, in Carol's arms. He was sixty-two. He never won the world heavyweight title, but "for a guy with no talent and a big smile, I did OK," he once said.

"Gritty," the *New York Times* called him. His fans adored him because they thought he was one of them. Always the underdog, he ignored the odds and the naysayers and just kept plugging along.

Those fans showed up in droves for LeDoux's funeral. About a thousand people packed Mount Olivet Lutheran Church in south Minneapolis. Jesse Ventura was there. Senator Amy Klobuchar paid her respects, as did the entire Anoka County Board. Members of the Twin Cities retired sporting elite attending the funeral included Twins great Tony Oliva; North Stars player, coach, and executive Lou Nanne; Senser; Quilici; North Stars player and Wild broadcaster Tom Reid; and Bob Stein, the former University of Minnesota football star who played for the Kansas City Chiefs' Super Bowl IV champions and was the Minnesota Timberwolves' first president.

Bob Lurtsema and Chuck Daszkiewicz were pallbearers—and the pallbearers, in keeping with LeDoux's spirit, wore Hawaiian shirts. Chico and Diane Resch read from the Scriptures. Diane called her longtime buddy "a character, and a person with character."

Karla Blomberg, president of Wishes & More, recalled a football game in which a big Wisconsin lineman was heckling the Minnesota crowd. LeDoux yelled to him, "You wanna go three rounds?" Then he added, "And you're buying the first two."

Bob Dolan praised his friend, saying, "He taught us all how to laugh, he taught us how to cry, that it was all right to cry, he taught us how to live and, in the end, he taught us how to die with dignity.

"His legacy is his charity work."

It was more than that. John Carney, LeDoux's army buddy, flew in from Boston to pay tribute to the friend who used to close the base pool to get in a couple hours of golf. Old friends Jim Rocca and David Martodam came to benefits featuring LeDoux. At the conclusion of the memorial service, Lou Hokanson, the Minneapolis boxer who sparred with LeDoux, rang a bell ten times, the final ten-count for LeDoux.

If LeDoux was going down for the count, his entire corner needed to be there with him.

Pastor Randy O'Brien told the story of LeDoux's championship fight with Larry Holmes, how the fight was stopped after Holmes thumbed LeDoux's eye. "What's an eye when you've given your heart?" O'Brien said, quoting LeDoux. The congregation nodded in agreement. LeDoux made noise with his fists, but as a tireless crusader for charity, he always opened his heart.

The day after LeDoux died, George Foreman read his obituary online in the *Star Tribune*. Foreman was so moved, he called the reporter who wrote the piece. "What a warrior!" Foreman said. Foreman did not attend LeDoux's funeral service but was very emotional in recalling the man he beat in 1975. "You just don't know the value of a real good man until we lose one."

LeDoux never won that coveted championship belt, but O'Brien, the pastor, guessed that LeDoux was probably wearing a crown in heaven.

The people's champion didn't need a crown when he visited Crosby-Ironton, the gym on Seventh Street and Hennepin Avenue, or the King of Clubs in northeast Minneapolis, or played with his grandchildren.

But he did wear a ring. A big ring. The kind of ring you see on the fingers of players who have won a World Series or Super Bowl. It was a ring commemorating his WBC championship fight with Holmes. The ring was inscribed: "LeDoux vs. Holmes, July 7, 1980."

It also quoted Sandy.

"They can't take it away," the inscription said, "because we ran our own race."

Afterword

THE GREATEST AND MORE

$\mathcal{S}$cott LeDoux considered himself a boxing historian, and there's nothing like living history. The only man to go toe-to-toe with eleven heavyweight champions was a great storyteller. LeDoux spoke of these champions with reverence, humor, and, in some cases, awe. Regardless of the outcome of each individual battle, LeDoux savored the experiences of stepping into the ring with men who became boxing legends. So did his fans, who often stopped him to ask what it was like to fight Larry Holmes, Ken Norton, or George Foreman, among others. With humility and enthusiasm, LeDoux, in his typical no-holds-barred style, shared anecdotes and opinions concerning the men who wore the belt he so coveted. Here are excerpts from our interviews and his memories of fellow boxers.

Muhammad Ali

The last time I saw Ali [in 2006] was in Vegas, and he was struggling. He recognized me, and he did that face, where he bites his lower lip. He was shaking, but I had the sense that he knew everything that was going on. Doesn't matter. He's still The Greatest, maybe the greatest who ever lived. I think he could have beaten Mike Tyson, peak for peak. He had such great legs, such great movement. You couldn't hit him when he was younger. He'd have knocked Joe Louis out. Joe was a shuffler. He was slow, but he had fast hands. He could put combinations together, but he couldn't have beaten Ali.

Ali is such a nice man. He's living in Scottsdale, Arizona, and every time I think about him, I think I need to make a greater effort to see him.

When I fought him in the exhibition in Chicago, he was puffy, probably twenty pounds overweight. He didn't care anymore. He was just making money. I bloodied his nose, his mouth. He hit me all over. The one thing I remember distinctively was the left hook. I was waiting for the right hand, and he hit me with the left hook. And I was thinking after the round, "How did he do that?"

But he didn't care when he fought me. I should never, never, never have gotten close enough to hit him, if he cared. He was done. The old Ali would have danced away from me. I'm realistic. The reason he was the greatest was he always found a way to win.

The rope-a-dope was such a con. He really was getting hit, and he was taking punches. But he would shake his head like he wasn't getting hit. What a shot he could take! He was just as big and strong as George [Foreman].

Guys like Ali have it every night. Guys like me have it once or twice in a career.

He didn't care when he got in the ring with Leon [Spinks] the first time, and Leon beat him. That got Ali's attention. Look what he did to Leon in the rematch.

I was at the Holmes fight, and I knew Holmes was going to beat him because Ali was, uh, old.

Ali was more than the greatest fighter. He was the greatest promoter I'd ever seen. He knew when to turn it on and turn it off. He could be your friend, a very kind man, and then turn on you if it would sell tickets. It was all part of being Muhammad Ali. I didn't always get along with Don King, but I had great admiration for him as a promoter. But do you think there could have been a Don King without Ali?

Frank Bruno

That was the real tallying point for me, when I knew I was done. Bruno knocked me down and split my eye, really badly. It is one of the only real bad scars I have from boxing. He could hit. Like I said, I earned frequent flyer miles during that fight.

Gerrie Coetzee

He was a tough guy, but I never had a shot, not with the referee telling me the day before the fight that Gerrie Coetzee is someday going to be the world champion. I was so disillusioned by boxing from what happened over there that I don't think I could evaluate Coetzee fairly. What happened over in South Africa and the way I was treated really took it out of me.

George Foreman

It was one of those early losses when I realized I had a lot to learn. George did more than cut my eye. He blasted me. I went down and got back up. Then he split it for twelve stitches.

In the first round, he used the left jab. I thought to myself, "I don't want to see the right hand." But I did. He hit me all over. And then I hit him and bloodied his nose.

In the second round, I was moving in on him, moving in and out and tagging him. Gil Clancy [Foreman's legendary trainer] told us years later that [Foreman] came back to the stool after the second round and was really discouraged. And Clancy had to pump him up. He told George, "He's ready to go." That's when George came right out and hit me with the right hand, cut me for twelve stitches. I went down, got back up at the count of nine, and they stopped the fight because of the gash.

I realized then that I could go a long way. I realized that I could fight with him because I stuck him with the jab. I hit him with some right hands to the body and some right hands to the chin. I wasn't his equal, but that let me know I was competent.

The difference in abilities wasn't that large. There wasn't that big a gap. The difference was that George hit harder than any heavyweight I ever faced or ever saw. When he hit you, it really felt like a house had just fallen on you.

It wasn't until I got into my forties and fifties that I realized how good I was. I could spar with guys and not get hit. And against George Foreman I learned how hard of a punch I could take. Other than Ali, who hasn't he hit that he couldn't take out?

.

Larry Holmes

You know, this was one of the fights where I was not afraid because I knew he wasn't a punishing puncher, not a devastating puncher. I was in great shape, in great condition, and I knew I could absorb anything he had.

He could not break an egg, as far as I'm concerned.

My goal was to get him to the end of the fight and then finish him off because I knew I was in better shape and I had endurance beyond anyone else. I knew that he was going to outpoint me. I also felt I could stop him in the late rounds, if he got tired. I needed to go to the body early, to punish him.

What I didn't anticipate was his boxing ability and his ability to avoid punches to the body and keep his left jab. He had a great jab. Not a hard jab, but a great jab. He had an eighty-one-inch reach, I had a seventy-eight-inch reach. He wasn't very coordinated, but he had movement. You couldn't trap him.

In the fight before ours, he thumbed Leroy Jones in the eye. Tore his retina. I was at the press conference afterward, and Leroy Jones was crying, saying, "All this guy does is stick thumbs in my eyes." [A detached retina forced Jones to temporarily retire from boxing after he fought Holmes.]

He got the thumb in my eye in the seventh, and they stopped the fight in the eighth round.

Some guys use their heads, their elbows, their feet, their laces. They shove you away, but then they lace you across the face. That deters your thinking because it burns, it stings. Larry was the best when it came to using his thumbs.

I think Larry has always been bitter that he wasn't recognized as the great champion he was. I agree that he was a great champion, there's no question about that. He held the title for seven years. He was good, and he did a lot of good things, and I have always been impressed with him over the years. Larry held his own with everybody and did what he had to do to win.

I wish Larry would give up on the race card that he claims constantly because it really isn't good for boxing. He plays that race thing all the time, and that isn't part of my vocabulary, and he has to move on to other things.

Lennox Lewis

[LeDoux sparred with Lennox Lewis in the fall of 2000, while LeDoux did commentary for ESPN2. LeDoux was nearly fifty-two years old; Lewis was twenty-five and in his prime as the undisputed world champion.]
When he came out of his corner, he could hit me. He had such long arms. He was fast, he was strong, he had great balance.

I talked to him and wanted to train with him. I sparred with him for a few days, and we put the piece on ESPN. He hit me in the head, and I hit him with a right-hand swing, which was my favorite punch to the body. Then he started going to the body with me. He just hurt me.

He was a very nice man, very courteous, polite. Very impressive.

Lennox Lewis, to me, was a tremendous fighter, and what impressed me the most was he got beat and came back to knock out the guys who beat him, and you have to give him his due. There isn't anybody who is dominating like Lennox Lewis did for so long.

[Lewis avenged his loss to Oliver McCall with a fifth-round TKO, won a unanimous decision over Evander Holyfield eight months after the pair fought to a draw, and knocked out Hasim Rahman in four rounds seven months after being knocked out by Rahman. Lewis also defeated ex-champions Mike Weaver, Frank Bruno, and Mike Tyson. Like Gene Tunney and Rocky Marciano before him, Lewis retired as champion.]

Ken Norton

Oh, he was ripped. When I saw him, I asked my manager, "Joe, can I fight with a T-shirt on?" Oh, he was just cut.

Papa Joe told me, "Early in the fight, he's going to have his way with you. He's going to be at the top of his game, and you've got to be focused on getting past the fifth round. You've got to stay focused on wearing him down and getting him tired."

In the fifth round, I remember ducking a big hook and hitting him with the right hand. And that was the turning point.

I never perceived fighting Ken Norton and knocking him down twice. We were on the same card together [in 1975, at the St. Paul Civic Center]. I was fighting Scrap Iron Johnson, and he was fighting Jose Luis Garcia. I sparred with him. After the sparring, he gave me that fight. He kept firing those big left hooks, and I kept ducking them. I could see every punch coming. I don't want to criticize him, but he was the most unorthodox fighter I ever fought. He straddled. He kept his legs far apart. So every time I wanted to get him off balance, I'd just run in and give him a shoulder block. I hit him, so I knew I could kick his butt.

I did a lot to him, but I never wanted to get hit with his uppercut because he knocked Duane Bobick out with it. So, in the fifth or sixth round, I was trying to push him away, and he came up with an uppercut and—oh, my God! He lifted me up, both feet off the ground. I didn't get knocked out, but he crushed me with that uppercut.

Greg Page

I was throwing my jab. I wasn't bringing it back. I was leaning out, and he was just reaching over and nailing me.

He could have been a great fighter. He had a lot of skills. He just couldn't motivate himself to train.

Leon Spinks

I didn't know that much about Leon, mostly just what I'd seen on television. He'd won the gold medal, and he had a lot of press. The fight was at the Aladdin in Las Vegas, and it was pretty exciting because all the press was there to cover Leon. And I was just a fighter, you know.

Leon was quicker, and I was able to use the tools I had learned along the way. I hit him with elbows, then the left hook. He never figured it out. He was what I expected. I had sparred with a middleweight, Doug Demmings, and Leon wasn't as fast.

He didn't hurt me at all. He was just fast. Otherwise, nothing.

I liked Leon, thought he was a good kid. We fought to a draw, but I thought I won. Of course, there's no way I could have won a decision since Leon had already signed to fight Ali for the title. But what do I know? Look what happened when he fought Ali.

After the fight, I was in the dressing room, getting dressed, and Leon walked in. He came over, and I thought, "Boy, what is he going to do?" He walked over and said, "You're one tough son of a bitch." And he shook my hand. We had a war. Back in the day, you had respect for each other. Now, it's all about you.

Leon called me a couple of years ago, out of the blue. He's a nice kid.

Mike Tyson

You could feel his fist. He bloodied my nose during training camp and cut me for eight stitches over my left eye. He cut me with a right hand. The next day, that's when I found out his gloves were tampered with.

We were training in Vegas, but Mike stayed at a budget hotel, a little room where you could cook. He was different. Hardly ever spoke. But I like Mike. He's a very smart guy, but he's just a product of his upbringing.

The cops found him on the street when he was twelve years old, beating up an adult to get money to eat. Think about that. How terribly sad.

Mike Weaver

It was a terrible situation. After the fight, I saw the video. He had rubber-soled shoes. I saw one of his guys get up in the ring and sweep it. He took all the resin out of the ring so I couldn't get a grip. I was on skates. I'd fire a right hand, and my back foot would slip out. It was terrible. I kept telling Joe, "You gotta rub my shoes up. Rub my shoes up!" From that point, I went with rubber-sole shoes.

But he hit me hard. He cut me on the cheek, just split the skin. He really was a tremendous puncher. He boxed really well. Good combinations.

People don't realize how hard he hit. Just because he didn't knock me out doesn't mean he couldn't hit.

ACKNOWLEDGMENTS

*T*wo days after graduating from college, I was given my first assignment as a professional journalist: interview a promising amateur boxer from Easton, Pennsylvania, named Larry Holmes. I was twenty-one years old, working for *The Trentonian*, the morning daily for Trenton, New Jersey, and Holmes, nicknamed the Easton Assassin, fought as an amateur for the Trenton Police Athletic League team. Holmes's amateur trainer, Percy Richardson, explained the art of covering boxing to me: "When you're covering a fight, always wear dark clothes and never sit in the front row," he said. "There are bleeders and there are snotters, and you don't want to be near any of them."

I was intrigued by this brutal sport but even more so by the characters. I spent an afternoon with the great champion Joe Frazier in 1973 at the Clover Leaf Gym in Philadelphia, weeks before his second fight with Muhammad Ali. I expected a brute, but Smokin' Joe could not have been more cooperative or friendly. I was stunned.

In the summer of 1980, not long after Holmes successfully defended his title against Scott LeDoux, I was in New York covering a baseball series for the *Minneapolis Star* between the Twins and Yankees. I hopped on the hotel elevator with Patrick Reusse, who worked for the St. Paul papers at the time, to attend a press conference announcing an Ali–Holmes title fight. The elevator stopped, and the door opened, and in stepped Ali and Don King, both dressed to the nines. King, who held a jeweled walking stick, stopped the elevator for a couple of minutes and began spewing one-liners, using us as a warm-up audience. We laughed out loud, and Ali giggled throughout, letting the great promoter be the King of comedy. Then King pressed the elevator button, and we were on our way. A free show with Don King and Muhammad Ali—what could be more entertaining?

Years later, I found out.

Anoka County, just north of Minneapolis, was bidding for a new Minnesota Vikings stadium, and Scott LeDoux was a county commissioner. After a meeting, I cornered LeDoux. He expected a question about the stadium. Instead I asked him, "What was it like to get punched in the head by George Foreman in his prime?"

LeDoux told me, using his line about being hit so hard that his ancestors in France felt it. Then I asked him about stepping into the ring with Ali. And Ken Norton. I was curious, that's all.

That's how it started. We recorded three dozen audio interviews and had dozens of other conversations. Coincidentally, Larry Holmes was the last boxer I interviewed for this book.

Scott LeDoux could not have been more gracious, and the same can be said for his family. Thank you to Carol LeDoux, Molly and Tim Lappin, Josh and Bridgette LeDoux, Judy and Wayne Wynn, and Denise Thompson.

Scott's friends and his boxing brethren answered the bell when I called for help—and this guy had a lot of friends. Thanks to Chuck Daszkiewicz for playing analyst while we watched video of Scott's fights. Thanks to Bob Dolan for behind-the-scenes stories. And thanks to Diane and Glenn Resch for putting Scott's life into perspective.

Thanks also to Jerry Blackledge, Karla Blomberg, Duane Bobick, John Carney, John Davies, Jim DeJarlais, Vern Emerson, Dan Erhart, George Foreman, Julie Galle, Craig Gallop, Bobby Goodman, Stephen Grossman, Brad Gunn, Lou Hokanson, Larry Holmes, Richie Junghans, Bob Lurtsema, Jim Malosky, David Martodam, Randy Nauman, Denny Nelson, Ken Norton, Brian O'Melia, Arnie Palmer, Tony Palumbo, Frank Perpich, Katherine Perpich, Carol Polis, Frank Quilici, Gordy Racette, Tim Rath, Jim Rocca, Doug Rollins, Steve Schussler, Joe Senser, Bob Smith, Dr. Eric Sorenson, Bob Stein, Mike Tyson, Jesse Ventura, and Chuck Wepner.

Sandy Date and John Wareham, my former colleagues at the *Star Tribune*, provided me with archival material. During my thirty-five years at the *Minneapolis Star* and *Star Tribune*, I worked with many talented people. Among those who wrote the articles that form the backbone of the story of Scott LeDoux's boxing career are Larry Batson, Bruce Brothers, Dick

Cullum, Bob Ehlert, Mike Gelfand, Doug Grow, Bill Hengen, Howard Sinker, Patrick Reusse, and Joe Soucheray.

Erik Anderson, my editor at the University of Minnesota Press, never lost faith in this project. His enthusiasm, keen eye, and unquestioned support were blessings that cannot be minimized. Thanks also to the Press's Kristian Tvedten for guidance, to managing editor Laura Westlund for suggestions, and to copy editor Mary Keirstead for patiently working with an author who is challenged by computer technology and dyslexia.

A belated and heartfelt thank-you to the late and legendary Gil Spencer, my first-ever editor, a great teacher, and the most fearless journalist I've ever met.

I would be remiss without acknowledging the emotional roller coaster I clung to during this project. It was difficult listening to Scott tell me about Sandy's illness and death. During the process of the reporting and writing of this book, we lost Scott. And then I lost my beautiful bride. Thanks to Clyde Bailey, Charley Barniskis, Tim Bauer, Andy Birch, Rabbi Norman Cohen, Bob Cosgrove, George Dreckmann, David Eden, Michael and Janet Enson, Jim Kern, Rosie Mahoney, Greg Meyer, Richard Meyer, Bill O'Meara, Joe Quick, Deirdre Ryan, John Schulz, David Smith, Theresa Westling, my Syracuse buddies (particularly Doug and Nancy Carney and Gordon Celliers), and Jeff Strickler—especially Jeff—for listening to me.

Most of all, thanks to Sarah and Sam Levy for making your mother and me proud.

NOTES

1. The Great Milford Mining Disaster

Page 1: Named by Adams's wife: "Cuyuna, The Lost Range," *Grand Rapids Herald Review*, February 28, 2014. Railroad company employee Cuyler Adams was out with his St. Bernard, Una, surveying property that he owned near Deerwood. Whether Adams actually discovered ore has been debated for a century. "Cuyuna Range," Miningartifacts.com.: In 1903 Adams formed the Orelands Mining Company.

Page 2: By 1918, the twenty-seven Cuyuna mines: "Cuyuna Range," Miningartifacts .com.

Page 2: Minnesota native Garrison Keillor talks: *A Prairie Home Companion*, Prairie home.publicradio.org.

Page 3: His father, an expert blaster: D. J. Tice, "The Milford Mine Disaster, 1924," in *Minnesota's Twentieth Century: Stories of Extraordinary Everyday People* (Minneapolis: University of Minnesota Press, 1999).

Page 3: "Everything was working": Tice, "The Milford Mine Disaster"; Aulie Berger, *The Milford Mine Disaster: A Cuyuna Range Tragedy* (Virginia, Minn.: W. A. Fisher Company, 1994).

Page 4: Forty-eight men worked: Connie Pettersen, "Failure to Learn? Destined to Repeat . . . Part I, The Accident at Milford Mine," *NewsHopper* (Brainerd/Aitkin, Minn.), March 11, 2006.

Page 4: "Water?" his buddy: Pettersen, "Failure to Learn?"

Page 4: A fraction of a second later: "Forty-One Miners Meet Death in Milford Mine," *Crosby Courier* (Crosby, Minn.), February 8, 1924.

Page 4: "For God's sake, run": Pettersen, "Failure to Learn?"

Page 4: For four hours that warning signal: Pettersen, "Failure to Learn?"

Page 4: Frank Hrvatin Jr., days shy: Pettersen, "Failure to Learn?"

Page 5: "When the women found out": Chao Xiong, "Mining Memories," Minneapolis *Star Tribune*, July 31, 2002.

Page 5: "An act of God?": Greg Gordon, "Still Mining the Case," Minneapolis *Star Tribune*, August 9, 2005.

3. "I Thought I Had Done Something Bad"

Page 15: Only 2,600 people: U.S. Census Bureau, 1960, *Number of Inhabitants: Minnesota*, www2.census.gov.

Page 15: Fast-forward a half century: U.S. Census Bureau, 2010 *Census Interactive Population Search*, http://www.census.gov/2010census/popmap/ipmtext .php?fl=27.
Page 15: Grabbing the greatest amount: *Minneapolis Tribune*, January 7, 1949.
Page 16: "It was the last thing": Bob Ehlert, "Scott LeDoux: He's Hung Up His Gloves, but Not the Memories," *Minneapolis Star Tribune*, Sunday Magazine, March 3, 1985.

4. When Lightning Struck

Page 26: The rising star: This famous quote was found via several sources, among them: "Sonny Liston, the Ali Poll," www.ali.com; Elizabeth Victoria Wallace, *The Hidden History of Denver* (Charleston, S.C.: History Press, 2011), 88. Sir Henry Cooper, the British champion, was no slouch, as a young Cassius Clay discovered in 1963 at London's Wembley Stadium. Cooper, weighing twenty-seven pounds less than Clay, stunned his young opponent with a left hook that sent Clay reeling into the ropes. Clay stood up, dazed. Then came the controversy that British fight fans still talked about a half century later. Clay's trainer, Angelo Dundee, apparently administered smelling salts to his future and undefeated champion, violating British rules. Dundee was also accused of splitting Clay's gloves, making it easier for the young American to cut his foe. Clay came out for the fifth round, opened a gash under Cooper's eye, and the fight was over. When the two met in 1966, the now-heavyweight champion won again. The fight was stopped in the sixth round—again, a deep gash under Cooper's eye forcing the referee to stop the match.

5. The Last Place on Earth

Page 27: The city has claimed: In attempting to determine who claims the title as Minnesota's walleye capital, www.highwayhighlights.com reports that Isle's big walleye statue used to have a sign below it that read, "Mille Lacs, Walleye Capital of the World," but this sign has since vanished. The walleye is positioned outside of a bank, posed in midleap, about fifteen feet tall.
Page 31: By the end of the nineteenth century: www.downtownduluth.com.
Page 31: But the sinister side of Highway 61: Title song from Bob Dylan's 1965 masterpiece, *Highway 61 Revisited*, Columbia Records.
Page 31: "I heard all the stories": Paul Levy, "Sailors in Port," *Minneapolis Star Tribune*, Sunday Magazine, August 9, 1987.
Page 33: "How much longer": Resch and Nystrom are best remembered for helping the New York Islanders launch a National Hockey League dynasty. But before the Islanders won four consecutive Stanley Cup titles, from 1980 to 1983, they captured the hearts and imaginations of hockey fans in Long Island and beyond. The Islanders, playing in just their third season, became one of only five teams in American sports history to crawl out of a 3–0 hole to win. But the Islanders' 1975 playoff run didn't end in Pittsburgh, where the team won game seven on the road. The Isles fell behind

defending Stanley Cup champion Philadelphia, 3–0, before winning three straight to force a game seven against the Flyers. Chico Resch's spectacular diving save on a penalty shot by the Flyers' Bill Barber in game four, which the Islanders won in overtime, was a key in turning the series around. The Flyers ultimately won the series. But by the time the Islanders won the first of their four consecutive Stanley Cups, in 1980, Resch's spot in Islanders lore was frozen for all time. Winner of the NHL's Bill Masterton Memorial Trophy in 1982, for perseverance and sportsmanship while with the Colorado Rockies, Resch retired in 1987, a three-time All-Star. He eventually moved to the broadcast booth and wowed a whole new generation of fans with his commentary during New Jersey Devils games. The most famous of the other three-games-to-none comebacks came in the 2004 American League Championship Series, when the Boston Red Sox buried the eighty-six-year-old legendary Curse of the Bambino in finally beating the New York Yankees. The first team to win a game seven after trailing, three games to none, was the NHL Toronto Maple Leafs, who shocked the Detroit Red Wings in 1942. The Philadelphia Flyers, down three games to none to Boston in 2010, stunned the Bruins en route to the Stanley Cup finals. During the 2014 Stanley Cup playoffs, with his team trailing three games to none, Los Angeles Kings goalie Jonathan Quick allowed San Jose just five goals in the last four games as the Kings eliminated the Sharks. Los Angeles went on to beat the New York Rangers to win the Stanley Cup.

6. "I've Had Enough"

Page 38: "I'd like to keep on fighting": *Duluth News Tribune*, January 1968.
Page 38: "You get a lot of personal satisfaction": *Duluth News Tribune*, January 1968.
Page 38: "When I fought Herrin": *Duluth News Tribune*, January 1968.
Page 39: "A big smile spread": Associated Press, February 20, 1968.
Page 39: "Just looking at LeDoux": *Duluth News Tribune*, February 25, 1968.
Page 39: There were awkward moments: *Duluth News Tribune*, February 21, 1968.
Page 40: "We're not going to throw": *Duluth News Tribune*, February 21, 1968.
　Gallop told the *Crosby-Ironton Courier* on February 21, 1968, that LeDoux would skip the national tournament in Salt Lake City because of his lack of experience.

7. Sandy

Page 42: Dick Young, the legendary: Dick Young, column, *New York Daily News*, July 3, 1980. Young could not say enough about Sandy, comparing her smile to that of June Allyson, a Hollywood star in the 1940s and 1950s and among the first actresses to star in her own TV show.
Page 43: "He asked me what I thought": *New York Times*, June 6, 1980.
Page 43: But there was no doubt: *New York Times*, June 6, 1980.

8. Papa Joe

Page 46: As a teenager: Joni Astrup, "One Man's Journey: Scott LeDoux Tells How He Gave His Life to Christ," *Star News* (Elk River, Minn.), June 16, 2004.

Page 46: "None of those Commies": Minneapolis *Star Tribune*, November 17, 1988.

Page 47: "If I had reenlisted": Eric Jorgensen, "Scott LeDoux: The Fighting Frenchman," *Cyber Boxing Zone Journal*, April 2000.

Page 48: Doc merely shrugged: Jorgensen, "Scott LeDoux."

Page 48: He turned pro in 1974: Curt Brown, "The Not-So-Sweet Science," Minneapolis *Star Tribune*, August 5, 1990. Danny Needham, known as the St. Paul Terror, earned the crown of Lightweight Champion of the Northwest, according to the *Cyber Boxing Zone*.

Page 49: Over the years: Jorgensen, "Scott LeDoux."

Page 49: Daszkiewicz was a throwback: Brown, "The Not-So-Sweet Science."

Page 49: "This," Daszkiewicz told a visitor: Brown, "The Not-So-Sweet Science."

Page 50: "Before giving them their cut": Pam Schmid, "Veteran Boxing Promoter Dies," Minneapolis *Star Tribune*, October 8, 2003.

Page 52: George Glover, a sheet-metal worker: Minneapolis *Star Tribune*, December 23, 1994.

9. The Great White Shadow

Page 53: "I want to be recognized": Minneapolis *Star*, October 9, 1972.

Page 54: "For us, a ghetto": Douglas S. Looney, "He's Not Pretty, He's Just Persistent," *Sports Illustrated*, May 9, 1977.

Page 54: With his boxing résumé: Bob Ehlert, "What Does a Guy Do Who Beat Up People for a Living?" *Minneapolis Star Tribune, Sunday Magazine*, May 10, 1987.

Page 54: Bobick said it was actually: Ehlert, "What Does a Guy Do Who Beat Up People for a Living?"

Page 54: For instance, just minutes: "LeDoux Takes 8th Mitt Step," Bill Hengen, *Minneapolis Star*, October 9, 1974.

Page 55: "If he had gotten up": Hengen, "LeDoux Takes 8th Mitt Step."

Page 55: "They ran in this Brown on us": "LeDoux to Fight in Rochester," *Minneapolis Tribune*, January 22, 1975.

Page 55: "Before the next round": "LeDoux to Fight in Rochester."

Page 56: LeDoux could have done worse: Ehlert, "What Does a Guy Do Who Beat Up People for a Living?"

Page 56: "I've challenged him": Bill Hengen, "Bring on Rod–LeDoux," *Minneapolis Star*, January 30, 1975.

Page 56: "Scott's making a lot of noise": Hengen, "Bring on Rod–LeDoux."

Page 57: "Wallace may be too clever": Dick Cullum, "LeDoux Is Matched with Dallas Ring Veteran," *Minneapolis Tribune*, February 23, 1975.

Page 57: Ben Sternberg, the promoter: Cullum, "LeDoux Is Matched with Dallas Ring Veteran."

Page 57: Daszkiewicz tried to justify: Cullum, "LeDoux Is Matched with Dallas Ring Veteran."

Page 57: "He butted me": *Minneapolis Star*, March 15, 1975.

Page 57: LeDoux's manager, Arnie Palmer: Dick Cullum, "Boxing," *Minneapolis Tribune*, March 26, 1975.

Page 58: What stung most: *Minneapolis Star*, March 15, 1975.

Page 58: But there were complications: Dick Cullum, column, *Minneapolis Tribune*, April 8, 1975.

Page 58: The intensity: Bill Hengen, column, *Minneapolis Star*, April 8, 1975.

Page 58: When Duane Bobick: Dick Cullum, "Boxing," *Minneapolis Tribune*, April 9, 1975.

Page 59: "I assume that LeDoux": *Minneapolis Tribune*, April 22, 1975.

Page 59: Indeed, LeDoux and Bobick: "Revised Figure," *Minneapolis Tribune*, April 30, 1975.

Page 60: "Right now": Larry Batson, "LeDoux Seeks Meat on Table before Pie in Sky," *Minneapolis Tribune*, April 20, 1975.

Page 60: "The bell rang": Patrick Reusse, "Gym Fulfills Glover's Dream to Keep Boxing Alive," Minneapolis *Star Tribune*, April 16, 1998.

Page 60: After the fight: Bill Hengen, "LeDoux the Fox," *Minneapolis Star*, April 24, 1975.

Page 60: "I thought LeDoux tired": Dick Cullum, "LeDoux, D. Bobick Win Bouts," *Minneapolis Tribune*, April 25, 1975.

Page 61: "We'd love to get in": Batson, "LeDoux Seeks Meat on Table."

Page 61: "This fight is hot now": Sid Hartman, "Duane Bobick Wants LeDoux," *Minneapolis Tribune*, April 25, 1975.

Page 61: "We're ready to fight": Hartman, "Duane Bobick Wants LeDoux."

Page 61: But after the Bobick fight: Hengen, "LeDoux the Fox."

Page 61: As the weeks passed: *Minneapolis Tribune*, May 14, 1975.

Page 61: "One thing is certain": "LeDoux's Managers Rejected in Bid for Boxing Franchise," *Minneapolis Tribune*, May 23, 1975.

Page 62: "When the bell rang": Dick Cullum, "Scrap Iron Says LeDoux Can Take Bobick," *Minneapolis Tribune*, November 15, 1975.

Page 62: Regardless, Johnson wasn't impressed: Bill Hengen, "Norton, LeDoux Next Possibility," *Minneapolis Star*, November 14, 1975.

Page 63: LeDoux's camp agreed: Bill Hengen, "LeDoux, Stander Camps Request," *Minneapolis Star*, December 5, 1975.

Page 63: Daszkiewicz was asked: Larry Batson, "LeDoux Says Bout Is a 'Good Matchup,'" *Minneapolis Tribune*, December. 7, 1975; Hengen, "LeDoux, Stander Camps Request."

Page 64: "I've discarded whatever": Batson, "LeDoux Says Bout Is a 'Good Matchup.'"

Page 64: "I hope me and Ron": Joe Soucheray, "LeDoux, O'Connor Win," *Minneapolis Tribune*, December 11, 1975.

Page 64: "We will be prepared": Bill Hengen, "Did LeDoux Really Win? Norton Next," *Minneapolis Star*, December 11, 1975.

10. One for the Record Books

Page 67: Brenner told insiders: Dick Cullum, "N.Y. Bids for Bobick Bout with Le-Doux," *Minneapolis Tribune*, January 4, 1976.

Page 67: "Everything's set except": Bill Hengen, "Pro Boxing Here to Try Saturday," *Minneapolis Star*, January 23, 1976.

Page 68: The promoters then turned: Dick Cullum, "Connecticut Boxer to Be Replaced as LeDoux Opponent," *Minneapolis Tribune*, February 4, 1976.

Page 68: "We feel that women": Bill Hengen, "LeDoux Finally Gets Opponent; Name's Carson," *Minneapolis Star*, February 5, 1976. Gunn went on to tell Hengen that "there is no reason they [women] should be accompanied by someone to receive a half-priced ticket."

Page 68: After knocking out Carson: "LeDoux at Crossroad as Middleton Fight Set for March 9," *Minneapolis Tribune*, February 22, 1976.

Page 68: "It's time for me": Dick Cullum, "LeDoux Thinks Fight May Be Turning Point," *Minneapolis Tribune*, March 9, 1976.

Page 68: The Middleton fight presented: *Minneapolis Star*, March 10, 1976.

Page 69: "It was a good heavyweight fight": Dick Cullum, "LeDoux Gets Fight Decision," *Minneapolis Tribune*, March 10, 1976.

Page 69: LeDoux made demands: Dick Cullum, "LeDoux Signs to Fight Bobick—If He's Willing," *Minneapolis Tribune*, April 1, 1976.

Page 69: Sternberg was promising: Bill Hengen, "LeDoux–Bobick Fight Nearer," *Minneapolis Star*, April 1, 1976.

Page 69: "The time has passed": Cullum, "LeDoux Signs to Fight Bobick."

Page 69: On April 5, after a year: "Fight Fans Get Biggie," *Minneapolis Star*, April 6, 1976.

Page 69: "I may as well tell you": *Minneapolis Tribune*, April 6, 1976.

Page 69: LeDoux countered: *Minneapolis Tribune*, April 6, 1976.

Page 70: "If LeDoux wins decisively": *Minneapolis Tribune*, April 15, 1976.

Page 70: "I've worked many rounds": "LeDoux Spars 10 Rounds Preparing for Duane Bobick," *Minneapolis Tribune*, April 16, 1976.

Page 71: On to the fight: *Minneapolis Tribune*, April 18, 1976.

Page 71: Bobick countered: Dick Cullum, column, *Minneapolis Tribune*, April 19, 1976.

Page 71: LeDoux: "He has always portrayed": *St. Paul Dispatch*, April 21, 1976.

Page 71: Sternberg was salivating: "Fight Fans Get Biggie," *Minneapolis Star*, April 6, 1976.

Page 72: "I believe I have the heart": Bill Hengen, "Bobick to Trim LeDoux," *Minneapolis Star*, April 21, 1976.

Page 72: As the state-record crowd: Bill Hengen, "Top Crowd Hails LeDoux," *Minneapolis Star*, April 23, 1976.

Page 72: "That LeDoux is a tough": Hengen, "Top Crowd Hails LeDoux." The head-line for Hengen's report ignored the winner of the fight, although Hengen certainly gave Bobick his due. But it was typical of the afternoon *Minneapolis Star*. Although the *Star* and *Tribune* were housed under one roof and owned jointly by the Cowles family, the *Star* often sought a second-day approach to stories. Without the same deadline constraints as the morning *Tribune*, *Star* reporters had the luxury of time, allowing them to do in-depth interviews while their *Tribune* counterparts were feverishly filing reports. The *Star*'s experimental, feature-like approach to news ended in 1982, when the *Star* and *Tribune* merged as a morning paper.

Page 72: Under a headline: Hengen, "Top Crowd Hails LeDoux."

Page 73: "He's a tough man": Dick Cullum, "Bobick Tops LeDoux for 35th Victory," *Minneapolis Tribune*, April 23, 1976.

Page 73: "Bobick is a sharp puncher": Hengen, "Top Crowd Hails LeDoux."

Page 73: "I knew he'd be tough": Cullum, "Bobick Tops LeDoux for 35th Victory."

Page 73: "What I don't like": Cullum, "Bobick Tops LeDoux for 35th Victory."

11. A Foreman Grilling

Page 75: Paddy Flood, a fight manager: Mark Kram, "Oh, to Be Young and 200 Pounds," *Sports Illustrated*, May 31, 1976.

Page 76: Half of his fights: Kram, "Oh, to Be Young and 200 Pounds."

Page 76: "I think I would have won": "LeDoux Drops 10-Round Decision," *Minneapolis Tribune*, June 27, 1976.

Page 76: "Wait a minute!": Jorgensen, "Scott LeDoux."

Page 77: "They tell me to be cool": Larry Holmes with Phil Berger, *Larry Holmes: Against the Odds* (New York: St. Martin's Press, 1998), 91.

Page 78: "Frazier won't get nailed": Dick Cullum, "LeDoux vs. Bobick Draws Heavy Receipts, Interest," *Minneapolis Tribune*, April 22, 1976.

Page 78: "Scott insisted": Sid Hartman, column, *Minneapolis Tribune*, August 12, 1976.

Page 79: "When you go in the ring": Bruce Brothers, "LeDoux Hoping to Move on Foreman after Five," *Minneapolis Tribune*, August 8, 1976.

Page 80: Foreman saw the fight: Associated Press, August 11, 1976.

Page 80: "I know the crowd": Associated Press, August 11, 1976.

Page 80: Some of the central New York: *Utica (N.Y.) Daily Press*, August 13, 1976.

Page 80: "If you gave George Foreman": *Utica Daily Press*, August 10, 1976.

Page 80: LeDoux, justifiably the underdog: "Don Riley's Eye Opener," *St. Paul Pioneer Press*, August 6, 1976.

Page 80: King loved the rhetoric: *Utica Daily Press*, August 10, 1976.

Page 81: "The very first round": Jorgensen, "Scott LeDoux."

Page 81: As Ron Lyle: Jess E. Trail, "Speaking of Ron Lyle," July 7, 2005, doghouse boxing.com.

Page 82: "He was loud-mouthing me": Associated Press, August 15, 1976.

Page 82: "It's been a good year": Bill Hengen, "LeDoux Loss Predictable," *Minneapolis Star*, August 16, 1976.

12. A Hair-Raising Fix

Page 84: "We will show": Mark Kram, "Keeping the Fight Game Afloat," *Sports Illustrated*, January 3, 1977.
Page 84: "If you're going to be remembered": Kram, "Keeping the Fight Game Afloat."
Page 85: "Any kind of title": Kram, "Keeping the Fight Game Afloat."
Page 85: "Promoter Don King": *Minneapolis Tribune*, January 13, 1977.
Page 86: "We are up against": Associated Press, February 14, 1977.
Page 87: "I started to get bumped": Bill Hengen, "Dispute Clouds LeDoux's Future," *Minneapolis Star*, February 14, 1977.
Page 88: LeDoux went over the ropes: Patrick Reusse, "LeDoux Remembers Hair-Raising Cosell Tale," Minneapolis *Star Tribune*, April 25, 1995.
Page 88: "You could see the toupee": Reusse, "LeDoux Remembers Hair-Raising Cosell Tale."
Page 88: Roone Arledge: Roone Arledge, *Roone, A Memoir* (New York: HarperCollins, 2003), 171.
Page 89: Boudreaux, who had his foot: Associated Press, February 14, 1977.
Page 89: "Scott then really shouted": Hengen, "Dispute Clouds LeDoux's Future."
Page 89: "As a boxing fan": Associated Press, February 16, 1977.
Page 90: "Any challenge": Associated Press, February 16, 1977.
Page 90: "Who knows what happens": Hengen, "Dispute Clouds LeDoux's Future."
Page 90: "I'm not afraid": Joe Soucheray, column, *Minneapolis Tribune*, February 16, 1977.
Page 91: "I've always wanted": *Minneapolis Tribune*, July 8, 1977.
Page 91: Later that week: *Minneapolis Tribune*, February 18, 1977.
Page 92: "Yes, it was": Associated Press, March 3, 1977.
Page 92: "The publicity from the fight": Max Nichols, "LeDoux Wins by Losing," *Minneapolis Star*, March 14, 1977.
Page 93: "Nobody has done anything wrong": Robert H. Boyle, "Some Very Wrong Numbers," *Sports Illustrated*, May 2, 1977.
Page 93: King called LeDoux's claims: Associated Press, April 2, 1977.
Page 94: "People talk about kickbacks": Dave Anderson, "Scandal Nothing New to Boxing," *New York Times*, April 25, 1977.
Page 94: "How can I learn": Joe Soucheray, column, *Minneapolis Tribune*, February 16, 1977.

13. A Suspension, a Missing Mouthpiece, a Rematch

Page 96: "I plan to fight": "LeDoux Has Plan," *Minneapolis Tribune*, June 16, 1977.
Page 96: "It might be Duane": Bill Hengen, "LeDoux Heard 'Voices of Doom,'" *Minneapolis Star*, July 21, 1977.

Page 96: Prater's response: Bruce Brothers, "LeDoux, Prater Bait Each Other with Vocal Jabs before Their Fight," *Minneapolis Tribune*, June 22, 1977.

Page 97: "He was ready to go?": "Bruce Brothers, LeDoux TKOs Prater in Sixth," *Minneapolis Tribune*, June 24, 1977.

Page 97: "For a change": Bill Hengen, "LeDoux Solves Case of Missing Mouthpiece," *Minneapolis Star*, June 24, 1977.

Page 97: Of his soiled trunks: Brothers, "LeDoux TKOs Prater in Sixth."

Page 97: LeDoux called his six-month suspension: "LeDoux Asks for 2nd Chance at Bobick," *Minneapolis Tribune*, July 10, 1977.

Page 98: What happened: "LeDoux Will Fight Suspension," *Minneapolis Tribune*, July 8, 1977.

Page 99: "I feel my signed": "LeDoux Asks for 2nd Chance at Bobick."

Page 99: "Three days later, on July 12": Tom Briere, "Bobick, LeDoux Fight Approved," *Minneapolis Tribune*, July 13, 1977.

Page 99: Don Riley: Looney, "He's Not Pretty, He's Just Persistent."

Page 100: "If Bobick and his people": Looney, "He's Not Pretty, He's Just Persistent."

Page 100: *Sports Illustrated* dubbed: Pat Putnam, "Make Him 38 and One," *Sports Illustrated*, May 23, 1977.

Page 100: Indeed, when Bobick: Ehlert, "What Does a Guy Do Who Beat Up People for a Living?"

Page 100: "I lost the fight": "Duane Bobick: Sadness Prepared Me," February 3, 2008, TheSweetScience.com.

Page 100: "More likely an easier time": Dick Cullum, "Bobick Camp Says LeDoux Will Lose," *Minneapolis Tribune*, July 24, 1977.

Page 101: When asked what happened: Cullum, "Bobick Camp Says LeDoux Will Lose."

Page 101: "I throw the same": "Boxer LeDoux Thinks He'll Beat Bobick," *Minneapolis Tribune*, July 26, 1977.

Page 101: This time, emotion: Bill Hengen, "LeDoux, Bobick Prepared to Improve on First Fight," *Minneapolis Star*, July 27, 1977.

Page 102: "Before the fight": "Duane Bobick: Sadness Prepared Me."

Page 102: "I thought that I fought": Dick Cullum, "Bobick Follows His Plan, TKOs LeDoux in 8th," *Minneapolis Tribune*, July 29, 1977.

Page 102: "Fight him again?" Dan Stoneking, "Bobick's Victory Cut-Rate," *Minneapolis Star*, July 29, 1977.

Page 102: At least they knew: *Minneapolis Star*, August 3, 1977.

Page 102: "We know what": "LeDoux Will Face Leon Spinks in Nationally Televised Match," *Minneapolis Tribune*, October 4, 1977.

14. "To Be Somebody"

Page 105: Spinks learned to fight: "Leon Spinks Becomes a Somebody," *Time*, February 27, 1978.

Page 106: "I like it": Brian Doogan, "The Big Interview: Leon Spinks," October 1, 2006, timesonline.co.uk.

Page 106: "Everybody loves to steal them": Stan Grossfield, "'I Can Eat, Breathe, Sleep. I Ain't Gonna Pressure My Brother for Money,'" BN Village, May 3, 2006.

Page 106: "Spinks has never": "LeDoux Will Face Leon Spinks in Nationally Televised Match."

Page 107: "He's not a hard KO puncher": Associated Press, October 23, 1977. LeDoux had tremendous respect for Spinks. Decades later, the gloves LeDoux wore in the Spinks fight were hung prominently in the hallway of his home, along with several framed boxing photos of LeDoux. The Spinks gloves were autographed by Leon.

Page 108: "I'm sure they can find": "Snubs Ali," *Minneapolis Tribune*, October 25, 1977.

15. The Greatest?

Page 110: "Listen, Scott is not going in": Dan Stoneking, "Ali: Theater or Boxing?" *Minneapolis Star*, November 26, 1977.

Page 110: "It's a freebie": "LeDoux Has Nothing to Lose against Ali," *Minneapolis Tribune*, November 27, 1977.

Page 111: To make his point: *Minneapolis Tribune*, November 29, 1977.

Page 111: The day before the exhibition: *Chicago Sun-Times*, December 2, 1977.

Page 113: Ali shrugged it off: Vic Ziegel, "Ali, Spinks and the Battle of New Orleans," *New York*, October 2, 1978.

Page 113: "They're talking about LeDoux": "LeDoux Says, 'I'll Fight Spinks in Back Yard,'" *Minneapolis Tribune*, February 16, 1978.

16. Always King

Page 116: "We have the feeling": Bill Hengen, "Frazier–LeDoux Bout Here Is 50-50," *Minneapolis Star*, February 8, 1978.

Page 116: "We tried to match him": "Scott LeDoux—A Tale of Promises . . . Broken," M. Howard Gelfand, *Minneapolis Tribune*, February 18, 1979.

Page 117: "Why else would I": Gelfand, "Scott LeDoux—A Tale of Promises."

Page 117: "We have high hopes": "LeDoux Signs Exclusive Pact with Don King," *Minneapolis Tribune*, April 20, 1978.

Page 118: Bob Busse: Gelfand, "Scott LeDoux—A Tale of Promises."

Page 119: "A guy like Bobick": Gelfand, "Scott LeDoux—A Tale of Promises."

Page 119: His manager, Don White: Robert H. Boyle, ed., "Bum Dope," *Sports Illustrated*, November 17, 1978.

Page 120: "The idea of working": Tom Briere, "LeDoux May Give Stars Some Added Punch," *Minneapolis Tribune*, November 29, 1978.

Page 120: "They're going to stage": *Minneapolis Tribune*, January 10, 1979.

Page 120: Daszkiewicz had heard enough: *Minneapolis Star*, January 26, 1979.

Page 121: Said LeDoux: Gelfand, "Scott LeDoux—A Tale of Promises."

Page 121: "It's been a long year": Gelfand, "Scott LeDoux—A Tale of Promises."

Page 121: Daszkiewicz insisted: Dick Cullum, "LeDoux, Beattie Fight Set," *Minneapolis Tribune*, February 7, 1979.

Page 121: "I'm an old man": "Gelfand, "Scott LeDoux—A Tale of Promises."

Page 121: "It was so unfair": *Minneapolis Star*, February 21, 1979.

17. Six Months to Live

Page 123: At the prefight weigh-in: Ken Hissner, "Interview with Earnie Shavers—The Hardest Hitting Fighter in Boxing History," November 26, 2009, doghouseboxing.com.

Page 124: "I'm going to be": Bill Hengen, "LeDoux Likes Challenge of Lyle Fight," *Minneapolis Star*, April 19, 1979.

Page 124: "It was the turning point": Dan Levin, "Before the Shower, Deluge," *Sports Illustrated*, October 9, 1972.

Page 124: Lyle was paroled: Hengen, "LeDoux Likes Challenge of Lyle Fight."

Page 125: "I want to be world champion": Associated Press, April 19, 1972.

Page 125: "Once the ice is broken": Bill Hengen, "The Three Musketeers," *Minneapolis Star*, May 2, 1979.

Page 125: "There's no question": Bruce Brothers, "LeDoux to Fight Lyle in Gamble for Title," *Minneapolis Tribune*, May 12, 1979. LeDoux's personal scrapbooks were filled with photographs of him with celebrities. Sylvester Stallone, Robert Goulet, and David Brenner were among those he met several times. He never got over not meeting Frank Sinatra. "I was that close," he said many times. "I still can't believe it."

Page 125: "What does a white guy": Brothers, "LeDoux to Fight Lyle in Gamble for Title."

Page 126: The thirty-year-old LeDoux: Brothers, "LeDoux to Fight Lyle in Gamble for Title."

Page 126: "I thought they": "Lyle Beats LeDoux in Close Fight," *Minneapolis Tribune*, May 13, 1979.

Page 126: "[Lyle] deserves another shot": "Lyle Beats LeDoux in Close Fight."

Page 127: "I'm back in my hotel": Ehlert, "Scott LeDoux: He's Hung Up His Gloves."

18. Cold, Hard Cash

Page 134: But Harold Smith was after: Dean B. Allison and Bruce B. Henderson, *Empire of Deceit: Inside the Biggest Sports and Boxing Scandal in U.S. History* (Garden City, N.Y.: Doubleday, 1985), 18.

Page 134: This, apparently, was how Smith: Richard Hoffer, "The Second Time Around," *Sports Illustrated*, March 3, 1992.

Page 137: Seconds later, there was a pounding: Allison and Henderson, *Empire of Deceit*, 160–61.

Page 138: Ali would see Smith: Jeremiah Tax, "The Big Boxing Con: An Account of the Harold Smith Hustle of a Bank," *Sports Illustrated*, February 18, 1985.

19. Luck of the Draw

Page 139: "One of us": *Minneapolis Tribune*, June 3, 1979.

Page 139: "Norton is getting $250,000": Joe Soucheray, "LeDoux Uses Ban to Work on Haymaker," *Minneapolis Tribune*, August 10, 1979.

Page 140: There were potential problems: Bill Hengen, "It Looks like a Bell-Ringer at the Met," *Minneapolis Star*, July 23, 1979.

Page 141: "A better word": Bill Hengen, "LeDoux Battles Again," *Minneapolis Star*, July 13, 1979.

Page 141: "I told her": Hengen, "LeDoux Battles Again."

Page 142: "I'm not saying": Soucheray, "LeDoux Uses Ban to Work on Haymaker."

Page 142: "It's good we've got": Bob Fowler, "'Rocky' Road a Primrose Path?" *Minneapolis Star*, August 14, 1979.

Page 142: "I know that he's better": Joe Soucheray, "Norton Doesn't Joke Around—At Least in Ring," *Minneapolis Tribune*, August 15, 1979.

Page 143: "Sure, I got hit": Bill Hengen, "LeDoux Fight Plan Was Fit to Be Tied," *Minneapolis Star*, August 20, 1979.

Page 143: "You look at the television tape": Hengen, "LeDoux Fight Plan Was Fit to Be Tied."

Page 144: "I'm inviting LeDoux": Dick Cullum, "LeDoux Rallies for Draw," *Minneapolis Tribune*, August 20, 1979.

20. The Monroe Doctrine

Page 145: "We didn't know": "LeDoux's Hometown Supporters Bugged," Rob Tannenbaum, *Minneapolis Star*, August 23, 1979.

Page 145: Sammie Marshall: Dick Cullum, "Norton, LeDoux Spar," *Minneapolis Tribune*, August 17, 1979.

Page 146: Weaver, who early: *Minneapolis Tribune*, November 16, 1979.

Page 147: "I waited": Dick Cullum, "Spinks Brothers Join Met Fight Card," *Minneapolis Tribune*, October 26, 1979.

Page 147: "I slid all over": Jorgensen, "Scott LeDoux."

Page 148: The writers, he said: Doug Grow, "LeDoux's Back in the Shadows," *Minneapolis Star*, December 5, 1979.

Page 148: "Whenever I get down": Grow, "LeDoux's Back in the Shadows."

Page 149: "I'm God-sent": Bill Hengen, "Monroe Talking like Real Heavy," *Minneapolis Star*, March 6, 1980.

Page 149: "All we know": Dick Cullum, "LeDoux May Get Chance to Fight Ali," *Minneapolis Tribune*, March 7, 1980.

21. "What's an Eye When You've Given Your Heart?"

Page 152: "Only in America": Doug Grow, "Tears Help Heal LeDoux's Scars," *Minneapolis Star*, June 30, 1980.

Page 152: Nobody saw Sandy and Scott: Grow, "Tears Help Heal LeDoux's Scars."

Page 154: "I would have liked": "Holmes, LeDoux Trade Gibes," *Minneapolis Tribune*, June 19, 1980.

Page 154: "Someone says to me": *Minneapolis Tribune*, June 25, 1980.

Page 154: LeDoux called Holmes: Joe Soucheray, column, *Minneapolis Tribune*, July 4, 1980.

Page 154: "Let me tell you something": Doug Grow, "Scott LeDoux: White Hope... with Red Neck," *Minneapolis Star*, July 4, 1980.

Page 155: "Scott just lost his composure": "Holmes Not Really Mad," *Minneapolis Tribune*, July 5, 1980.

Page 156: Hartman offered: Sid Hartman, column, *Minneapolis Tribune*, July 7, 1980.

Page 156: "This is not going to be": Bill Hengen, "Holmes Isn't Fighting 'Rocky,'" *Minneapolis Star*, July 7, 1980.

Page 156: "My head," he said: Hengen, "Holmes Isn't Fighting 'Rocky.'"

Page 156: "He has a mean, wicked right": Howard Sinker, "Underdog Status Can't Dampen Enthusiasm in Crosby-Ironton," *Minneapolis Tribune*, July 6, 1980.

Page 157: "I'm telling you": Doug Grow, "Fans Wanted Scott's Blood," *Minneapolis Star*, July 8, 1980.

22. Last Rounds

Page 159: "There's no future in it": *Minneapolis Star*, March 26, 1981.

Page 160: "The only thing that's sore": "LeDoux Beats Sam in 10-Round Workout," *Minneapolis Tribune*, August 1, 1981.

Page 160: "I wasn't Joe's first choice": Joe Soucheray, "LeDoux Joins Old Folks' Rush to the Ring," *Minneapolis Tribune*, August 28, 1981.

Page 161: "It would have been a great fight": Ben Tighe, "'The Fighting Frenchman' Scott LeDoux," MinnesotaBoxing.com.

Page 163: "He made me so mad": Jorgensen, "Scott LeDoux."

Page 163: "I've never had any idea": *Minneapolis Tribune*, February 16, 1982.

Page 163: "I knew early": *Minneapolis Tribune*, February 26, 1982.

Page 164: "Four months ago": Joe Soucheray, "Scott, Sandy LeDoux Finally Able to Laugh at Life," *Minneapolis Star Tribune*, August 4, 1982.

Page 165: "He's telling me": Jorgensen, "Scott LeDoux."

Page 166: "I really think": Jorgensen, "Scott LeDoux."

Page 168: "If you saw the two of them": "Vancouver Boxer Wins Decision over LeDoux," *Minneapolis Star Tribune*, September 25, 1982.

Page 169: "When I go out": *Minneapolis Star Tribune*, November 19, 1982.

Page 170: "I knew I was done": Jorgensen, "Scott LeDoux."

23. Game Seven

Page 173: A year later: "Proceeds of Run to Honor Paula Leu," *Minneapolis Star Tribune*, August 7, 1984.

Page 174: "'Sara Smile' was playing": Ehlert, "Scott LeDoux: He's Hung Up His Gloves."

Page 175: "We cried so many times": Ehlert, "Scott LeDoux: He's Hung Up His Gloves."

Page 175: "I've got no regrets": Joe Soucheray, "LeDoux Leaves the Ring, Still on His Feet," Minneapolis *Star Tribune*, June 17, 1983.

Page 180: "I felt terrible": Patrick Reusse, "LeDoux's Wife Is Putting Up the Good Fight Now," Minneapolis *Star Tribune*, November 17, 1988.

Page 180: "Boxing can turn you": Reusse, "LeDoux's Wife Is Putting Up the Good Fight Now."

Page 181: "We're lucky": Reusse, "LeDoux's Wife Is Putting Up the Good Fight Now."

24. Down for the Count

Page 187: "I think all of us": Dan Barreiro, "LeDoux, at 42, Wants Some of the Action," Minneapolis *Star Tribune*, May 10, 1991.

Page 187: The second Tyson: Patrick Reusse, "LeDoux Returns to Ring with Pride Intact," Minneapolis *Star Tribune*, June 4, 1991.

Page 189: "I'll look in the mirror": Nolan Zavoral, "A New Arena: Scott LeDoux's Life Is Taking Shape with Challenge of Border to Border," Minneapolis *Star Tribune*, June 3, 1990.

25. Crucial Confrontation

Page 193: He said he lost touch: Brian O'Melia, inducted into the New Jersey Boxing Hall of Fame in 2000, said he knew little about LeDoux before they fought at the Minnesota State Fairgrounds in St. Paul. "I'd been told that Scott was a dirty fighter," O'Melia said. "That wasn't the case, at least not when we fought. He beat me, plain and simple. I was an OK fighter. There were a few fights that the refs had to stop because they thought I was hurting my opponent's hands. But when I fought Scott, I didn't know how far he'd go, but I wasn't surprised that he fought for the title. He was a real tough guy. You couldn't hurt him."

26. Something to Prove

Page 200: "I have name recognition": Darlene Prois, "LeDoux Steps into Anoka County Ring," Minneapolis *Star Tribune*, July 23, 2004.

Page 201: "It's tough for me to say no": Michael Rand, "Ex-boxer Has Reason to Get Back in Ring," Minneapolis *Star Tribune*, October 12, 2005.

Page 201: The Boogeyman: John Branch, "Derek Boogaard: A Brain 'Going Bad,'" *New York Times*, December 5, 2011.

Page 202: "Sometimes I worry": Minneapolis *Star Tribune*, February 21, 2008.

27. Funeral for a Friend

Page 203: "How many people die": Minneapolis *Star Tribune*, August 19, 1997.

Page 204: Years later, while toiling: Patrick Reusse, "His Toughest Fight," Minneapolis *Star Tribune*, August 19, 1997.

Page 204: "Boxing was big": Patrick Slack, "Hall of Fame Boxer Duane Bobick Faces His Greatest Fight," *Morrison County Record*, February 12, 2012.

Page 205: "I've accomplished way more": Rand, "Ex-boxer Has Reason to Get Back in Ring."

INDEX

Nafstad, Rog, 158
Nanne, Lou, 120, 209
Nassau, the Bahamas, 162
National Association of Counties, 204
National Cancer Institute, 180, 181
National Hockey League, 120, 201
NBC, 115, 134, 143, 145
Needham, Danny, 48
Nelson, Denny, 37, 57, 81, 143, 144, 149, 175
Nelson, Lehne, 188–92
New York, 58, 64, 91–93, 100, 117, 123, 132, 140, 152, 180
New York Daily News, 42, 152
New York Islanders, xii, 151
New York Magazine, 113
New York Times, 92, 209
Nobles, James, 202
Nomellini, Leo, 29
North Dakota State, 29
Northern Bar, 50, 51
Northside Gym, 49
Norton, Ken, xi, 13, 19, 57, 64, 65, 78, 85, 90, 99–101, 113, 116, 117, 123, 132–34, 136, 138–45, 148, 151, 159, 173, 176, 181, 203, 205, 207, 209, 211, 215, 216
Nystrom, Bobby, 33

O'Brien, Dr. Jerry, 157
O'Brien, Pastor Randy, 210
Ocasia, Osvaldo, 153
O'Connor, Dan, 202
Oliva, Tony, 209
Olympics, 54, 78, 84, 99, 102, 105, 107, 141, 147
O'Melia, Brian, 62, 85, 193, 194
ore, 1–5, 8, 20, 110
Orlando, Florida, 61
Osowiecki, Greg, 68
O'Sullivan, Chester, 98

Page, Alan, 173
Page, Dennis, 162
Page, Greg, 147, 160–63, 203, 216

Palmer, Arnie, 51, 57, 58, 61, 79, 95, 108
Papa Joe's A Go Go, 50
Parkinson's disease, 203
Patterson, Floyd, 169
Pawlenty, Governor Tim, 201
Paychex, Inc., 176
Penninger, Larry, 53
Pep, Willie, 25, 181
Perkins restaurant, 205, 206
Perpich, Frank, 2, 15, 194
Perpich, Gloria, 4, 5
Perpich, John R., 5
Perpich, Katherine, 1, 2, 5
Perrault, Jim, 202
Peterson, Ron, 62
Pilot Air Freight, 186, 199
Polis, Carol, 89, 94
Prater, Tom, 85, 96, 97
Providence, Rhode Island, 76, 83, 84
Puckett, Kirby, 179
Pullens, Arthur, 53

Quarry, Jerry, 68
Queen Elizabeth Sports Centre, 162
Quilici, Frank, 168, 208, 209

race, 125, 137, 153–55, 202
Racette, Gordon, 167–69, 175, 176
Rahman, Hasim, 215
Rainforest Café, 177
Randolph, Leo, 84
Rath, Tim, 176, 190
Rather, Dan, 93
Reid, Tom, 209
Reiter, George, 69
Renaud, Larry, 56
Resch, Diane, 17, 22–24, 35, 41–43, 70, 151, 180, 189, 194, 198, 207, 209
Resch, Glenn (Chico), xii, 8, 20, 32–33, 35, 43, 44, 151, 180, 198, 207, 209
restraining order, 190
Rhodes, Governor Jim, 77
Riley, Don, 80, 99
Ringling Bros. Circus, 115

Paul Levy is an award-winning journalist who worked for the Minneapolis *Star Tribune* for thirty-five years. He interviewed Richard Nixon, the Dalai Lama, and Muhammad Ali, among many others. He is the author of the children's book *The Turtle Who Lost His Shell* and has written for the *New York Times*, *Reader's Digest*, and *Sports Illustrated*.